C000195127

'THE **BLOODIEST** THING THAT **EVER** HAPPENED IN FRONT OF A CAMERA' CONSERVATIVE POLITICS, 'PORNO CHIC' AND **SNUFF**

Stephen Milligen

A Headpress Book

CONTENTS

"Beware of false prophets that come to you in sheep's clothing,
but inwardly they are ravening wolves."
Matthew 7: 15

"Murder is a crime. Describing murder is not.
Sex is not a crime. Describing it is."
Gershon Legman

"The great enemy of the truth is very often not the
lie — deliberate contrived and dishonest — but the
myth — persistent, persuasive and unrealistic."
John F. Kennedy

ACKNOWLEDGEMENTS

THIS MANUSCRIPT WAS ORIGINALLY INTENDED TO BE A SHORT ARTICLE, things just got a bit out of hand, quite a lot out of hand really.

I've known about the snuff movie myth for years, but I did not believe it and did not feel the need to investigate any further. Some people seem predisposed to believe hearsay that reinforces a bleak and inhumane assessment of society, possibly reflecting their own disappointment and disillusionment at the world they see around them: a persistent problem for Christian moralists throughout history. The willingness to believe the worst and the persistence of the myth made me reconsider. Eventually I began to wonder when and where the snuff panic began, who started it, and why.

In a poem, *Letter to the author of the book, The Three Impostors* (1770), the French philosopher Voltaire made the observation: "If God did not exist it would be necessary to invent him." A century later Fyodor Dostoevsky wrote *The Brothers Karamazov (*1880), and as part of a discussion littered with descriptions of brutality and torture of children one character states, "I think that if the devil doesn't exist, but man has created him, he has created him in his own image." To which the other character retorts "Just as he did God, then?"[1] A concise summary of the human need to create images of good and evil to explain, and personalize events and behaviour which are beyond their comprehension. The two figures that have dominated Christian moral thought for centuries, God and Satan, adversaries in a historical soap opera, played out a contrived conflict between good and evil. Serving as a moral barometer, their function is to maintain the existing social order, but as religious belief receded before the advances of science, theological assumptions were challenged, paradigms questioned and value systems undermined. Confronted with these challenges conservative protestors escalated their claims and the severity of their rhetoric.

Social changes in the 1960s and challenges to the status quo led

---

1   Fyodor M. Dostoevsky, *The Brothers Karamazov*, trans. Constance Garnett, Encyclopaedia Britannica Inc., Chicago and London, 1952: 123.

conservatives to campaign against symbolic threats such as drugs and pornography, and culminated in an outrageous and outlandish accusation by one very prominent group of anti-obscenity crusaders that has persisted for decades without any evidence being produced to substantiate it. The claim that performers were intentionally killed during the making of pornographic films, 'snuff movies', to satisfy the jaded and depraved appetites of a decadent society was announced by Citizen's for Decent Literature (CDL) to further their own political agenda. The claim was obviously a lie, but over time its repetition has assured it a mythical status and led to further repetition and, amongst willing audiences, blind acceptance. 'Snuff' movies exist in this social drama as a 'moral panic', a modern evil and symbolic threat to the social order, a warning of the threat posed by decadence and degeneracy and a way to re-establish traditional values.

The research for this manuscript would not have been possible but for the help and expertise of a number of other people. Along the way Scott Stine, Kathleen McCracken, Liz Young, Joanne Knox, Sorcha Ni Fhlainn, Tony Feenan, Brian Carville, Whitney Strub, Ciaran Dalligan, Derek Shields, Gary McMurray and Darren Topping provided help with materials and ideas, and Jenny Allen provided patience and sense of humour. Special thanks are owed to Tom Brinkmann and David Kerekes for the generous loan of articles and FBI documents.

INTRODUCTION

The *Bloodiest* Thing That *Ever* Happened In Front Of A Camera

In 1976 the United States celebrated the 200ᵀᴴ anniversary of the Declaration of Independence. This foundational document asserted autonomy and freedom from British rule and, in its bicentennial year, the media and politicians aggressively exploited it as an immensely important symbolic event. Across the nation celebrations were organized which paid tribute to American traditions and achievements. National history was sanitized and national character idealized for a spectacle designed to make the American public feel good after more than a decade of divisive social unrest, economic problems and high-profile political abuses. Religious belief and traditional values were emphasised, marking a period of resurgent right-wing conservative ideology.

In the same year, one of the most important symbolic events was the release of a low-budget independent film entitled *Snuff* (Allan Shackleton, 1976), which caused a national outcry and became the most controversial film of the decade. *Snuff* also played a pivotal role in the conservative backlash against the liberalisation of sexual values and the mainstream acceptance of sexually explicit adult material. Released with an X rating, the film was advertised in a way that evoked an image of sexual extremes reminiscent of the Marquis de Sade. Purporting to show the real murder of an actress purely for the entertainment and titillation of the audience, the film epitomized all of the excesses prophesied by conservatives as the consequence of the social and moral decay of the 'sexual revolution'.

The late 1960s and early 1970s were a tumultuous time in American society during which conservative values were challenged by liberal ideas. 'The Sexual Revolution', reported heavily by the news media in 1963 and 1964 culminating in a cover story by *Time* (24 January 1964), implied a radical shift in attitude and behaviour, but the changes

1

in values really began several years before.[1] In Tom Smith's opinion "The metaphor of a Sexual Revolution captured the imagination of a generation of Americans, but poorly describes and generally exaggerates the changes in the sexual mores of Americans."[2] According to Smith the Sexual Revolution was an "uprooting of sexual morality" that reflected changes in attitude and behaviour which threatened conservatives and therefore challenged advocates of repressive Puritan ideas and caused traditionalists to lament libertine hedonism.[3]

Enveloped in this cultural conflict, traditional values and practices were being eroded by inevitable social changes. A generational gap seemed to sharply contrast opinions and beliefs, disillusionment was rife and many difficult questions were asked about American society. Even before the Watergate scandal Charles A. Reich, Professor of law at Yale, asserted, "there is a lawlessness and corruption in all the major institutions of our society."[4] In his *People's History of the United States* (1980) Howard Zinn also noted the social problems of the early seventies: "the system seemed out of control — it could not hold the loyalty of the public."[5] Irresponsible and indifferent, society was pervaded by a blinkered hypocrisy that refused to acknowledge obvious social problems, as across the nation extreme poverty contrasted with opulence and luxury.[6]

The source of dissatisfaction was identified by Reich, who opened his book *The Greening of America* (1970) with the observation, "America is dealing death, not only to people in other lands, but to its own people."[7] Promising that a revolution was coming, instigated by a new generation, Reich wrote: "Their protests and rebellion, their culture, clothes, music, drugs, ways of thought and liberated lifestyle are not a passing fad or a form of dissent and refusal, nor are they in any sense irrational."[8] Many Americans felt that since they were not in control of

1   Tom W. Smith, "The Polls — A Report: The Sexual Revolution?" *Public Opinion Quarterly* 54 (1990): 415.
2   Ibid: 419.
3   Ibid: 416.
4   Charles A. Reich, *The Greening of America*, Penguin, Harmondsworth, Middlesex, 1971: 13.
5   Howard Zinn, *A People's History of the United States*, Longman, New York and London, 1980: 528.
6   Reich, *The Greening of America*: 13–15.
7   Ibid: 11.
8   Ibid: 11.

the machinery of their society they needed a new culture;[9] new ideas invited reflection and re-examination, and offered personal choices for change. Reich identified the "loss of self, or death in life" as the most devastating impoverishment in contemporary America:

> Beginning with school, if not before, the individual is systematically stripped of their imagination, their creativity, their heritage, their dreams and their personal uniqueness, in order to style them into a productive unit for a mass technological society. Instinct, feeling and spontaneity are repressed by overwhelming forces.[10]

Obviously this is a dehumanizing process, and one that would inevitably impact on society and meet with resistance.

Critiques of society, politics and sexuality appeared in many contemporary films such as the sarcastic observations found in one of the segments in *Everything You Always Wanted to Know About Sex But Were Afraid to Ask* (Woody Allen, 1972). In Allen's film the deranged Dr Barnardo (John Carradine) claims credit for discovering how compulsive masturbation leads to a career in politics, reflecting a common perception of politicians. However, more developed critiques are found in other Woody Allen films such as *Sleeper* (1973), where Allen satirizes the problems of contemporary American society as well as paying homage to slapstick comedy.

Owner of a health food store in Greenwich Village, Miles Monroe (Woody Allen) is cryogenically frozen in 1973 after routine surgery and revived in 2173. The twenty-second century, however, is radically different to the one in which he lived; it is a utopia of right-wing ideas where official dogma and enforced discipline prevail. After a nuclear war in the twenty-first century the tumultuous, promiscuous and democratic society he remembers was obliterated and replaced by a fascist state, the American Federation. All of the population are frigid, relying on technology for sexual gratification, an ominous forewarning of the consequences of militarism, conservative ideology and moral crusades in the 1960s and 1970s. Told that his re-awakening was illegal and, if caught, his punishment would be to have his brain

---

9   Ibid: 12.
10   Ibid: 16.

"electronically simplified," Monroe is horrified because his brain is his second favourite organ. When he is also told that those who resist the reprogramming are exterminated for the good of the state Monroe is prompted to ask, "What kind of government you guys got here? This is worse than California!" which was under the governorship of Ronald Reagan when Monroe was frozen.

Several scenes in the film are used to lampoon contemporary events and satirize American society. Ignorant of twentieth-century history Dr Tryon (Don Keefer) asks Monroe to identify some photographic artefacts that survived a nuclear war. Sarcastically Monroe identifies Bela Lugosi in one picture and claims he was mayor of New York, suggesting that the real mayor of New York was a blood sucker. After being shown a picture of evangelist Billy Graham, Monroe explains that he was "very big in the religion business" and knew God personally, adding that Graham's relationship with God was so close that they were rumoured to go on double dates together and some people suspected a romantic link.

A news broadcast made by President Richard Nixon has also been preserved and is an important topic of discussion for those trying to understand the past. The doctors speculate Nixon was a president who did something so awful that all records about him were destroyed, a bleak appraisal that Monroe confirms. He also adds that Nixon was considered so untrustworthy that, even while president, each time he left the White House Secret Service agents had to check the silverware, to make sure it had not been stolen.

Other contemporary films commented on the moral hypocrisy of politicians and the political system in relation to sexual morality. Most of *Shampoo* (Hal Ashby, 1975) takes place within a frantic forty-eight hours and follows the activities of George (Warren Beatty), a womanizing hairdresser who has sex with many of his female clients. Attending a 'Nixon for President' party with his girlfriend (Goldie Hawn), George finds that several of his lovers are also present, creating an awkward situation. Numerous sound bites from Republican political speeches committing Nixon to put a halt to permissiveness, sharply contrast with the conduct of his supporters at the party.

The illegal activities of Nixon's administration were exposed during the Watergate investigation and his resignation address is incorporated into an early scene of the *Rocky Horror Picture Show* (Jim Sharman,

1975), broadcast on the radio as the conservative and sexually repressed Brad (Barry Bostwick) and Janet (Susan Sarandon) drive through a thunderstorm. Nixon's resignation tarnished his administration and the political excesses called into question the traditional values he claimed to champion. The radio broadcast foreshadows Brad and Janet's visit to Dr Frank-N-Furter's castle where their traditional sexual values are challenged. Frank-N-Furter (Tim Curry) is an updated Dr Frankenstein, a sexual scientist, who creates his own Adam, an Adonis not a monster, to help relieve his "tension." The bisexual Frank-N-Furter's singleminded pursuit of "absolute pleasure" is a hedonistic inversion of the traditional Christian philosophy of abstinence and monogamy.

Sleeper likewise satirizes the sex-politics debates of the day. After being shown a picture of Norman Mailer, Monroe (Woody Allen) notes that the writer donated his ego to the Harvard Medical School and, identifying a feminist bra burning protest, he plays down the significance of the act when he mockingly observes, "notice it's a very small fire." Shown a *Playboy* centrefold Monroe explains that the women in the magazine did not really exist, they were actually blow-up dolls made from rubber. Nonetheless, he still wants to take the centrefold with him for further study and promises he will submit a full report later.

There is no partisan political ideology behind Allen's satire, and at the conclusion of *Sleeper* Monroe criticises *all* political systems. Confused by his stance Luna Schlosser (Diane Keaton) asks him what he does believe in, to which Monroe retorts "sex" and "death," quipping, "at least after death you're not nauseous." The irony is unfortunate since *Snuff* sought to exploit public curiosity about pornography in a film that promised a new twist on sex and death, causing nationwide, and later international, outrage.

In *The Politics and Poetics of Transgression* (1986) Peter Stallybrass and Andrew White observe: "what is socially peripheral is so frequently symbolically central."[11] Nowhere was this more evident than the obscenity debate, which was a major ongoing issue for Middle America. From the 1930s to the mid 1960s the motion picture production code enforced a set of standards that Hollywood filmmakers had to

11   Peter Stallybrass and Allan White, *The Politics and Poetics of Transgression*, Cornell University Press, 1986: 5.

adopt if their work was to get the approval of conservative moralists. Section II of the Production Code stipulated, "Excessive and inhumane acts of cruelty and brutality shall not be presented. This includes all detailed and protracted presentation of physical violence, torture and abuse." The Code also determined that the sanctity of marriage and family life was to be respected: "No film shall infer that casual or promiscuous sex relationships are the accepted or common thing," and the subject of adultery could be addressed as a topic, but never condoned. "Scenes of passion" were only to be used when essential to the plot and not presented in any way that could "stimulate the baser emotions." Rape was not to be shown graphically, only suggested if essential to the storyline. Abortion, prostitution and white slavery were all to be avoided, as were venereal diseases and "Sex perversion or any inference of it [was] forbidden." But changes within the film industry and throughout American society during the 1950s and sixties undermined the power of the Production Code — and the depiction of sex and violence grew progressively more graphic.

Beginning in 1957 and continuing throughout the 1960s decisions made by the Supreme Court relaxed legal definitions of obscenity, sparking numerous anti-smut organisations that exaggerated the prevalence of pornographic material and the danger it posed in the course of their crusades. Simultaneously, sensing an opportunity, business entrepreneurs exploited the new freedoms by developing a legitimate market for adult entertainment which eventually culminated in a short lived era of 'porno chic,' during which middle-class Americans openly consumed adult orientated books, magazines and films. Throughout the 1960s conservatives felt they were losing the ongoing legal battle to establish the social boundaries for adult materials. Numerous local crusades across the nation warned of the consequence: an apocalyptic chain of events beginning with the proliferation of obscene material that would eventually destroy American society, turning children into corrupt and degenerate sex criminals, and as adult materials became prevalent and more acceptable anti-obscenity groups became more desperate.

The wave of 'porno chic' announced in the *New York Times* in

1973 had, by 1976, become a 'porno plague' according to *Time*.[12] As a consequence of various social crusades a public perception of pornography developed and John B. McConahay identified the three dangerous myths about pornography that emerged in the 1970s: "belief in the increase in violence in pornography, the existence of snuff films, and the availability of child pornography."[13] Anti-obscenity crusaders created and aggressively promoted all of these myths to advance their political agenda.

Released in the wake of 'porno chic' and prompted by the mainstream success of *Deep Throat* (Gerard Damiano, 1972) and the judicial retrenchment of *Miller v. California* (1973) in the Supreme Court, the low-budget sexploitation film *Snuff* provided militant feminists and conservative moralists with a focus for their attacks on pornography. In 1976 the release of *Snuff*, a film with no credited cast or crew, called into question the realism of the events depicted by claiming that a woman *had* in fact been murdered in the course of filming, providing feminists and anti-obscenity activists with an easy target.

As a form of popular entertainment, cinema is based on the understanding that the audience suspends disbelief to become engrossed in the spectacle on-screen, yet remains secure in the knowledge that the people and events they are watching are not real. The idea of filming a real murder for the purpose of entertainment and financial gain was not new in the 1970s. In response to a contemporary film *Les Incendiairies* (George Méliès, 1906)[14] Guillaume Apollinaire wrote a short story entitled 'Un beau film' (published on 23 December 1907) that parodied the censorship of Méliès' work.[15]

Apollinaire's story is recounted by one Baron d'Ormesan, a

---

12 "The Porno Plague," *Time* (5 April 1976): 46–51.
13 John B. McConahay, "Pornography: The Symbolic Politics of Fantasy," *Law and Contemporary Problems* 51 (No.1, 1988): 62–65.
14 Also known as *Histoire d'un Crime*, the film was about a criminal who sets fire to a farm but is caught in the act by the police and subsequently beheaded. At the time of its release the film was suppressed because the final scene was considered too graphic. Georges Méliès (b.1861–d.1938) was one of the pioneers of cinema. Mainly associated with fantasy films he also made advertising films and melodramas, but experimenting with the medium he was one of the first filmmakers to present nudity on screen with *Après le Bal* (1897).
15 Guillaume Apollinaire, *The Wandering Jew and other stories*, trans Remy Inglis Hall, London, Hart Davis, 1967: 172–175.

wealthy aristocrat who, along with a few associates, has established the International Cinema Company (ICC) with the aim of finding newsworthy films to exhibit. Several notable sequences of film footage are acquired by the company but d'Ormesan also wants to see the commission of a crime of the "right quality" which could be distributed by ICC. Accepting that it is unlikely that such a piece of film could be found legitimately the filmmakers organize to make their own.

Six perpetrators are involved in perpetrating and filming the crime. They begin by abducting a young elegantly dressed couple, followed by the kidnapping of an older gentleman in evening dress to complete the cast. All of the captives are taken to a villa (rented anonymously) where a photographer is waiting with his camera. The cooperation of the older gentleman is acquired after d'Ormesan assures him that he will not be harmed if he follows instructions and kills the young couple. Yielding, the gentleman's only request is that he would like to be masked while carrying out the murders, to protect his identity.

The story continues: Despite his part as co-conspirator, d'Ormesan describes the shooting of the footage as a "dismal scene."[16] The young woman is first to die, stabbed in the heart after a brief struggle, while the young man is murdered quickly afterwards, his throat slit from ear to ear. Although the two victims are partially undressed by their captors before filming commences, there is no nudity and no sexual activity during the film. Surprisingly competent, the gentleman carries out the role of assassin "almost professionally" and his mask is not disturbed during the murders. Later, the filmmakers remove the evidence of their activities in the villa and release the gentleman assassin to return to his club to gamble.

The discovery of the murder causes "a terrible scandal," the victims being "the wife of a Minister of a small Balkan state, and her lover, the son of a pretender to the crown of a North German principality."[17] The scandal is reported widely and some newspapers publish a special edition due to public interest. Predictably, when the film is released amid the hysteria it is a huge financial success in Europe and America. The police however do not suspect that the film is an actual recording

16 Ibid: 173.
17 Ibid: 174.

of the murder, even though it is advertised as such.

Needing to close such a high profile case the police arrest and charge a Levantine who is unable to provide an alibi for his whereabouts on the night of the murders. He is subsequently convicted and sentenced to death. In a cynical act of opportunism the film company send a photographer to record the execution of the scapegoat, and the new scene in turn is added to the existing murder footage and reissued achieving further financial success. Apollinaire's story closes two years after the ICC is dissolved and d'Ormesan has received more than a million francs as his share of the profits (only to lose it all at the races).

The idea of real murder being passed off as fake was notably exploited by Herschell Gordon Lewis in *The Wizard of Gore* (1970). The wizard, Montag the Magnificent (Ray Sager), delivers a monologue to his audience pointing out that in the past the roman arena catered to those who wished to see a violent and bloody spectacle, then wryly asserts, "Today, television and films give us the luxury of observing grisly accidents and deaths without anyone actually being harmed." Then Montag distorts the situation when he hypnotizes his audience into believing that the murders he commits onstage are just theatrical effect. As Robert Kolker points out in *A Cinema of Loneliness* (1988), 'snuff' movies would require the conventional understanding that films are *not* reality to be revised:

> The question would no longer involve a viewer becoming a prisoner to an illusion of reality — or of attending a documentation of reality — but being guilty of assenting to the actual event of murder. The only real meaning of such films would emerge from the moral choice of attending them or not.[18]

Amidst the advertisements for *Snuff* and the media debate many people *did* attend, making the film a box office success in a number of cities. Paul Schrader, who wrote and directed *Hardcore* (1978), understood the fascination:

18 Robert Phillip Kolker, *A Cinema of Loneliness: Penn, Kubrick, Scorsese, Spielberg, Altman,* Oxford University Press, Oxford, 1988: 199.

Movies are a flexible medium. It's easy to simulate death on film, which is partly why people think snuff films exist. They've seen simulated versions and believe they're genuine. I think it's conceivable these films exist, but whether they do or not is less important than the public's belief that they do — their willingness to believe in an evil fantasy. That's what's interesting here.[19]

In the 1970s, it was largely due to the apocalyptic rhetoric of anti-obscenity group Citizens for Decent Literature (CDL)[20] and militant feminists, that the 'evil fantasy' found a wide audience. The story and characters in *Snuff* were not compelling, and the special effects were unconvincing. For all of the hype and hysteria the film was not the first time a reputedly 'real' murder had been caught on film, nor was it the first time sex and murder were addressed in fictional settings.

Throughout the 1960s Mondo movies attracted audiences with the promise of exotic spectacles, graphic violence, and occasionally documented human death.[21] Elsewhere, in the art-house film *Blowup* (Michelangelo Antonioni, 1966) a photographer accidentally takes a series of pictures of a murder in progress, but the body disappears, the incriminating film is stolen and the mystery never solved. The thematic connections between sex and death were thoughtfully explored in *Peeping Tom* (Michael Powell, 1960) and *Charlotte* (Roger Vadim, 1974), but *Snuff* went further. Publicity for *Snuff* claimed the film documented the murder of an actress for sexual titillation and in doing so extended the anti-obscenity myth that pornography corrupts people and turns them into sexual deviants and depraved killers.

19 Rider McDowell, "Movies To Die For," *San Francisco Chronicle* (7 August 1994) This World section: 9.
20 Citizens for Decent Literature was founded in 1956 but in 1962 it became 'Citizens for Decent Literature and Motion Pictures' and in the early 1970s it changed its name to Citizens For Decency Under the Law. However, despite the changes it maintained the acronym CDL.
21 Mondo films are usually feature-length films that invariably promise to show authentic footage of unusual or shocking events, mainly pertaining to sex or violence, from around the world. In Mondo a narrator that is rarely reliable usually guides the film's viewers through the unfamiliar and disjointed material. The films try to justify themselves by claiming to be educational, but they rarely are. The popularity of *Mondo Cane* gave the genre its name, spawned numerous imitators, and created a wave of pseudo-documentaries that exploited public ignorance and curiosity while satisfying a thirst for sex and violence. For a detailed discussion of Mondo films see Mark Goodall *Sweet & Savage: The World Through the Shockumentary Film Lens*, Headpress, London, 2006.

As an idea, 'snuff' would not have been be so outrageous if it referred exclusively to a murder caught on film. In documenting events for educational and informative purposes television and Mondo movies had already shown that was possible. However, murder as the climax of a pornographic film, done purely for entertainment, was a shocking idea and an awful comment on the moral standard of American society. Allan Shackleton exploited public curiosity and aroused the anger of militant feminists in his advertising campaign for *Snuff*, in the same way as the pioneering '40 Thieves' exploited the conservative sexual morality of the 1950s and sixties to sell films. His campaign was a success primarily because of the protest by women's groups that drew more attention than the advertisements, making *Snuff* the most controversial film of the decade.

The term 'snuff', as a euphemism for death, had existed in the English language for more than 100 years, but in the 1960s it received new and disturbing prominence.[22] In newspaper reporting of the Manson Family murders, allegations circulated in the tabloid press that some of the killings had been filmed as part of a cult ritual, and the rumour became firmly embedded in popular culture. According to Sgt. Don Smyth (LAPD vice squad) the idea of 'snuff' films originated during the investigation into the Tate-LaBianca murders in 1969 when "The media was mistakenly informed that the Manson people had taken home movies of the murders." The press used the term 'snuff film' to describe these supposed films and the name stuck.[23] Ed Sanders embellished the idea of 'snuff' films in his sensationalized Manson exposé *The Family* (1971) to include ritualistic murders with sexual elements, and Smyth also noted "The present-day connotation — the idea of filming an unsuspecting actress' murder with the intent to distribute commercially — that was added later."[24] This was an elaboration created by anti-obscenity activists CDL.

In the early 1970s Raymond Gauer, national spokesman of the prominent anti-obscenity organisation CDL, expanded the definition

---

22 Paul Beale dates the phrase 'snuff it' as a euphemism for 'to die' to the late nineteenth century. Paul Beale (Ed.), *A Dictionary of Slang and Unconventional English*, Routledge and Kegan Paul, London, 1984: 1107.
23 Smyth quoted in McDowell, "Movies To Die For," *San Francisco Chronicle* (7 August 1994) This World section: 8.
24 Smyth quoted in ibid.

of the term 'snuff' to suit his own political agenda when he used it as a reference to a specific type of pornographic film with explicit sex scenes where an unsuspecting actress was actually murdered on screen as the film's climax. If 'snuff' movies really existed, as he claimed, then no one could doubt that permissiveness in American society had reached the nadir of decadence. It would also be impossible to deny that national values had been corrupted to the extent that in the pursuit of individual freedom and self-realisation people had turned away from traditional values and religion and instead used drugs and watched pornographic films. His rhetoric was repeated in speeches, articles and mass mailed fundraising letters for CDL, even prompting an FBI investigation. The term resurfaced in newspaper reports late in 1975, a few months prior to the release of *Snuff,* and was further adapted and promoted by militant feminists during the 1970s and eighties as evidence of the amoral and exploitative adult film industry.

The debate around *Snuff* magnified an existing piece of propaganda into a moral panic and eventually into an urban legend. As a consequence it developed into a contentious symbolic topic of debate, often used by moral conservatives and militant feminists in their rhetoric. In *Killing for Culture* (1993) David Kerekes and David Slater note the paradox, "Snuff as a commercial commodity is a fascinating, but illogical concept. It reads well in crime fiction and, from the journalistic angle, it is one of the all-time great moral panics to feed the people; a malleable and terrifying superstition."[25] But, in practical terms, it is absurd. The surrounding panic primarily benefited conservative politicians and anti-obscenity activists, whilst a number of filmmakers exploited the possibility that 'snuff' films exist.

It is not a coincidence that when 'snuff' movies are discussed it always in relation to heterosexual pornography, never gay porn. Anti-obscenity activists such as CDL were obsessed by the corruption of young men by pornography, turning them into deviants, rapists and murderers who attacked vulnerable women, a cherished icon in conservative America and one that was sure to attract sympathy and support. Beginning with the idea that all pornography is abusive to women, 'snuff' movies were, to CDL and militant feminists, the logical

25 David Kerekes and David Slater, *Killing for Culture: An Illustrated History of Death in Film from Mondo to Snuff*, Annihilation Press, 1993: 310.

consequence of the industry and the ultimate example of woman hating. In fact, no one had obtained, or even seen, such a film. The idea of 'snuff' is the idea of pornography taken to an extreme, an embodiment of a breakdown in social values where real explicit sex and violence are presented solely for the purpose of entertainment. The panic surrounding 'snuff' films had philosophical implications for American culture, where everything is a commodity in the economic market. When everything is for sale, the only question is — 'at what price?'

Above: George Putnam illustrates
Perversion for Profit

Chapter One

PERVERSION FOR PROFIT

Citizens for Decent Literature and
the Crusade against Porn

THE STORY OF 'SNUFF' MOVIES BEGAN ALMOST TWO DECADES BEFORE THE American bicentennial with the establishment of the anti-obscenity organisation Citizens for Decent Literature Inc. (CDL) in staunchly conservative Cincinnati, Ohio, by Charles H. Keating Jr. on 1 November 1958. Reflecting on the entrenched traditionalism that kept the city of Cincinnati lagging behind the rest of the nation, Mark Twain allegedly said, "I'd like to be in Cincinnati when the world ends, because it will happen ten years later there."[1] Decades later Larry Flynt and his supporters described Cincinnati as "The state where the dumb come to die." Even in the 1970s, it was a reactionary stronghold.[2]

According to one version of the story, while attending the Milford Retreat for Catholic men in 1956 Charles H. Keating Jr., a former Navy pilot, lawyer, businessman, champion swimmer and family man with six children, was asked by Reverend Nicholas Gelin, along with an FBI agent, a business executive, and two rug salesmen who shared the same beliefs, to do something about the "filth flooding our newsstands."[3] However, in an article for the *Nation* (5 July 1965) Norman Mark recounts a different version of Keating's reason for becoming an anti-obscenity activist. Taken from a CDL pamphlet, Mark's story describes how one day in 1956 Keating saw some boys at a newsstand looking at magazines featuring nude women and abnormal sexual behaviour, prompting him into action.[4] Whatever the reason, Keating accepted

---

1   Twain quoted in Michael Binstein and Charles Bowden, *Trust Me: Charles Keating and the Missing Billions*, Random House, New York, 1993: 78. There is some doubt about whether the comment was made by Twain. Kim A. McDonald, "Many of Mark Twain's Famed Humorous Sayings Are Found to Have Been Misattributed to Him," *Chronicle of Higher Education* (Sept. 4, 1991), A8.
2   Larry Flynt, *An Unseemly Man*, Bloomsbury, London, 1997: 127.
3   Keating quoted in Binstein and Bowden, *Trust Me*: 87.
4   Norman Mark, "The Anonymous Smut Hunters," *Nation* (5 July 1965): 5. In *Catholic Digest*

the moral responsibility and became active, giving talks about the dangers obscenity posed to American society. On the way to his first big anti-obscenity talk Keating went to a cigar store and bought $50 of adult books and magazines to use as examples of the $500 million porn industry. His first direct action against pornography came when he participated in a raid on a small candy store owned by an elderly woman. Emphasising the store's proximity to a school to justify the arrest he noted that the shop also sold sex toys. During the trial Keating, as the prosecuting attorney, even used 'expert' witnesses to prove that obscene materials were harmful and the old woman was convicted, fined $100 but, most important, publicly shamed.[5] For Keating public displays of morality were *essential*.

The significance of CDL is largely unacknowledged by historians and the organisation's influence on American culture largely unappreciated. Linking the sectarian Catholic groups and the anti-Communists of the Old Right with the broader conservative ideology of the New Right, CDL created a continuum in right-wing politics. Whitney Strub gauged the organisation's influence and importance saying, "CDL taught modern conservatives how to profit from perversion by playing off public ignorance and fear and how to harness that fear for political gain. In doing so, CDL helped foster a transformative shift from which American politics has yet to recover."[6]

When Keating incorporated Citizens for Decent Literature he urged the public to read classics, not smut. The same day the organisation was established, CDL put on workshops for police, prosecutors and clergy from fifteen states on how to tackle obscenity.[7] From then on Keating was never one to miss a chance to lecture on his favourite subject

---

(January 1963) Keating identified CDL's origin as being in the Jesuit retreat but when testifying before the congressional Hearings on *The Mailing of Obscene Matter* (1958) he reported that the creation of CDL stemmed from a meeting in Autumn 1955 where a small group of businessmen identified a problem and decided on a course of action. Intending to network with civic, religious and fraternal organisations they aimed to create an "aroused public opinion" and ensure that existing obscenity laws were enforced. Whitney Strub, "Perversion for Profit: Citizens For Decent Literature and the Arousal of an Antiporn Public in the 1960s," *Journal of the History of Sexuality* 15:2 (May 2006): 265. The only certainty is that Keating altered the story of CDL's origin depending on his audience so he could tell them what they wanted to hear.

5   Binstein and Bowden, *Trust Me*: 87.
6   Strub, "Perversion for Profit," *Journal of the History of Sexuality* 15:2 (May 2006): 265.
7   Binstein and Bowden, *Trust Me*: 87–88.

whenever the opportunity arose. By February 1959 CDL had attracted the attention of 500 communities who requested information and a meeting was convened in Cincinnati to appoint a steering committee aimed at establishing a national organisation.[8]

At a national level like-minded politicians aware of the value of anti-obscenity rhetoric voiced similar concerns to CDL. In 1959 Representative Kathryn E. Granahan (Democrat, Pennsylvania), chair of a House Post Office subcommittee, called for a nationwide campaign by "decent-minded citizens," to take action against "smut and filth." She asserted, "The peddling of smut to children is a heinous crime that must be stopped," but that in many instances communities "are seemingly unaware of the size and seriousness of this problem."[9] This sentiment was echoed a few months later by Keating at the ninth annual communion breakfast for Roman Catholic employees of Best & Co. at the Waldorf Astoria, where he condemned juvenile delinquency and traced its roots to newsstands where "cancerously filthy literature" was freely available.[10] Still a local, or at best regional, organisation CDL needed to expand its membership to become a nationwide force with political influence. The word 'smut' is synonymous with 'obscenity' but in CDL speeches and publications Keating emphasised the use of the latter, and words like 'pornography,' because they carried legal connotations. *Printed Poison* (1960) clearly demonstrated the legalistic vocabulary used by Keating when he said, "I don't know what smut means, and I don't think anyone else does either," but 'obscenity' and 'pornography' were used because they "occur in the law."[11]

Despite the superficial authority derived from the language used, from the outset there were serious problems with the claims made by CDL because they were usually based on speculative estimates

8   "War on Smut begun by a Citizens Group," *New York Times* (26 February 1959): 33. The committee was composed of Mrs C.R. Addington (Coral Gables, Florida), Robert Bowers (Memphis), Mrs. Walter A. Craig (Philadelphia), James M. Flanagan (St. Louis), Mrs. John B. Hoffman (St. Paul), Leo C. Renaud (Boston), Paul S. Rose (Salt Lake City), Sherman Titens (Cleveland), and Robert Foy and Charles Keating (Cincinnati).
9   "Pornography Scored," *New York Times* (19 May 1959): 18.
10   "Crime Laid to Reading Fare," *New York Times* (28 September 1959): 34.
11   Keating quoted in Strub, "Perversion for Profit," *Journal of the History of Sexuality* 15:2 (May 2006): 267. Strub also notes that CDL literature and rhetoric appropriated a sexual vocabulary from pornography, repeatedly calling for an 'aroused' public, to support their crusade. Strub, "Perversion for Profit," *Journal of the History of Sexuality* 15:2 (May 2006): 261–262.

about the size of the pornography business. Postmaster General Arthur Summerfield estimated that pornography was a $500 million a year industry. However, CDL assumed he was only talking about adult materials sent through the mail so they doubled his estimate to include non-mailed items and used the figure of $1 billion in their speeches and literature. Soon Summerfield began quoting the CDL figure of $1 billion, citing them as an authority. But when CDL saw Summerfield estimating $1 billion, assuming once more that it was only for adult materials in the mails, they doubled it again, arriving at a figure of $2 billion. If the $2 billion estimate were true then every family in America would have to spend $50 annually buying porn — a substantial expenditure in 1950s society. In contrast Peter Jennison, executive director of the National Book Committee, estimated that the pornography business was worth about $25 million annually.[12] Keating claimed his statistics came from an estimate of how much the gross annual intake for pornographic films was (in the US and Canada), and then added in his estimate of the purchase of adult books and magazines. What his estimates are based on is unclear but, when he added his two estimates, he came up with a figure of $2 billion.[13] Despite the obviously unscientific approach of the CDL estimates they were frequently cited as authoritative and helped legitimise anti-obscenity crusades across America.

The case of *Samuel Roth v. United States* (24 June 1957) was a legal watershed, with the Supreme Court setting new standards for obscenity prosecutions that would cause debate for more than a decade. Samuel Roth, the accused, operated a business in New York City, publishing books, magazines and photographs, and the twenty-six charges brought against him were based on circulars used to advertise his products. He was convicted on four counts of violating federal obscenity statutes.[14]

Writing the majority decision affirming Roth's conviction, Justice William J. Brennan acknowledged "sex and obscenity are not

12 Edwin A. Roberts Jr., *The Smut Rakers: A Report In Depth On Obscenity and the Censors*, The National Observer, Silver Spring, Maryland, 1966: 116.

13 Ibid: 117.

14 The prosecution of obscene material was a relatively recent legal development. In Britain the *Obscene Publications Act* (1857) gave courts the power to seize and destroy offending materials by making the sale of such material a statutory offence, but it did not define 'obscenity'. It was in the case of *R. v. Hicklin* (1868) that a test for obscenity was proposed. The 'Hicklin Test', as it was known, identified that objectionable material was obscene because it tended to 'deprave and corrupt'. The same subjective test was applied in American courts.

synonymous" and asserted "Obscene material is material which deals with sex in a manner appealing to prurient interest." This was a crucial distinction to make. He added "Sex, a great and mysterious motive force in human life, has indisputably been a subject of absorbing interest to mankind through the ages; it is one of the vital problems of human interest and public concern." Brennan referred to the Supreme Court decision in *Thornhill v. Alabama* (1940), which stated "The freedom of speech and of the press guaranteed by the Constitution embraces at the least the liberty to discuss publicly and truthfully all matters of public concern without previous restraint or fear of subsequent punishment," and that "Freedom of discussion, if it would fulfil its historic function in this nation, must embrace all issues about which information is needed or appropriate to enable the members of society to cope with the exigencies of their period." He also referred to the instructions given by the judge in the original Roth trial, who directed the jury,

> The test is not whether it would arouse sexual desires or sexual impure thoughts in those comprising a particular segment of the community, the young, the immature or the highly prudish or would leave another segment, the scientific or highly educated or the so-called worldly-wise and sophisticated indifferent and unmoved.

The test was to be based on the perception of the average person, thereby establishing the idea of a national standard by which contentious material might be judged. The test, which became known as the Roth Test for obscenity, states:

> The test in each case is the effect of the book, picture or publication considered as a whole, not upon any particular class, but upon all those whom it is likely to reach. In other words, you determine its impact upon the average person in the community. The books, pictures and circulars must be judged as a whole, in their entire context, and you are not to consider detached or separate portions in reaching a conclusion. You judge the circulars, pictures and publications which have been put in evidence by present-day standards of the community. You may ask yourselves does it offend the common conscience of the community by present-day standards.

Concurring with the majority decision Chief Justice Earl Warren acknowledged that the "line dividing the salacious or pornographic from literature or science is not straight and unwavering." He went on:

> The conduct of the defendant is the central issue, not the obscenity of a book or picture. The nature of the materials is, of course, relevant as an attribute of the defendant's conduct, but the materials are thus placed in context from which they draw colour and character. A wholly different result might be reached in a different setting.

Because Roth was obviously "plainly engaged in the commercial exploitation of the morbid and shameful craving for materials with prurient effect," Warren believed the conviction was correct, and that "State and Federal Governments *can* constitutionally punish such conduct." (Emphasis added.) This was an opinion from which anti-obscenity crusaders took great encouragement.

Justice William O. Douglas dissented from the Court's decision because he believed that the Roth Test

> gives the censor free range over a vast domain. To allow the State to step in and punish mere speech or publication that the judge or the jury thinks has an undesirable impact on thoughts but that is not shown to be a part of unlawful action is drastically to curtail the First Amendment.

He was not convinced by the rhetoric of conservative moralists and challenged their basic assertion because "it is by no means clear that obscene literature, as so defined, is a significant factor in influencing substantial deviations from the community standards." Despite the rhetoric of politicians and anti-obscenity crusaders, no definitive link between obscene literature and deviance had been established. Douglas also noted, with considerable irony, that

> When those who know so much about the problem of delinquency among youth — the very group about whom the advocates of censorship are most concerned — conclude that what delinquents read has so little effect upon their conduct that it is *not* worth investigating in an exhaustive study of causes, there is good reason for serious doubt

concerning the basic hypothesis on which obscenity censorship is defended. (Emphasis added.)

Believing that the "common conscience of the community" standard was in conflict with the First Amendment protections for freedom of speech and that the standard set would not be acceptable to the American people if it were applied to other areas such as religion, economics, politics or philosophy, Douglas asked "How does it become a constitutional standard when literature treating with sex is concerned?" He was not in favour of selectively applying the First Amendment and for the rest of his career on the Supreme Court Douglas remained an advocate of free expression, and a determined opponent of censorship.

While the legal definition of obscenity was vague and open to interpretation, technological developments provided new opportunities for the developing adult entertainment industry. Alongside the publication of adult materials in printed form, in the late 1950s 8mm film equipment became a popular format and during the next decade portable projectors revived the stag movie. By the end of the 1960s pornographic films had discovered a new popularity.[15] The people who made pornographic loops were usually small-scale businessmen who had little money. They would entice whoever they could, using money, drugs or by appealing to a kinky sense of sexual adventure, to appear in their films. Performers, sometimes underage, were hired as cheaply as possible to keep costs down because the producers did not expect to make a large profit.[16] The popularity of 8mm adult film loops both added a new dimension to the obscenity debate and paved the way for full-length adult feature films.

Each new technology presented a fresh challenge to CDL, but the rigid morality espoused by the organisation ensured that, despite lacking any scientific evidence and in sharp contrast with Justice Douglas, CDL were determined believers in the corrupting effect of pornography. The organisation set criteria for membership and screened applicants, who had to be over twenty-five years of age

15   Joseph W. Slade, "Violence in the Hard-Core Pornographic Film," *Journal of Communication* (Summer 1984): 160.
16   John B. McConahay, "Pornography: The Symbolic Politics of Fantasy," *Law and Contemporary Problems* (v.51 No.1, 1988): 64.

and have family and church affiliations. CDL also sought people who could "handle such [explicit] material over an extended period of time without being adversely affected."[17]

In their self-appointed role as moral guardians CDL read and viewed pornographic materials that were analysed and summarized before being made available to prosecutors and legislators. This meant that it would be possible for CDL staff members to indulge in their own smutty interests while sanctioned by their job to do so, and then hypocritically condemn the same materials to maintain their respectability.[18] Charles Keating owned an extensive collection of pornography that he used as evidence in the course of his crusade. To shock his audience he would display his most exotic and sensational material. When one journalist tried to interview him, Keating produced some colour pictures of women having sex with pigs, his latest imports from Denmark.[19]

CDL chapters were active in cities across America in the late 1950s and early 1960s but grassroots protests were often out of line with official CDL rhetoric and it was evident that the headquarters had little or no control over the local chapters.[20] Possibly as a consequence, in the 1960s CDL tried to focus their membership, aiming to attract only those who were committed. Hangers-on were rejected, ironically because Keating was concerned that a citizens' movement could attract fanatics and earn his organisation a bad name.[21] Keating admired J. Edgar Hoover, a national symbol of law enforcement, and wrote to the FBI Director (16 September 1960) asking him to address a CDL meeting scheduled for February 1961, but Hoover was advised to decline.[22] The FBI Director was reluctant to associate himself with CDL because Keating had previously come to the attention of the FBI

---

17 David Corn, "Dirty Bookkeeping," *New Republic* (2 April 1990): 14. See also Binstein and Bowden, *Trust Me*: 95–96

18 Flynt, *An Unseemly Man*: 123.

19 Binstein and Bowden, *Trust Me*: 120. Ironically, according to Binstein and Bowden, in the basement of the FBI headquarters in Washington there was a screening room where Hoover and his colleague Clyde Tolson would retire to watch pornographic films. Because of FBI seizures the selection of films available to Hoover would be almost limitless. Binstein and Bowden, *Trust Me*: 92. Postmaster general Arthur Summerfield also kept a library of obscene materials that he used to demonstrate to the press and politicians the need for stronger anti-smut laws. Roberts Jr., *The Smut Rakers*: 63.

20 Strub, "Perversion for Profit," *Journal of the History of Sexuality* 15:2 (May 2006): 276.

21 Roberts Jr., *The Smut Rakers*: 103.

22 Binstein and Bowden, *Trust Me*: 90–91.

when, in 1956, he was legal representative of Research Laboratories of Colorado Inc., a company that submitted a fraudulent application to get access to Atomic Energy Commission information.[23] The resulting investigation did not lead to charges being brought even though the Cincinnati office seriously considered the possibility. A few years later Keating wrote to Hoover (28 August 1963) requesting copies of a child molester poster but as a consequence of the earlier investigation the FBI was reluctant to give CDL any support.[24]

When CDL did incorporate other anti-obscenity crusaders specific requirements had to be met. For example, when in January 1966 F. Michael O'Brien's 'Operation Cleansweep' was granted chapter status by CDL, O'Brien began paring down the membership to a core group, in line with CDL practices. Despite this the organisation's mailing list in the mid 1960s was reported to contain almost 6,000 names.[25]

Keating described the CDL strategy, saying

what we would like to see is just a handful of very dedicated people who are able to communicate with the community the sense of our objectives. It is a very simple concept: To arrest, prosecute, and convict those who are committing the crime of selling obscenity.[26]

However, the obscenity issue was much more complicated than Keating would acknowledge, and subject to politically motivated misuse.

Local organisations were often too zealous in their rhetoric and actions, generating bad publicity and tarnishing the reputation of CDL. Despite the screening processes for membership there were also blatantly political misuses of the obscenity issue. In 1963 two CDL members in California, Assemblyman E. Richard Barnes and Superintendent of Schools Max Rafferty, opposed Wentworth and Flexner's *Dictionary of American Slang* (1960), a serious reference work, which Rafferty condemned as "a practicing handbook of sexual

---

23 Ibid: 86. Ironically the FBI investigation into Research Laboratories of Colorado coincided with Keating's attendance at the Milford Retreat where he claimed to have been asked to address the problem of smut.
24 Ibid: 91, 89. See also Stephen Pizzo, "Keating's Trouble With the Government Began Back in fifties," *National Mortgage News* (18 November 1991): 10.
25 Roberts Jr., *The Smut Rakers*: 102.
26 Keating quoted in ibid: 102.

perversion."[27] Keating tried to distance CDL from Rafferty's claims, stating that his organisation had no part in the incident: "I think that in their official capacities they would be justified in looking at the book if it tends to negate culture or education. But this is quite different from a CDL action."[28] Rafferty's objections were probably designed to embarrass a political opponent; however, the controversy did not adversely affect the book, and in fact it helped double the sales,[29] which raised questions about the effects of CDL's anti-obscenity crusade.

While Rafferty focused on condemning one book for his own political gain Keating was making his contribution to a more general conservative crusade against obscenity in American society. The threat was articulated by a number of prominent figures and was consistently emphasised as a serious challenge to the national morality, especially to the young. In his "Demoralization of Youth" article in *Christianity Today* (6 July 1959) Yale sociologist Pitrim Sorokin alleged,

some 50 million pieces of obscene advertising annually mailed mainly towards teenagers in the $500 million-a-year pornographic business in this country certainly contribute a tangible share to the growth of juvenile delinquency, to the too early and too erotic sexual life of the 'wild' portion of our youth and the cultist cynicism, vandalism, and sterile rebellion of our beatniks.[30]

A few months later, in the *Law Enforcement Bulletin* (January 1960), FBI Director J. Edgar Hoover emphatically concurred:

The time for half-hearted oblique action against depravity is past. Although this despicable trade reaps $500,000,000 a year, this diabolical business is costing the nation much more than money. It is robbing our country and particularly our younger generation of decency — it is a seedbed for delinquency among juveniles and depravity among all ages.[31]

27 Rafferty quoted in ibid: 29.
28 Keating quoted in ibid: 104.
29 Ibid: 30–31.
30 Sorokin quoted in Estes Kefauver, "Obscene and Pornographic Literature and Juvenile Delinquency," *Federal Probation* 24 (1960): 6. Sorokin later became a CDL member.
31 Hoover quoted in "FBI Chief Urges Drive to Bar Smut," *New York Times* (2 January 1960):

Hoover continued his polemic, declaring "This truly shocking and shameful state of affairs is made even more deplorable by the knowledge that sex crimes and obscene literature often go hand in hand."[32] Neither Keating, Hoover, or Sorokin had any evidence to support their claims but they continued making public statements and asserting their opinions as fact.

As part of the Subcommittee to investigate juvenile delinquency in the 1950s Senator Estes Kefauver became aware, while investigating the presumed link between crime and horror comics, that young people could purchase obscene material.[33] Subcommittee members were concerned by what they saw as the increasing sadism, masochism and fetishism in pornography, and "Many witnesses felt that torture, maiming and killing have been tragic consequences." Anti-obscenity crusaders continually made the accusation that sexual deviance would lead to murder. The portrayal of abnormal sexual behaviour as normal, the Subcommittee felt, would "diminish the chances of impressionable young people to form socially desirable attitudes which would carry over into maturity."[34] Kefauver singled out pornographers that produced sadomasochistic material as "particularly noxious" because they were operating *within* the law.[35] Dr William P. Riley, the vice president of CDL, claimed that the court system catered to "a vociferous minority" while ignoring anti-obscenity activists.[36] A few years later he condemned opponents of CDL as "homegrown leftists" naming publisher Ralph Ginzburg, psychologist Dr Albert Ellis, Hugh Hefner and the ACLU as "people who want to destroy the Judeo-

---

25. Hoover claimed playing cards, films, magazines, comic books and other pornographic products constituted obscene and vulgar literature.

32 Hoover quoted in ibid: 25.

33 Kefauver, "Obscene and Pornographic Literature and Juvenile Delinquency," *Federal Probation* 24 (1960): 5. In 1950 Senator Estes Kefauver (Democrat, Tennessee) was chairman of the committee hearings on organized crime that moved to Chicago, but left after only a few days of secret meetings. Years later it was alleged that Kefauver fled the city because Sidney R. Korshak, a labour lawyer and business advisor to several large corporations with ties to organized crime, was reported to have in his possession infra-red photographs of Kefauver in a compromising position with a young woman. The Chicago Mafia had supplied the woman to Korshak, and the camera planted in a room at the Drake Hotel. Seymour Hersh, "The Contrasting Lives of Sidney R. Korshak," *New York Times* (27 June 1976): 20.

34 Ibid: 9.

35 Ibid: 6.

36 "Stiffer Smut Laws Urged At Forum," *New York Times* (14 May 1961): 62.

Christian concepts upon which the world has been built."[37]

The big profits and small penalties were identified by Kefauver as an attraction for entrepreneurs entering the porn business, and he emphasised that traffickers sometimes enticed "young boys and girls" to pose for pictures or perform in films. Describing the participants as criminals, he noted that they were attracted because of a "large and eager market, the lure of extremely high profits, and the knowledge that weak, ineffective laws will allow [them] to escape with a short sentence or pitifully small fines."[38] The weak sentences and minor financial risks were,

> a major factor in opening the floodgates for a $½ billion annual mail-order business in all kinds of filthy and vile books and photographs, motion pictures, and other material not fit to come into the American home. No avenue of commerce is free from this illegal traffic and the United States mails, as the greatest communication system in the world, has been fastened on by the purveyors of filth to an unbelievable extent.[39]

Faced with an ever-increasing threat from porn, Kefauver believed that the American public had to be alerted and mobilized to fight against degeneracy and reassert traditional values.

Use of the word 'citizens' suggests a grassroots populist movement, but CDL was comprised of a mixture of middle-class and professional occupations that was reflected in the organisation's naïve but elitist rhetoric. CDL stated publicly that it did *not* want to arouse public opinion on the subject of obscenity;[40] rather, the emphasis for motivation was put on "a firm and now confirmed belief in the basic Judeo-Christian principles upon which this Nation was founded and by which most of its people live; a belief, in short, in the Constitution of the United States."[41] This was in sharp contrast to the beliefs of Justice Douglas

---

37 "Head of Anti-Smut Group Castigates 'Leftist' Foes," *New York Times* (16 March 1964): 63.
38 Kefauver, "Obscene and Pornographic Literature and Juvenile Delinquency," *Federal Probation* 24 (1960): 4.
39 Ibid: 6.
40 Roberts Jr., *The Smut Rakers*: 101–102.
41 Richard Kyle-Keith, *The High Price of Pornography*, Public Affairs Press, Washington, D.C., 1961: 90.

in *Roth* (1957), who gave the First Amendment full support and took a positive view of the general public when he asserted "I have the same confidence in the ability of our people to reject noxious literature as I have in their capacity to sort out the true from the false in theology, economics, politics, or any other field." For all of its populist rhetoric, elitist ideology and promotion of middle-class morality, CDL was the most effective pressure group "largely because it knows how to lean on local prosecutors and because its leaders know the law,"[42] and despite claims to the contrary, CDL rhetoric was always intended to shock and outrage.

Initially CDL addressed members of influential religious and civic organisations in the Cincinnati area, making them aware that pornographic magazines were available in the locality, not just in large cities like New York and Los Angeles. Once pornography was established as a pertinent social and political issue the religious and civic groups would co-operate with CDL.[43] Speakers from CDL emphasised that the war on obscene material was a fight for God and traditional American values, and against Communism. In his speeches Charles Keating called CDL a religious crusade and claimed

> The question posed by this onslaught of evil is not one involving freedom or censorship. The question is the survival of Judeo-Christian civilization. If the decent citizens of this nation continue lethargic and apathetic in the face of this pernicious enemy, the families of Western Civilization will live under the anarchy of the libertine, and 'the plum soon thereafter will become ripe for plucking' by Communism.[44]

CDL's methods were very successful. Using pamphlets, circulars, newsletters, talks by guest speakers, and *The Accused*, a Loretta Young TV show, to promote their ideas, the organisation quickly attracted national attention.[45] Before congressional hearings on the Mailing of Obscene Matter (1958), Keating reiterated his warning that pornography was "capable of poisoning any mind at any age and of

42 Roberts Jr., *The Smut Rakers*: 101.
43 Kyle-Keith, *The High Price of Pornography*: 90.
44 Keating quoted in Mark, "The Anonymous Smut Hunters," *Nation* (5 July 1965): 6.
45 Kyle-Keith, *The High Price of Pornography*: 91.

perverting our entire younger generation."[46]

To promote the organisation's ideas CDL produced a number of one-off publications in the early 1960s, such as *Criminal Obscenity Convictions in Which United States Supreme Court has Denied Review, 1957–1958* (1960), *Fight Newsstand Filth: The Law is Your Weapon* (1960), and *Printed Poison: A Community Problem* (1960). The organisation also published two regular newsletters, *Vanguard: Young Adults Newsletter* and the *National Decency Reporter* (from 1963–1985). In 1962, during an appeal against an obscenity conviction for Henry Miller's *Tropic of Cancer,* CDL distributed a pamphlet containing what they considered to be the nineteen most offensive passages from the novel. Defence attorney Elmer Getz noted the paradox "This pamphlet, which was supposed to show how bad the book was, had no plot, no redeeming qualities. While fighting pornography, CDL had actually created a piece of pornography."[47]

In 1962 CDL became a national organisation, and two years later it claimed 200 chapters, growing to 300 by 1965. However, the organisation never clearly stated what constituted a 'chapter'. It could be 100 people, all of whom were active in an anti-obscenity campaign, or a solitary individual involved in a letter writing campaign.[48] At the same time, CDL had three mechanisms to remove the organisation's dependency on grassroots activism. The first was the *National Decency Reporter* magazine, which was distributed across America; secondly the series of public service films produced to raise awareness of the threat of pornography; and finally the *amicus curiae* briefs submitted to the Supreme Court that focused CDL activities on legal change. The organisation's leadership took control and established a single unified voice but stifled any opportunity for debate within CDL.[49]

As a national organisation CDL provided information and assistance to local groups and organized symposiums to share their concerns about pornography. One of the ways they dealt with problems was to organize letter-writing campaigns,[50] a tactic aggressively exploited throughout

46   Keating quoted in Eric Schlosser, *Reefer Madness and Other Tales from the American Underground*, Allan Lane, London, 2003: 132.
47   Mark, "The Anonymous Smut Hunters," *Nation* (5 July 1965): 6–7.
48   Ibid: 5.
49   Strub, "Perversion for Profit," *Journal of the History of Sexuality* 15:2 (May 2006): 277.
50   Louis A. Zucher Jr. and R. George Kirkpatrick, *Citizens For Decency: Antipornography Crusades*

the 1960s and 1970s to raise funds. Letters from CDL members to city officials condemning the effects of pornography ranged from a polite 'thank you', in anticipation of subsequent criminal prosecutions, to hate mail. Many of the letters were written by CDL youth group members and warned of the dangers posed by pornography, even though the organisation asserted no one in the youth group would be exposed to obscene materials.[51]

Behind the dogmatic anti-obscenity rhetoric CDL employed more sophisticated legal logic. In the *Nation* Norman Mark noted that the organisation was

> against 'smut', but prints no lists or guidelines for merchants — thus avoiding charges of prior restraint. It is for legal action, but tries hard not to become a party with the prosecution — thus avoiding costly countersuits. It says it is against boycotts, although it has been frequently accused of suggesting them at meetings of the membership. It is for orderly judicial processes, although it has been accused of trying to influence judges and prosecutors by such tactics as letter writing and courtroom packing.[52]

While the tactics used by CDL were contentious, and of dubious legality, they were undoubtedly effective.

Directed by Keating, CDL rhetoric appealed to the anti-communist sympathies of conservative Americans, not generally known for being interested in social issues, expanding the organisation's audience. In January 1958, while appearing before the Judiciary Committee to testify about the threat posed to American society by pornographers mailing obscene matter, Keating claimed that every act of juvenile delinquency was a consequence of pornography and, furthermore, that the increasing availability of obscene material was part of a Communist plot to destroy America. Keating explained to the Committee that the plan was "to print and deposit for mailing and delivery obscene, lewd, lascivious, and filthy books." To him the reason for this strategy was clear: "The enemies of our country recognize the effects of

---

as *Status Defence*, University of Texas Press, Austin and London, 1976: 43–44.
51 Mark, "The Anonymous Smut Hunters," *Nation* (5 July 1965): 5.
52 Ibid.

pornography upon our country and our youth." During the hearings he even expressed a desire to prosecute Grace Metalious' mainstream bestseller *Peyton Place* (1956).[53] However, many Americans did not see the threat immoral literature posed.

The following year Keating travelled to Chicago (15 October 1959) to give a speech in which he again exaggerated the threat of pornography. He warned, "If, God willing … your child escapes direct contact with the pernicious influence in the minds of this junk … he still will be exposed to the evil influences in the minds and breasts of his companions."[54] Keating thus encouraged insecurity and paranoia amongst those who already accepted the threat of smut. Addressing children, Keating endorsed chastity, denounced pornography, and explained how Communists were trying to use obscene materials to undermine American morals and values. To dramatize his ideas he wove sensational and shocking homilies into his speeches. One such story, which he told to high school girls in Cincinnati, recounted an incident involving a young mother run down by a car as she crossed a street pushing her baby in a pram. The cause of the accident, according to Keating, was the Bermuda shorts worn by the young woman, and the sight of her exposed legs distracted the driver's attention. At the end of his talk he requested that all of the girls make a pledge never to wear Bermuda shorts.[55] In 1964 Keating addressed students at Highland High School (Salt Lake City) warning them "The masters of evil are here," evidenced by "various filthy material" which he had purchased earlier at a local newsstand. To highlight the danger Keating read sections from several books such as *Lesbian Lust*, *The Gay Boys* and *Sex Rampage* to the students.[56] If the children were not already familiar with pornography before his presentation, Keating made sure they were by the end of it.

CDL also arranged that youth groups only had access to the organisation's own literature and some sympathetic *Reader's Digest* articles to help reinforce their opinions, but no information that contradicted the CDL agenda or questioned censorship.[57] Speeches

---

53 Keating quoted in Binstein and Bowden, *Trust Me*: 87–88.
54 Keating quoted in ibid: 94.
55 Ibid: 95.
56 Corn, "Dirty Bookkeeping," *New Republic* (2 April 1990): 14.
57 Roberts Jr., *The Smut Rakers*: 105–106.

written by members of CDL youth groups conscientiously recited the organisation's ideology and distorted FBI statistics, which indicated ever-increasing crime levels, along with claims of increases in illegitimate births and an upsurge in venereal disease,[58] all of which emphasised a decline in morality. A member of CDL Youth delivered a speech entitled "Happiness" which read:

> Happiness is a new book, with shining brightly colored pictures.
> Obscenity is hot clammy hands ripping furiously through pages of death.
> Happiness is a new baby brother.
> Obscenity is a baby with only a mother.
> Happiness is a child's imagination — tall giants and puddles with rainbows.
> Obscenity is a perverted mind with a morbid preoccupation with sex.
> Happiness is a boyfriend that you introduce to your parents.
> Obscenity is a guy that you meet on the street corner.
> Happiness is joy, life, love.
> Obscenity is distortion, exploitation, death.[59]

Simplistic and naïve, the speech reflects the conservative values promoted by CDL, but ignores the social changes that were ongoing in a constantly changing nation.

At least one author recognised the hypocrisy of CDL and other anti-obscenity groups and published a sexually explicit satire of them. The cover of the adult novel *Youth Against Obscenity* (1965), a fictional memoir, mocked the moralistic rhetoric of many anti-obscenity youth groups that hid their decadent lifestyles. The cover text of the novel emphasised the difference between public and private behaviour, stating "in the crowded auditoriums they preached and screamed about obscenity in magazines, but on secluded beaches and mirrored bedrooms they enjoyed their sex in about every imaginable way — trading and swapping partners at will..." However, conservatives across America did not question the motives of CDL leaders or the members' private conduct. Public conduct and apocalyptic rhetoric dominated and the war against smut was the sole focus.

---

58   Ibid: 115.
59   Reproduced in ibid: 115.

CDL took over as a national moral conscience of America in 1965 when Monsignor Thomas Little announced that the Catholic League of Decency was to undergo a series of changes. The name was changed to the National Catholic Office for Motion Pictures (NCOMP) and a National Centre for Film Study was established to educate audiences. Instead of rating films NCOMP produced a monthly newsletter of reviews and presented an annual award for filmmaking.[60] In contrast, around the same time, John W. McDevitt, Supreme Knight of the Knights of Columbus and an honorary member of CDL, compared the threat 'smut' posed to the nation with the threat of Communism but concluded that pornography, eating away at the heart of American life, was the greater danger.[61]

Pennsylvania Supreme Court Justice Michael Musmanno delivered a speech at the 1965 CDL convention expressing concerns about declining standards of decency leading to a modern day Sodom and Gomorrah.[62] A few years earlier when he testified before the Subcommittee on Postal Operations in 1962 Musmanno perplexingly lamented, "I cannot understand why a ponderous problem is made of definition of words. Obscenity — how can anyone doubt what it means? And yet [the courts] go into fine legal argumentation as to what it includes, and so on."[63] For him, as a conservative moralist, what constituted 'obscenity' was obvious, but as a judge he should have recognized that obscenity, as a social construct, changes as society's values change. Musmanno's comments were later reported in the *National Decency Reporter* (November–December 1965) under the headline "Justice Musmanno electrifies decency forces in NYC." Charles Keating praised Musmanno's speech because it "held the convention spellbound with its intellectual beauty."[64]

Musmanno made extravagant allegations, such as claiming "Magazines with pictures and sketches that would disgrace oriental harems are sold to children as if they were as innocuous as bags of popcorn" — thereby corrupting the youth of America and ensuring

60   Carolyn See, *Blue Money*, David McKay and Company, New York, 1974: 159–160.
61   Roberts Jr., *The Smut Rakers*: 115.
62   Ibid: 114.
63   Musmanno quoted in *The Obscenity Report: Pornography and Obscenity in America*, Macgibbon and Kee, London, 1970: 13.
64   Keating quoted in Roberts Jr., *The Smut Rakers*. 113.

a continuing decline in moral values. He attributed blame for the availability of obscene materials to the government, through the postal service that he condemned for "running a first-class sewer" which "pipes into the purest of households, the most impeccable families, a stream of debauchery, sensuality and prurience which could contaminate and degrade even a house of assignation." Like Charles Keating, Musmanno blamed government prosecutors for the availability of obscene materials, especially district attorneys who "sit inertly on the river bank, wrapped in the ultimate contentment of their lassitude and enjoying to the fullest degree the irresponsibility of their incorruptible incompetence." This was an outrageous allegation for a judge to make, but only one of many made by Musmanno. Voicing his support for CDL and the campaign against obscenity, he declared:

> I congratulate you for participating in this great crusade to drive into oblivion the dirty-fingered authors who store their morals in the sewer, refresh their brains with ditchwater, dip their pens into the gutter and produce the imbecilic filth which is corrupting standards of decency on a scale never before known since the days of Sodom and Gomorrah.

He continued his tirade against obscene material with emotive imagery and more exaggerated rhetoric:

> I congratulate you on this crusade to drive into bankruptcy, ignominy, and, if necessary, into prison the wealth-wallowing purveyors of that filth whose dollars are stained with the tears of mothers who have seen their daughters deceived, seduced and shamed, and who have watched the[ir] sons entering on the path of licentiousness because of unholy impulses stirred by those whose only god is greed and whose motivation is avarice.[65]

Richard E. Barnes, a California assemblyman who had protested the *Dictionary of American Slang* a few years before, also addressed the conference and put the threat of obscene material into a global perspective when he said:

---

65   Musmanno quoted in ibid: 113.

Don't tremble in fear of an atomic bomb but tremble at the contemplation of Freedom's demise from this planet. Tremble at the thought of what is planned for your children and the world's children if Twentieth Century barbarism enslaves the earth's teeming millions ... we do not need to stand supinely by while these predators, and purveyors of filth infect and infest our youth.[66]

John W. McDevitt later elaborated on Barnes' claims, pointing out that the US military could defend the nation from "bombs from Peking, rockets from Moscow, or missiles from Havana," but the threat of pornography, which went largely unchallenged, threatened to teach the "sad and oft repeated lesson of history" that "in vain does a bronze shield defend the heart of a country if the innermost core of the nation's heart is eaten away by the dry rot of immorality."[67] The image of moral decline and the downfall of civilization was a regular theme in the speeches at CDL conferences; the fight against obscenity was a fight for freedom and the continuation of traditional American values.

The *Perversion for Profit* documentary (1965) produced by CDL was a clear statement of the organisation's beliefs and agenda. From the outset of the film, the presenter George Putnam, a notable TV news broadcaster in California, made his ideology clear with predictably sensational and contentious opinions presented as fact. "A floodtide of filth is engulfing our country in the form of newsstand obscenity," he warned. "It is threatening to pervert an entire generation of our American children." No matter who bought the obscene material from newsstands, between seventy-five per cent and ninety per cent ended up in the hands of children, according to Putnam, and, once corrupted, it was "practically impossible" to adjust back to 'normal' attitudes. In the course of the film Putnam repeatedly refers to "deviants" and "unnatural sex acts" and how pornography depicts abnormal practices as normal. To heighten the anxiety of parents Putnam claimed that even if children were not reading filthy literature they were constantly

---

66 Barnes quoted in ibid. 114.
67 McDevitt quoted in ibid. 115. The alternative to an open and liberal attitude towards sexuality is to repress sexual instincts and thereby make the people more productive and of greater use to the state, an idea to which, according to Wilhelm Reich in *The Sexual Revolution* (1936), Hitler was committed.

exposed to other people who were reading it. In typical CDL rhetoric he asserts:

> Never in the history of the world has the merchants of obscenity, the teachers of unnatural sex acts, had available to them the modern facilities for disseminating this filth — high speed presses, rapid transportation, mass distribution — all have combined to put the vilest obscenity within the reach of every man, woman, and child in the country.

Citing a number of professional bodies and government agencies Putman asserted that the availability of pornography was causing the moral decline in America, adding that moral decay weakened the national resistance to Communism. To reinforce the sense of urgency he claims that sixteen of the nineteen major civilizations in history vanished because of moral rot and decay.

Because it was a profitable enterprise, a $2 billion a year industry by CDL estimates, the volume of explicit material and shocking nature of the content were all escalating. Putnam exaggerated, claiming that the vast majority of material was too obscene to show or quote from and that the material in *Perversion for Profit* had to be censored. Whitney Strub noted the irony of the CDL film saying: "Whereas lurid exploitation posters often promised explicit content the films failed to supply, CDL reliably provided graphic depictions of sexuality."[68] CDL delivered in its films what the exploitation producers could not.

Trying to identify the CDL crusade with a moral majority under attack from a corrupt and deviant minority, Putnam contended:

> The nakedness, the nudity of these magazines is defended and foisted

---

68 Strub, "Perversion for Profit," *Journal of the History of Sexuality* 15:2 (May 2006): 280. The film was funded by a $40,000 donation from the Purex Co. [Raymond I. Parnas], "Obscenity regulation and enforcement in St. Louis and St. Louis County," *Washington University Law Quarterly* 98 (1968): 108. While Putnam described himself as a lifelong Democrat he maintained a very conservative stance on many issues. At a roast to celebrate Putnam's fiftieth year in broadcasting former president Richard Nixon noted his significance saying, "Some people didn't like what he said; some people liked what he said. But everyone listened to George Putnam. That is why he has been one of the most influential commentators of our times." Dennis McLellan, "George Putnam, Longtime LA newsman, dies at 94," *LA Times* (13 September 2009) online at http://www.latimes.com/news/obituaries/la-me-putnam13-2008sep13,0,210512.story

upon the people by a vociferous minority in our society. They lack the moral standards and values of our Judeo-Christian heritage. They not only oppose the principles of that heritage, which has given us our rich institutions and laws, but they advocate their overthrow.

Quoting from Pitrim Sorokin, Putnam characterized contemporary magazines on newsstands as depicting "the world as a sort of human zoo inhabited by raped, mutilated and murdered females and by he-males outmatching in bestiality cavemen, and out-lusting the lustiest of animals. Male and female alike are hardened in cynical contempt of human life and values." His distorted generalization and apocalyptic rhetoric were designed to magnify the concerns of his audience, using fear to prompt action, a hallmark of CDL campaigns.

Putnam showed examples of obscene magazines that could be bought openly on newsstands to highlight his contention that porn is misinformation that weakens the nation's youth. In the first instance, 'girly' magazines such as *Adam*, *Gent* and *Bachelor*, were reported to sell fifteen million copies per month. They featured provocative pictures of nude women in sexually suggestive poses "calculated to stimulate the reader" and, according to Putnam, encouraged breast and sodomy fetishes. 'Nudist' magazines, such as *Sundial*, *Nude Living* and *Sunshine and Health*, he contended, would not continue to be printed if they were only for nudists because there would not be sufficient demand. Continuing a practice used by CDL representatives at meetings and public talks, in *Perversion for Profit* magazines are made to look more suggestive and explicit by pasting black strips over photographs to cover the genital regions of models even if they are wearing bikinis.[69] In the most sensational claim of the film Putnam alleges that a young boy told a court that he raped and killed a five-year-old girl after being stimulated by a nudist magazine. To make matters worse, simultaneously in Washington a judge was granting a second class-mailing permit to the same nudist magazine. Increasingly severe yet unscientific accusations linking pornography to violent sex crime had already circulated for decades without substantiation. Such claims were intended to generate outcry, incite public anger, and gather

69   Mark, "The Anonymous Smut Hunters," the *Nation* (5 July 1965): 5.

support for anti-smut crusades. Exploitation entrepreneurs, always looking for an opportunity to make money, even sought to exploit anti-obscenity rhetoric in films such as *The Sinister Urge* (Ed Wood Jr., 1959). Posing as an exposé of the smut film racket, the film dramatized sensational and unfounded allegations about the corrupting influence of porn made by anti-obscenity groups. By showing adult films turning a normal young man into a ruthless sex killer terrorizing women, smut pictures were demonised as a menace to society.

Putnam described 'physique' magazines such as *Olympic Arts*, *Male Physique*, *Adonis*, and *Grecian Build Pictorial* as a "terribly sad indictment of our society." Misguided children, he argued, take them as instruction guides for body development but exposure turns young men into homosexuals, a term which Putnam spits out with venom. The magazines, he cautioned, also lead on to other deviances such as transvestism, sadism and masochism. The worst category is the cheap pocket novel, containing sleazy stories where "nothing is left to the imagination," and once familiar with the books teenagers seek out similar works from the same publishers. Taking time to read a passage from Don Elliot's *Sex Jungle* (1960) because of the philosophy it reveals, Putnam chose to emphasise the excitement felt by the sixteen-year-old narrator and the link made between violence and sex.[70]

For most of the presentation in *Perversion for Profit* Putnam positioned himself beside the national flag and in front of a map of the United States, and concluded his presentation with the words, "Oh God deliver us, Americans, from evil." Wrapped in traditional imagery, his message is directed to the insecure and uninformed.[71] The film enabled CDL to spread their ideology to existing audiences and to win new converts for many years. CDL's pre-eminence as the national anti-smut organisation was reinforced the same year when representatives were invited to testify before a congressional subcommittee.

In September 1965 Keating and James Clancy, chief counsel for CDL, testified before a subcommittee investigating "noxious and obscene matter and materials" where they claimed that pornography was part

---

70 'Don Elliot' was a pseudonym used by award winning science fiction writer Robert Silverberg.
71 CDL produced 'educational' films such as *I'd Rather Have A Paper Doll* where a marriage is ruined by a husband's desire for porn, and specifically recommended for high school audiences was *Pages of Death*, a dramatic reconstruction of a sex crime committed by a sixteen-year-old boy after exposure to pornographic books and magazines.

of a communist conspiracy to undermine American society. As was his habit Keating produced examples of pornographic materials. Amongst them were *His Brother's Love* (1965), a novel about homosexuality, *Sensational Step Daughter* (about incest), *Fiseek Art Quarterly* (which featured pictures of erections), and *Jaybird Safari* (featuring pictures of male and female genitals in contact), all of which he had purchased for forty-five dollars the previous night from newsstands around Washington, D.C. In his comments Keating emphasised "this filth is available practically anywhere in Washington, or New York, or Los Angeles ... for that matter, practically anywhere in the United States."[72] The prevalence of obscene publications was a serious matter because "these magazines are the catalytic agents to warp and twist the minds of youth and destroy their souls and wreck their lives."[73] Before the subcommittee, despite the presence of women and young members of CDL, he read extended summaries of chapters of *Lust in Leather* (1964), detailing Satanic orgies, lesbianism, drug use, bondage, sodomy and adultery. To further illustrate his point Keating tried to read a number of pages of *Love's Lash* into the transcript of the proceedings, but was stopped by the Committee chairman, John H. Dent Jr. (Democrat, Pennsylvania), who asked him to just mark the relevant passages.[74] Despite this excess, the panel accepted Keating's opinions without question.

By 1965 CDL had expanded its title to Citizens for Decent Literature and Motion Pictures, an acknowledgement of technical developments, but it still concentrated on paperback books, magazines and tabloid newspapers.[75] When journalist Edwin Roberts Jr. visited Cincinnati to research material for his book *The Smut Rakers* (1966) Keating gave him a personal tour of the city. Taking him to King's News, a local bookstore, Keating bought adult paperbacks and magazines totalling $28.30. Amongst the magazines, whose cover price was $2.50 at a time when most magazines were twenty-five cents, were *Bizarre Life*, *Jaybird Journal*, *Black Magic* and *Tip Top*. Roberts noted that Keating "knew just which books and magazines to choose. His selections represented

---

72   Keating quoted in Binstein and Bowden, *Trust Me*: 94–95.
73   Keating quoted in ibid.
74   Ibid.
75   Mark, "The Anonymous Smut Hunters," *Nation* (5 July 1965): 5.

some of the most tawdry publications available over the counter any place in the country."[76] Years of experience ensured Keating knew his audience and how to find the most controversial pornography available.

However, obscure and sensational books and magazines were not the ultimate target for CDL. They were just building blocks in Keating's crusade, a crusade designed to draw public attention to and evoke outrage at extremes of pornography and pass them off as representative examples of the industry as a whole, all the while recruiting more grassroots members for CDL. Keating's primary target was made clear in an editorial for the *National Decency Reporter* (January 1966) when he wrote:

> Hugh Hefner, with his philosophy and his *Playboy* magazine, defiles decency and contaminates our youth. He reduces our women to the status of animals, desirable for their physical characteristics only — to playthings for men, to be used to satisfy their lustful desires and then cast aside. This licentious tramp batters the ramparts of decency with his magazine which is being read monthly by 1,860,000 college men — and in addition, by 5,710,000 more of our male citizens. A cancer in our midst — and yet what parent or minister effectively rises to the challenge.[77]

Before *Playboy* began publishing in 1953 the only way for many American men to see a woman's breast exposed was to read a copy of *National Geographic*, "safe in the knowledge that it could never be accused of sexual exploitation."[78] The 'Playmate' quickly became a familiar icon of 1950s America, an ideal woman with sanitized sexuality who was completely nonthreatening. *Playboy* was CDL's prime target partly due to its superficial presentation of women as playthings, but primarily because of its influence on American culture.[79] Whilst the organisation viewed it as a "salacious and lewd magazine,"[80] the

---

76 Roberts Jr., *The Smut Rakers*: 100–101.
77 Keating quoted in ibid: 104.
78 Russell Miller, *Bunny: The Real Story of Playboy*, Corgi, London, 1985: 64.
79 Roberts Jr., *The Smut Rakers*: 104.
80 "Report of Commissioner Charles H. Keating Jr.," in *The Report of the Commission on Obscenity and Pornography*, Bantam, New York and London, 1970: 615. J. Edgar Hoover viewed *Playboy* readers as "moral degenerates" and reading the magazine was grounds for dismissal from the FBI. Victor S. Navasky, *Kennedy Justice*: Atheum, New York, 1971: 142.

popularity of *Playboy* meant it was beyond CDL's reach.

Even though CDL was less than ten years old the organisation had drawn criticism from commentators who were concerned about the methods being used. In the *Nation* (5 July 1965) Norman Mark criticized the tactics used by CDL to achieve its aims and claimed that CDL was confused with the well-established Catholic Legion of Decency (CLD) or the National Office of Decent Literature (NODL) — giving it more respectability and influence than it deserved.[81] In *The Smut Rakers* Edwin Roberts Jr. concluded:

> The story of CDL is a story of good intentions, and efficient use of the law, imaginary statistics, repeated inconsistencies, and overheated metaphors. In general its rambunctiousness is not likely to attract the more thoughtful members of the community. And its use of adolescents to parrot the CDL line is downright disturbing.[82]

Despite receiving criticism the organisation was growing in membership and political influence, and by 1967 claimed 300 chapters nationwide.[83] However, insulating itself from criticism, CDL members rarely engaged in debate with adversaries, because when they did they did not fare well. At the organisation's national conference in 1969 lawyers Stanley Fleishman and Irl Baris, both of whom had acted as defence counsel in prominent First Amendment cases, debated obscenity issues with Charles Keating and James Clancy. Challenging allegations made by CDL to the effect that pornography undermined morality and destroyed lives Baris asked Clancy "Have you been corrupted, or are you a superman?" Unused to such questions Clancy eventually replied, "I'm steeled against this stuff, but yes, it has ... lowered my morals." Baris sarcastically retorted, "Then why don't you stop collecting it?"[84] But in front of a crowd of hostile CDL members Fleishman and Baris were only making a personal point.

In 1967 DeWitt Wallace, publisher of *Reader's Digest* magazine, gave CDL $36,000, enabling the organisation to employ Raymond Gauer as

81 Mark, "The Anonymous Smut Hunters," *Nation* (5 July 1965): 7.
82 Roberts Jr., *The Smut Rakers*: 117.
83 Corn, "Dirty Bookkeeping," *New Republic* (2 April 1990): 14.
84 Clancy and Baris quoted in Strub, "Perversion for Profit," *Journal of the History of Sexuality* 15:2 (May 2006): 265.

a full-time national director, a post that made him responsible for co-ordinating the organisation's activities across America. *Reader's Digest* recognized the contemporary concern provoked by the obscenity issue and as well as supporting CDL published a number of articles sympathetic to the aims of the organisation.[85] It was Gauer in his role as national director of CDL who began circulating stories about pornographic 'snuff' movies, in which actresses were murdered for sexual titillation in the early 1970s. Predictably, like Keating, Gauer needed a reason to embark on a campaign against obscene material, a justification for his personal crusade.

One Sunday night in the late 1950s Raymond Gauer was walking to a Chinese takeaway near his Hollywood home. He was shocked to find that a sex shop had opened, displaying racks of paperbacks and magazines, displays of dildos, vibrators, French ticklers, lubricants and cock rings. Whilst he admitted being excited by what he saw, Gauer was also disgusted; he experienced a clash of his natural human instincts and his strict Catholic upbringing that he needed to resolve. At home later that night Gauer felt he was being summoned by God to confront and overcome the allure of pornography.[86] Deciding to take action, the following day he wrote a letter of complaint to the Chamber of Commerce noting the presence of the store. Within a week he received a letter of thanks from the Chamber of Commerce and a promise that the police would be notified.

A few days later Gauer read in a newspaper that the shop had been

---

85   Joseph F. Kobylka, *The Politics of Obscenity: Group litigation in a time of Legal Change*, Greenwood Press, New York, 1991: 49. Orland K. Armstrong began his own crusade against obscenity in the late 1950s and wrote several anti-obscenity articles for *Reader's Digest* in the mid-1960s; "Must our movies be obscene?" *Reader's Digest* (November 1965): 154–156; "The damning case against pornography," *Reader's Digest* (December 1965): 131–134; "Filth for profit: The big business of pornography," *Reader's Digest* (March 1966): 73–76; "Victory over the smut peddlers," *Reader's Digest* (February 1967): 147–154; and "Landmark decision in the war on pornography" *Reader's Digest* (September 1967): 93–97. As a consequence of his experience with an anti-smut group in Florida in 1970 Armstrong founded the Springfield Citizens' Council for Decency. In the same time period several other anti-obscenity articles were published in *Reader's Digest*: Senior editor and regular contributor Clarence W. Hall published "Poison in print — and how to get rid of it," *Reader's Digest* (May 1964): 94–98; and Charles H. Keating wrote two articles "The Report that shocked the nation," *Reader's Digest* (January 1971): 37–40, and "Green light to combat smut" *Reader's Digest* (January 1974): 147–150. According to Gay Talese it was DeWitt Wallace who later used his political influence to organise for Gauer and James Clancy to meet with senators during the Abe Fortas confirmation hearings. Gay Talese, *Thy Neighbor's Wife*, Doubleday, New York, 1980: 370.

86   Gay Talese, *Thy Neighbor's Wife*, Doubleday, New York, 1980: 368–369.

raided.[87] Encouraged by the effect of his letter, and impressed by the consequential feeling of power, Gauer began to spend his free time driving around LA noting the names and addresses of sex shops in the city. In the downtown area alone he found six sex shops in close proximity to the City Hall and the LAPD headquarters. Outraged that such places were being tolerated he wrote to the Mayor, Norris Poulson, and a few days later the vice squad raided the businesses, arresting a number of sales clerks and confiscating several tons of adult materials. Shortly after the raid Gauer came to the attention of CDL and during one of Keating's speaking engagements in LA the two men were introduced. Finding that they shared the same abhorrence of pornography, Gauer was incorporated into the organisation where he quickly rose through the ranks, and by 1967 was head of the LA chapter of CDL.[88]

Outside CDL Keating had other important interests to occupy his attention. The American Financial Corporation (AFC) was a business developed by Keating and Carl Lindner in Cincinnati. Between 1960, when it was conceived, and 1972, AFC's average compounded growth rate in earning was consistently more than twenty per cent. As the company grew it acquired numerous other businesses, banks and even the Cincinnati *Enquirer* newspaper, which gave Keating an outlet for his political agenda.[89] AFC did not create any products; instead it bought up other companies and broke them down to recoup the initial investments. As AFC developed, new financial instruments were created and a complex maze of subsidiaries grew up to confuse regulators and enable the executives to operate outside the established business community.[90] By July 1972, when Keating left his private law practice and joined Lindner at AFC as executive vice president, the company was estimated to be worth about $1 billion. A powerful regional economic entity, AFC made generous donations to

---

87 Ibid. When Carolyn See interviewed Raymond Gauer, circa 1973, he recounted a similar story about his introduction to decency activism. However, in the version he told to See initially it was a peep show on Hollywood Boulevard, which he entered and found shocking, but later Gauer told her that he had only stood outside the peep show and not entered. In both cases he sought to emphasise the effect of the letter he had written to the Chamber of Commerce. See, *Blue Money*: 160–161.

88 Talese, *Thy Neighbor's Wife*: 369–370.

89 Binstein and Bowden, *Trust Me*: 103.

90 Ibid: 116.

the Republican Party,[91] enabling Keating to buy political influence and expand his crusade nationwide.

In October 1967 Congress set up the President's Commission on Obscenity and Pornography for which Keating had repeatedly called, but before the Commission's final report was published in 1970 several political events ensured that the obscenity debate was distorted and politicized by supporters of Richard Nixon and other conservatives. This series of events began with the nomination of Abe Fortas as Chief Justice of the Supreme Court, was continued by the election of Richard Nixon as president of America, and culminated in the Manson Family murders. The swift condemnation of the *Report of the President's Commission on Obscenity and Pornography* (1970) was a restatement of traditional conservative values, and was followed by a period of 'porno chic' where adult material achieved mainstream respectability. This in turn was followed by the ruling in *Miller v. California* (1973), reversing a fifteen-year trend in Supreme Court decisions, and ushering in the end to the short-lived era of 'porno chic'.

91   Ibid: 107–108.

Abe Fortas

Chapter Two

THE FORTAS FILM FESTIVAL

Pornography as a Political Issue

METHODIST BISHOP OF LOS ANGELES GERALD KENNEDY LAMENTED SOCIAL changes in postwar America saying, "The atmosphere is wide open. There is more promiscuity, and it is taken as a matter of course now by people. In my day they did it, but they knew it was wrong."[1] A few years later *Newsweek* (13 November 1967) announced, "The old taboos are dead or dying. A new, more permissive society is taking shape."[2] After a series of civil rights and First Amendment decisions in the 1950s and sixties, by 1968 right-wing conservatives had identified an opportunity to shift the balance of the Supreme Court in favour of their own ideology. With the assistance of CDL a series of events were set in motion that had far-reaching consequences.

In the postwar years a number of films eroded the power of the Hollywood Production Code of self-imposed censorship. *The Moon is Blue* (Otto Preminger, 1953) was condemned by the Catholic Legion of Decency for using the word 'virgin', as was *The Man with the Golden Arm* (Otto Preminger, 1956) for drug references. *Time* pointed the finger at the film industry, looking for a scapegoat to be held responsible for the perceived moral decline of the nation: "Hollywood, of course, suggests more of morals and immorals to more people than any other single force."[3] American society was being "bombarded" with sexual images and individuals had to make choices about what was acceptable: "It is part and symptom of an era in which morals are widely held to be both private and relative, in which pleasure is increasingly considered an almost constitutional right rather than a privilege, in which self-denial is increasingly seen as foolishness rather than virtue."[4] Further

---

1   Kennedy quoted in "Morals: The Second Sexual Revolution," *Time* (24 January 1964): 42.
2   "Anything Goes: Taboos in Twilight," *Newsweek* (13 November 1967): 40.
3   "Morals: The Second Sexual Revolution," *Time* (24 January 1964): 43.
4   Ibid.

45

important films challenged the restrictive Production Code and eroded the symbolic power it carried, such as *The Pawnbroker* (Sidney Lumet, 1965), which was condemned by the National League of Decency, but despite revisions later the same year to reflect changes in contemporary cinema, the Code was challenged by *Who's Afraid Of Virginia Woolf?* (Mike Nichols, 1966), which caused such a commotion that the Code had to be rewritten again. Jack Valenti, president of the MPAA, defended contemporary cinema fare: "Films can't live in a vacuum. They relate to the temper of the times, the posture of today."[5] Reflecting the changing influence of the Production Code Geoffrey Shurlock, the seventy-three-year-old chief executor, said, "As far as I'm concerned the public makes up its mind" and conceded, "America has in time grown up to accept sex. All the taboos are beginning to break down, which is probably the most healthy thing that could happen."[6] In 1968 the film industry finally dropped the Production Code in favour of a ratings system.

English social commentator Malcolm Muggeridge believed the changes were an inevitable mark of decay: "As society ebbs, people reach out for vicarious excitement, like the current sex mania in pop songs and the popular press. At the decline and fall of the Roman Empire, the works of Sappho, Catullus and Ovid were celebrated. There is an analogy in that for us."[7] This was a bleak prediction for American society, especially for conservative moralists. "I would expect the pendulum to swing back," said British film producer Tony Richardson, somewhat more philosophically. "Another historical movement will occur, some major cataclysm, and society will need heroics, moral codes, ideals. All victories are limited; they are never total. Just when you think you have advanced for a time, you find you are mistaken."[8]

Campaigns by CDL and other anti-obscenity groups drew public attention to the issue of pornography with notable consequences. In 1968 the Post Office Department received 230,000 protests, triple the number received in 1963. One commentator noted, "there's one hell of a lot of letter writing going on with samples of the kind of thing the writer doesn't want his twelve-year-old to see."[9] Seizing the

5 "Anything Goes: Taboos in Twilight," *Newsweek* (13 November 1967): 40.
6 Ibid: 41.
7 Muggeridge quoted in ibid: 40.
8 Ibid: 43.
9 "Pornography: Time for a Halt," *Newsweek* (6 October 1969): 46.

opportunity, conservative politicians recognized public awareness and fear could be manipulated for their own partisan political advantage. William McCullough (Republican, Ohio) felt that the anti-smut protests were timely: "While we must respect the right of a citizen to expose himself to pornography if he so desires, we must also respect the right of Americans not to … have this obscene trash thrust upon them, unsolicited and unwanted through the mails."[10] Growing concern about obscene publications at a local level meant the issue became important on a national level, changing the balance of power in the Supreme Court and beginning a conservative backlash against smut.

On 13 June 1968 Supreme Court Chief Justice Earl Warren privately submitted his resignation to President Lyndon B. Johnson, but it was not publicized until a week later. The reason for the resignation was simple: Warren feared Richard Nixon would win the next election and, given the opportunity, appoint conservative judges to the Supreme Court. As soon as the resignation was announced Senator Robert Griffin (Republican, Michigan) and Senator John Tower (Republican, Texas) promised to block any 'lame duck' appointments.[11] Thus began a long drawn out campaign by conservatives to ensure that Warren's replacement would reflect traditional religious values and halt the progressive direction taken by the Court over the preceding fifteen years. The previous year, in his address to Congress (May 1968), Richard Nixon made his position on obscenity clear when he warned:

American homes are being bombarded with the largest volume of sex-orientated mail in history. Most of it is unsolicited, unwanted and deeply offensive to those who receive it. Mothers and fathers by the tens of thousands have written to the White House and the Congress … asking for Federal assistance to protect their children against exposure to erotic publications.[12]

On 28 June 1968 Strom Thurmond (Republican, South Carolina), a right-wing conservative, noted the arrangement between Johnson and

10 Ibid.
11 Nadine Cohodas, *Strom Thurmond and the Politics of Southern Change*, Mercer University Press, 1993: 392.
12 "Time for a Halt," *Newsweek* (6 October 1969): 46.

Warren, and vowed to prevent the president from appointing the next Chief Justice. A few days later he acknowledged that his opposition vote often stood alone, and that he was unable to prevent liberal justices from being appointed to the Court, but he emphasised that this was an opportunity for conservatives who complained about damage caused to the nation by the Supreme Court to give the next president the chance to change the court leadership, the implications of which could last for the next twenty years.[13]

When Raymond Gauer and a friend found out that Abe Fortas, Lyndon Johnson's nomination for Chief Justice, had defended Greenleaf Publications (California), a company which had published sexually explicit material, they took the information to DeWitt Wallace, director of *Reader's Digest*, who in turn urged them to take their lecture and slides to Washington, D.C. to coincide with Fortas' hearing.[14]

In his opening challenge to the Fortas nomination Thurmond claimed that Fortas was an unacceptable candidate because of his "long reputation as a fixer and his involvement with many questionable figures," a reference mainly to the close links between Fortas and Lyndon Johnson. His alignment with the "radical wing" of the Supreme Court by voting in the majority with Chief Justice Warren was also emphasised as an important issue, as was his aiding of communists and his support for decisions which "extended the power of the federal government and invaded the rights of the states, turned criminals loose on technicalities." The Fortas nomination was not popular amongst Southerners because he had advised Johnson on civil rights legislation from 1957 onwards and his influence led to the enactment of five civil rights bills that imposed federal legislation. Even though he had joined the Supreme Court in 1965, the year after the *Escobedo* decision (1964), he had sided with the majority in the *Miranda* decision

---

13 Cohodas, *Strom Thurmond and the Politics of Southern Change*: 393. After President Harry Truman made gestures towards civil rights in 1948 Thurmond began to exploit public concerns and campaigned for segregation and supported anti-miscegenation laws. In 1957 Thurmond mounted a twenty-four-hour eighteen-minute long filibuster (the longest in congressional history) trying to block a civil rights bill and in 1964 he wrestled a senator from Texas to the ground to prevent him from voting for the Civil Rights Act. Despite serving for forty-eight years in office Thurmond sponsored virtually no leading bills or initiatives. His defection to the Republican Party in 1968 led the way for other Southern Democrats and as a consequence the former Confederate states have been solidly Republican since.

14 See, *Blue Money*: 166–167.

(1966),[15] making him a target for the law and order lobby.

The committee hearings began on 16 July, and two days later Thurmond began questioning Fortas, spending two hours asking about cases that had already been decided. Fortas refused to answer many of Thurmond's questions because they pertained to cases yet to come before the Supreme Court, and defended himself by saying he hoped the American people would understand that his refusal to answer reflected a sense of constitutional duty and responsibility.[16] Thurmond's line of questioning went further when he challenged Fortas on the Supreme Court decision in *Mallory v. United States* (1957), asking how the Supreme Court could condone releasing a self-confessed rapist, even though Fortas was not appointed to the Court at that time.[17]

One of Thurmond's aides, James Lucier, thought that the senator's strategy was a disastrous mistake, and one which gave the impression that the line of questioning was simply a delaying tactic, *not* an attempt to investigate the views of Fortas. In Lucier's opinion Thurmond should have adopted a strategy which illustrated Fortas was a radical and a "legal moral relativist and thereby temperamentally unfit for the judiciary ... a political animal who does not possess the necessary independence and integrity to break off the connections and habits of a political past."[18] The turning point in the proceedings came when James Clancy, chief counsel for CDL, appeared as a witness before the Senate Judiciary Committee.

Prior to Clancy's arrival opposition to the Fortas nomination was making little headway, but his testimony provoked a public response and helped extend the duration of the hearings, thus delaying Chief Justice Warren's departure and preventing Lyndon Johnson from nominating

---

15 Cohodas, *Strom Thurmond and the Politics of Southern Change*: 392–393. The Supreme Court decision in *Escobedo v. Illinois* (1964) ruled that criminal suspects had a constitutional right to legal counsel during police interrogations under the sixth amendment. Two years later the Court's decision in *Miranda v. Arizona* (1966) added that any statements made by defendants in police custody during interrogation were only admissible at trial if the prosecution could demonstrate that the suspect had been informed of their right to consult with an attorney and the right against making statements to incriminate themselves prior to questioning. Defendants not only had to be informed of these rights but also acknowledge that they understood them. The two decisions had obvious widespread consequences for law enforcement and police procedure had to be changed to ensure that suspects were informed of their rights.

16 Ibid: 393–394.

17 Corry, "Strom's Dirty Movies," *Harper's Magazine* (December 1968): 35–36.

18 Lucier quoted in Cohodas, *Strom Thurmond and the Politics of Southern Change*: 394–395.

an alternative successor.[19] Clancy told the committee that the moral standards of America were being eroded, a situation contributed to by

a set of decisions by the US Supreme Court which completely throws caution to the winds, and is an open invitation to every pornographer to come into the area and distribute millions of copies — and I am not exaggerating — millions and millions of copies of what historically had been regarded in France as hardcore pornography.[20]

Thurmond asked Clancy during the hearing, "Other than being ashamed of the decisions, and ashamed to write in detail their reasoning," could there be any other reasons for the *per curiam* reversals? Clancy answered falsely, stating that there were no other reasons.[21] In his testimony Clancy claimed that after studying fifty-two recent Supreme Court decisions pertaining to obscenity he found that Fortas had cast the deciding vote against an obscenity ruling in forty-nine instances.[22] However, in his testimony Clancy did not clearly establish Fortas' judicial philosophy on obscenity. Most of the Supreme Court decisions relating to obscenity were unsigned, making it impossible to ascertain if Fortas had cast any of the deciding votes. Furthermore, Fortas was always said to have cast the deciding vote, but what did that really mean if there were four other justices voting in the same manner? His only signed opinion was in *Ginzburg v. United States* (1966), and in that he argued states *could* constitutionally enact legislation preventing panderers from distributing offensive material to minors.

Selected photographs were submitted by Clancy to support his accusations and in his testimony, prompted by Thurmond's questions, he repeated the unsupported allegation that pornography bred violence. The CDL strategy, through Clancy's accusations, was to make Fortas seem personally responsible for America's moral decline. To reinforce his challenge to Fortas' nomination Thurmond arranged for his colleagues on the committee and the press to see a copy of *O-7* that Clancy had brought with him. Despite his contentious opinions Clancy's

19 Laura Kalman, *Abe Fortas: A Biography*, Yale University Press, New Haven and London, 1990: 342.
20 Clancy testimony quoted in Kalman, *Abe Fortas, A Biography*: 342.
21 Strub, "Perversion for Profit," *Journal of the History of Sexuality* 15:2 (May 2006): 283.
22 Kalman, *Abe Fortas: A Biography*: 342.

testimony, which was not corroborated by any subsequent witnesses, went unchallenged. While in Washington Clancy also presented a thirty-minute slideshow called Target Smut that highlighted some of the pornographic films Supreme Court rulings had permitted to remain on display. These he screened privately for senators and the press.[23]

To substantiate the accusation that Fortas was soft on pornography, Senators opposing Fortas' nomination dug up a number of films which one of Nixon's aides sarcastically called the "Fortas film festival."[24] The anti-Fortas campaigners, led by Robert Griffin (Republican, Michigan), planned to show the films on Capitol Hill as well as to send copies to women's groups and civic organisations, all done with the intention of provoking public outrage. Kits containing excerpts from the Judiciary Committee hearings were sent to all Republican Senatorial candidates.

The film O-7 had been found obscene by the lower courts in California, but the Supreme Court overturned the verdict in Schackman v. California (1967) much to the annoyance of James Clancy. However, the single sentence justifying the decision was not a comment on obscenity. The verdict was reversed simply because the police officers confiscating the film did not have a valid search warrant.[25] On the day O-7 was first mentioned in the hearings Thurmond urged members of the press and Senators on the Judiciary Committee to see the film,[26] even though one of his aides described it as a "vulgar, filthy, subjective thing of a woman disrobing down to her panties."[27] Original stag films were shot on 16mm commercial stock but in the late 1960s, as technology developed, porn loops, shot on 8mm reels and lasting about ten minutes, became more widely available. These were used on either home projectors or coin operated booths in clubs and sex shops. Better quality porn loops were shot on Super 8 colour film and included sound.[28]

Similar to many other stag movies of the era O-7 showed a young woman writhing on a couch while gradually stripping off her garter belt, bra and panties. Jokes circulated on Capitol Hill claiming that

---

23   Ibid: 342–344.
24   "The Fortas Film Festival," Time (20 September 1968): 30.
25   Kalman, Abe Fortas: A Biography: 343.
26   John Corry, "Strom's Dirty Movies," Harper's Magazine (December 1968): 30.
27   "Judgement and the Justice," Time (2 August 1968): 15.
28   David Hebditch, and Nick Anning, Porn Gold: Inside the Pornography Business, Faber and Faber, London, 1988: 20.

the showing of stag films was the only way the Judiciary Committee could get all its members together, and prompted complaints by other Senators who felt left out of the fun. Before the films were screened Senator Phil Hart (Democrat, Michigan) pointed out that all the Senators assembled had seen similar stag movies thirty years before, challenging the moralistic rhetoric being used by Thurmond and CDL. Most of the press giggled at the film when it was shown because it had to be projected onto a wooden panel, as there was no screen in the room. At the Republican Capitol Hill Club rumours circulated that Thurmond wanted to show the stag films on the floor of the Senate, and some speculated that he had finally gone mad.[29]

In 1957 the Supreme Court ruled that nudity *per se* was not obscene and allowed *Garden of Eden*, a nudie documentary, to be shown legally. The decision catalysed a wave of nudie films by people like Russ Meyer, H. G. Lewis and Doris Wishman. Many people may not have liked the subject matter of sexploitation films but in a competitive industry it was often the only way for aspiring filmmakers to gain the necessary experience. While still a student at UCLA Francis Ford Coppola made his first film, *Tonight For Sure* (1961), an attempt to profit from the popularity of nudie films. He took his camera to several bars on Sunset Strip, edited the footage into a film, and convinced his father Carmen Coppola to write the score. Next Coppola was hired to shoot some 3D footage, a contemporary fad, which was spliced into an earlier English film, *Bellboy and the Playgirls* (1958), featuring stripper June Wilkinson. His early work in smut films contributed to his filmmaking education and prepared him for his later critically acclaimed work such as *Finian's Rainbow* (1968), starring Fred Astaire, and *The Godfather* (1972), which won Academy Awards for best picture, actor and screenplay. Following the *Garden of Eden* verdict, Ephriam Landon, a veteran lawyer and expert on censorship, believed that the more tolerant attitude prevailing in society meant, "Censorship of films and books has become simply a matter of taste." As a consequence he felt that:

> Today there's absolutely nothing you can't show or write about if it's
> done in good taste, absolutely nothing. If the courts judge something

---

29 Corry, "Strom's Dirty Movies," *Harper's Magazine* (December 1968): 30.

obscene, they are in effect making an aesthetic rather than a moral judgement. If the censorship rules of 1950 were in effect today, two out of every three films shown now would be banned.[30]

After the porn loops were shown to the Judiciary Committee *Time* reported that the "Senators were not titillated but shocked, and they left the showings in a grim mood."[31] *Newsweek* speculated that despite heavy criticism from several senators who had seen *O-7*, *O-12* and *Flaming Creatures* (Jack Smith, 1962) most of the rest of the senators would want to look at the films, generously asserting, "The motivation was not prurient interest but political."[32] Holding Fortas personally responsible for the films, Strom Thurmond was quoted in the Washington *Post* as challenging President Johnson to watch the four films and afterwards ask himself, "if he still favours Mr. Fortas' appointment to the second most important public office in the United States."[33]

After viewing *O-7* Senator Frank Lausche (Democrat, Ohio) said it was a "scandalization of the womanhood of the United States and of the world." As a consequence of watching the film, he announced, "If the nominee was my brother I would not vote for him."[34] Similarly, Senator George Murphy (Republican, California) was upset by the films, as was Senator Jack Miller (Republican, Iowa), an associate of CDL, and Senator Milton R. Young (Republican, N. Dakota) also attributed his opposition to the Fortas nomination to the films.[35] Outside Capitol Hill the "fanatically right-wing" Liberty Lobby produced a mass mailing accusing Fortas of being a revolutionary and a supporter of the porn industry,[36] and around the country the story featured prominently in many regional newspapers.[37] Holding Fortas personally responsible,

30 "Anything Goes: Taboos in Twilight," *Newsweek* (13 November 1967): 42.
31 "The Fortas Film Festival," *Time* (20 September 1968): 30.
32 "Fleshing Out the Case," *Newsweek* (12 August 1968): 22.
33 Thurmond's comment was originally quoted by Robert Albright, "LBJ Scares Tactics of Fortas Foes," *Washington Post* (7 September 1968) in Murray, *Fortas*: 481.
34 Corry, "Strom's Dirty Movies," *Harper's Magazine* (December 1968): 36.
35 Ibid.
36 "The Fortas Film Festival," *Time* (20 September 1968): 30–31.
37 Such as "Stripper film plays role in Fortas inquiry," Toledo (Ohio) *Blade* (25 July 1968): 2; "Strip-tease film joins controversy," Sumter *Daily Item* (25 July 1968): 1, 2A; "Strip film an issue," Fort Scott *Tribune* (25 July 1968): 1; Saul Friedman, "4 Films: 'The End' for Fortas," St. Petersburg *Times* (12 September 1968): 1, 6A.. Some newspapers carried full page anti-Fortas advertisements which emphasised the issue of pornographic films, for example "Stamping

both William Buckley and James Kilpatrick wrote editorials for the Washington *Evening-Star* demanding that the nominee be evaluated solely by his position on obscenity. Members of the public sent letters to Lyndon Johnson voicing concern and disappointment that the president would nominate a defender of smut peddlers.[38] The *National Decency Reporter* (July–August 1968) went further, warning that if Abe Fortas were confirmed as Chief Justice the Fortas Court would be so liberal that it would make the Warren Court seem like right-wing extremists.[39]

A Sergeant from the LAPD vice squad appeared before the committee, providing two additional films, *Flaming Creatures* and Jean Genet's *Un Chant d'Amour* (1950), and a selection of magazines as examples of 'obscene' materials permitted by the Supreme Court rulings.[40] Nudist magazines, similar to those condemned by CDL in *Perversion for Profit*, such as *Nudie-Fax, Friendly Female* and *Weekend Jaybird*, were presented to the Committee as further evidence of the consequences of permissive liberalism and to show the kind of materials that were found to be *not* legally obscene by the Supreme Court. Thurmond exaggerated the content of the magazines and described them as "foul, putrid, filthy, repulsive, objectionable and obnoxious."[41] While the Committee questioned deputy Attorney General Warren Christopher, Thurmond read and displayed a copy of *Nudie-Fax*, exactly the kind of magazine he was condemning as obscene, for all to hear and see. To emphasise what he was doing, one of Thurmond's assistants would prop up the magazine when it began to droop, one of many symbolic gestures orchestrated by Thurmond during the course of the hearings.[42]

The Washington *Post* (8 September 1968) published a sarcastic cartoon, mocking Thurmond's tactics, which showed Thurmond as the "Obscenator" standing in a doorway clutching a roll of film trying to attract the attention of a passer-by saying "Psst — Want to see some dirty pictures?" An editorial in the *New York Times* criticised the actions

out smut means stopping Fortas," (Florida) *Herald-Tribune* (15 September 1968): 4C.

38 Strub, "Perversion for Profit," *Journal of the History of Sexuality* 15:2 (May 2006): 283–284.

39 Edward de Grazia, *Girls Lean Back Everywhere: The Law of Obscenity and the Assault on Genius*, Vintage, New York, 1993: 526.

40 Corry, "Strom's Dirty Movies," *Harper's Magazine* (December 1968): 36.

41 "Judgement and the Justice," *Time* (2 August 1968): 15.

42 Corry, "Strom's Dirty Movies," *Harper's Magazine* (December 1968): 35.

of the Judiciary Committee during the Fortas nomination hearings "to pass out magazines and show movies and blame Mr. Fortas for their obscenity, real or otherwise, is to attack one man when the real target is the Supreme Court itself. That, of course, has been the aim of the demagogues all along."[43] *Time* magazine (20 September 1968) noted that berating the Supreme Court had become a popular preoccupation, and that it was being blamed for everything from rising crime rates, racial conflict and the loosening of morals to a general climate of permissiveness.[44] Attorney General Ramsey Clark identified partisan politics and a desire to roll back civil rights advances as the motivation behind some Senators' opposition to the Fortas nomination, and added, "If certain members of the Senate are as concerned about pornographic materials as they appear to be — and should be — they might work on legislation designed to control it, not attack the Supreme Court as if it caused lust."[45] Calling the protracted hearings before the Judiciary Committee a "constitutional crisis," Clark warned that the developing situation threatened the "system of government: separation of powers, [and] independent and uninhibited judiciary."[46]

Outside the hearings Thurmond used his radio broadcasts and an issue of his newsletter, *Strom Thurmond Reports to the People* (5 August 1968), to condemn Fortas. In "Fortas on Filth" Thurmond repeated the allegation that Fortas had been the swing vote in decisions overruling the lower courts and interpreting the Constitution in such a way that hardcore pornography was protected. He also claimed, in wild exaggeration, that while Fortas had been a member of the Supreme Court

state restrictions on filthy books and pictures have been virtually swept away ... The effect of the Fortas decisions has been to unleash a floodtide of pornography across the country ... This is not a question simply of girlie magazines and salacious literature. The new era of pornography

---

43 "The Fortas Nomination," *New York Times* (14 September 1968): 30.
44 "The Fortas Film Festival," *Time* (20 September 1968): 30.
45 Benjamin Welles, "Clark Declares Foes of Fortas Play Politics and Oppose Rights," *New York Times* (14 September 1968): 17; See also "Judgement and the Justice," *Time* (2 August 1968): 15.
46 Welles, "Clark Declares Foes of Fortas Play Politics and Oppose Rights," *New York Times* (14 September 1968): 17.

features photographs which leave nothing to the imagination and which appeal to the most perverted interests of mankind.[47]

Despite attempts by Johnson's administration to fight back against the obscenity accusations, there was little chance of success, and one president aide wrote in a memo with a note of resignation, "Thurmond tastes blood now." The popularity of Fortas declined sharply and subsequent allegations of financial impropriety, regarding a series of lectures delivered at American University, ended Fortas' nomination hopes.[48]

A telegram was sent to Fortas (10 September 1968) requesting he attend the Committee for more questioning. Fortas replied, declining the invitation. The Committee went ahead with the proceedings anyway. Thurmond requested that the Committee hear testimony about lectures given by Fortas at the American University Law School (in Washington). Finally, on 17 September the Committee voted 11–6 to send the Fortas nomination to the full Senate. There Griffin, Thurmond and other opponents launched into a filibuster to once more slow down the proceedings. On 1 October President Johnson asked Congress for a decision on the matter and, when the final results came in, Fortas was fourteen votes short. The following day Fortas requested that Johnson should withdraw his nomination.[49]

When it was publicized that Fortas had requested that the nomination be withdrawn, making him the first Chief Justice designate since 1795 to be denied the seat, Strom Thurmond announced, with his usual lack of tact, "This is the wisest decision Fortas has made since

---

47   Thurmond quoted in Cohodas, *Strom Thurmond and the Politics of Southern Change*: 395. Thurmond's moralistic stance was blatant hypocrisy. Noted for being "hornier than a bagful of rhinos" he was married twice, both times to South Carolina beauty queens. In one well-known story he reportedly seduced a female convict in the back of the car carrying her to death row. Even in old age Thurmond would grope and tickle female colleagues and staff. After Thurmond's resignation in 2002, aged ninety-nine, Senator John Tower (Republican, Texas) said, "When ol' Strom dies, they'll have to beat his pecker down with a baseball bat to get that coffin lid closed." Despite his racist political ideology rumours circulated for decades that Thurmond had fathered several illegitimate children with black women. The publication of Essie Mae Washington-Williams' memoir *Dear Senator* (2005) confirmed her as one of the illegitimate children. Pope Brock, "He Was A Notorious Bigot and White Supremacist," *Sunday Times Magazine* (3 April 2005): 50–53.
48   Strub, "Perversion for Profit," *Journal of the History of Sexuality* 15:2 (May 2006): 284
49   Cohodas, *Strom Thurmond and the Politics of Southern Change*: 395–396.

he has been on the Supreme Court" and added, "I suggest that Mr. Fortas now go a step further and resign from the court for the sake of good government."[50] An article in the *National Decency Reporter* (September–October 1968) proudly announced the defeat of the Fortas nomination and gave CDL credit for playing a key role in the confirmation process and helping to shape the future of American society. The CDL accusations broadened the attack on the reputation and career of Fortas, and using the issue of obscenity made the attack more accessible to the public, exploiting contemporary concerns. As a consequence the hearings identified CDL as a significant national organisation and gave Keating, Gauer and Clancy a taste of real legal and political power.[51]

A few months after the Senate hearings Yale Law School held a version of the Fortas film festival to show how foolish the senators present at the hearings had been in their criticism of Justice Fortas. *Flaming Creatures*, one of the contentious films, was described by one of the law students as "a harmless, stupid stag movie." John T. Rich, editor of the *Yale Law Journal*, attended the screening, noting, "I figured if Senator Strom Thurmond could see this movie, so could I."[52] But the Fortas film festival made it clear that anti-obscenity crusaders were aware of the growing popularity of pornographic films and showed they were prepared to make exaggerated claims about the dangers posed to American society to magnify the concerns of Middle America and gain support for their cause.

An article in *Time* (11 July 1969) observed, "An erotic renaissance (or not as some would have it) is upon the land. Owing to a growing climate of permissiveness — and the Pill — Americans today have more sexual freedom than any previous generation." Acknowledging the social changes within American society the article continued, "Aesthetically, pop sex may well reflect a stunting of the imagination, a dilution of artistic values, and a cultish attempt to substitute sensation for thought." Perhaps most worrying for conservatives and anti-obscenity crusaders, *Time* perceptively conceded, "In a sense, the creative arts and even their sleazy offshoots — blue movies, smut books, peepshows, prurient

---

50 Thurmond quoted in ibid: 396.
51 Strub, "Perversion for Profit," *Journal of the History of Sexuality* 15:2 (May 2006): 284.
52 "Yale Law School Holds 'Fortas Film Festival,'" *New York Times* (5 November 1968): 40.

tabloids — hold a public mirror to a society's private fantasies. A nation gets the kind of art and entertainment it wants and will pay for."[53] In a free market economy, the increasing popularity of adult materials reflected the desires of an expanding segment of society. In contrast, to conservatives the proliferation of pornography could legitimately be seen as a decay of basic traditional values, making the danger more immediate than ever before.

Art-house films were the respectable face of adult entertainment and featured nudity but also some serious social comment. With budgets of around $200,000 they were often imported and occasionally doctored (with additional sex scenes being added to spice them up further) to attract a wider audience.[54] After being exhibited at the Cannes and San Sebastien film festivals, *The Female* (Leopoldo Torre Niellson, 1961) was bought up by an American distributor and re-edited with extra sex scenes added. Released as a dirty art film, "This combination of art and sex is particularly effective in smaller situations where people will flock to see the same film in an art-house they would not go near in a sex house." *I Am Curious (Yellow)* (Vilgot Sojman, 1966), a 'serious' art-house film, was thought by those in the industry to take the "briefcase trade" away from hardcore houses, reflecting the poor quality of many low-budget sexploitation films.[55] Ironically, despite the controversy surrounding *I Am Curious (Yellow)* it did not contain the most explicit film footage being shown in America at the time. *Doktor Glas* (Mai Zetterling, 1968), rated M for 'mature' audiences and distributed by Twentieth Century Fox, contained a dream sequence that showed eight frames of close-up footage of male and female genitals during sex. The sequence lasted one-third of a second and would not be consciously picked up by the human eye.[56]

Sexploitation films were more common in American cinemas than art-house movies and were usually made on a budget of between $25,000 and $45,000, such as those by Russ Meyer. The films could be made in two versions, 'hot' and 'cool', and distributed accordingly

53 "Sex as a Spectator Sport," *Time* (11 July 1969): 51.
54 "Sexpix of $25,000–45,000 Negative Cost See Bright, Not Clouded, Future," *Variety* (16 July 1969): 17.
55 Kent E. Carroll, "N. Y. Overseated For Sex: Cheapies Fear Class Sin Pics," *Variety* (1 July 1969): 70.
56 "Inside Stuff — Pictures," *Variety* (16 July 1969): 17.

THE FORTAS FILM FESTIVAL

to draw the widest audiences possible. Meyer was frequently used as an example of how low-budget sexploitation films could be a critical and commercial success. Lee Hessel of Cambist Films criticized major studios for distributing films such as *Candy* (Christian Marquand, 1968) and *The Killing Of Sister George* (Robert Aldrich, 1968) across America on general release, hence provoking a "moral backlash" in provincial areas and creating difficulties for other filmmakers. Hessel also advised that with two different versions of *Vixen*, Russ Meyer could exhibit anywhere across America and make twice as much money. In the late 1960s Peter Kaufman of Jemco Films reported that sexploitation films made on a budget of $25,000 to $45,000 were doing better than ever. In America companies such as Jemco, Fountain Films, Olympic International and Entertainment Ventures were making about seventy-five to 100 films annually, in colour, with full synch sound, and of a similar quality to those of Russ Meyer. The last category of films were 'Cheapies.' They were often shot in a single long weekend and usually cost less than $25,000; some were even made for less than $8,000. But with a limited number of cinema screens and a relatively large number of films being produced, the market for exploitation films and cheapies was very competitive.[57]

Cinemas in New York, the major market for exploitation films, were said to be "over-seated" by the late 1960s, with insufficient "prurient interest ticket-buyers to support them all." Low-budget films found it difficult to recoup their costs in the face of stiff competition. About 350 cheap exploitation films were produced each year for the New York market, but that only lowered prices at cinemas and created a surplus of films for out-of-town exhibition. In an attempt to maximise profits some theatres even got into the film business by partially financing productions ($7,000–$10,000 budgets). There were technical considerations too and many of the cheapies were shot in 16mm and blown up to 35mm, giving the image less definition, but this had to be done because most drive-ins and exploitation cinemas only had 35mm projectors.[58]

---

57 "Sexpix of $25,000–45,000 Negative Cost See Bright, Not Clouded, Future," *Variety* (16 July 1969): 17. The term 'hardcore' is used in the article, but it is to describe nudity and simulated sex. The meaning of the term changed with time.
58 Carroll, "N. Y. Overseated For Sex: Cheapies Fear Class Sin Pics," *Variety* (1 July 1969): 70.

The commercial value of exploitation films was apparent in the number of cinemas exhibiting them. Across the United States between 250 and 300 cinemas showed exploitation films in 1966 compared to approximately 800 in 1969. Peter Kaufman proclaimed, "This is not a dying industry, it is probably the most profitable in the entertainment industry today;"[59] but to be successful films needed to present something new and unique. As a consequence the depictions of sex and violence constantly pushed the boundaries of acceptability. This was made more difficult because of major studio productions and pressure from police and local communities. Many independent film producers feared that as president, Richard Nixon would realign the Supreme Court and support conservative activists who wanted to restore regional or community censorship.[60]

In the *Nation* Andrew Boyd pointed out that Nixon's anti-obscenity rhetoric was an easy way of avoiding discussions of real issues such as the Vietnam War, foreign policy, inflation, race riots and unemployment. There was no debate on obscenity because no politician would campaign on behalf of pornography. It was a one-sided campaign where politicians only had to vie with each other to see who could most vocally denounce pornographers for corrupting the youth of America and undermining the national moral standard.[61] But CDL were unconcerned with wider social issues, maintaining a focus on the emotive obscenity issue and continuing to grow in political influence. By 1969 the honorary committee of CDL included four US senators and seventy Representatives.[62] With a political administration espousing

59 "Sexpix of $25,000–45,000 Negative Cost See Bright, Not Clouded, Future," *Variety* (16 July 1969): 17.
60 Carroll, "N. Y. Overseated For Sex: Cheapies Fear Class Sin Pics," *Variety* (1 July 1969): 1.
61 Andrew Boyd, "Porno Politics," *Nation* (9 November 1970): 452.
62 Corn, "Dirty Bookkeeping," *New Republic* (2 April 1990): 14. Amongst them was Donald E. 'Buz' Lukens (Republican, Ohio) who was convicted in June/July 1989 for contributing to the delinquency of a minor after being videotaped admitting to having sex with a sixteen-year-old girl. Lukens had been paying an African-American woman to have sex with her daughter, possibly since the girl was age thirteen. Lukens' unsuccessful defence tried to argue that he could not have contributed to the delinquency of a minor because she was already immoral. Defrocked Speaker Jim Wright (Democrat, Texas), whose career ended in general disgrace in the late 1980s, was also an honorary member of CDL. In October 1974 Wilbur Mills (Democrat, Arkansas), an honorary CDL member, was found in a compromising position with 'Fanne Fox', an Argentinean stripper. Intoxicated, and bleeding from a scuffle with Fox, Mills leaped from his car and ran into the nearby Washington Tidal Basin when police approached. Another supporter, Wayne Hays (Democrat, Ohio), was exposed in 1976 for having hired a secretary

traditional values, anyone identified as transgressing would be labelled a deviant. In the summer of 1969 one man became a symbol of everything conservatives had warned about and also accidentally gave rise to the belief that 'snuff' movies existed.

who could not type. Another of Keating's supporters was Bill Chappell (Democrat, Florida) who failed in a re-election campaign in 1988 after his involvement in a military appropriations scandal was revealed. Corn, "Dirty Bookkeeping," New Republic (2 April 1990): 15.

Helter Skelter

Chapter Three

THE MOST EVIL MAN IN THE WORLD

Charles Manson and the Rumours of 'Snuff'

CHARLES MANSON WAS, FOR MOST OF HIS LIFE, AN ANONYMOUS PETTY criminal of no distinction until late 1969 when he was labelled the 'most evil man in the world' by Los Angeles newspapers. Distorted reporting and sensational allegations relating to Manson created the initial snuff rumours — meaning films of ritual human sacrifices. Claims made about Manson were embellished during the early 1970s by CDL and later in the decade by militant feminists, changing the focus from ritualistic murder to pornographic films where the unsuspecting actress was murdered at the climax.

Implicated in several brutal murders at the homes of Sharon Tate and the LaBianca family in August 1969, Manson and his associates became notorious around the world. Newspapers quickly linked the two sets of murders and media coverage plunged LA into a panic where gun sales increased fourfold and members of the public, fearing for their own security, bought guard dogs and hired bodyguards.[1] Initially the police also believed that the LaBianca murders were a "carbon copy" of those at the Tate house, but later decided that the similarities were superficial and probably unconnected.[2]

When identified, Manson and his co-defendants, members of a group known as the Family, were depicted as the epitome of hippy counterculture excesses to an uninformed audience, and his 'cult' activities were taken as a direct attack on the traditional order of American society. To conservatives they were dropouts and runaways, shirking their responsibility to society, violating accepted standards of sexual behaviour with their communal lifestyle. A few months after Manson's arrest Paul O'Neill wrote in *Life*:

1   Thomas T. Noguchi and Joseph Di Mona, *Coroner To The Stars*, Guild, London, 1986: 129.
2   "The Night of Horror," *Time* (22 August 1969): 14–15.

> The Los Angeles killings struck innumerable Americans as an inexplicable
> controversion of everything they wanted to believe about the society
> and their children — and made Charles Manson seem to be the very
> encapsulation of truth about revolt and violence by the young.[3]

Media speculation and exaggeration surrounding the crimes
committed by Manson and the Family created a hysterical climate
where no act was too outrageous or obscene to be believed, an
atmosphere that contributed to the later 'snuff' panic. Publicly
demonised for every aspect of their unconventional lifestyle, Manson
and his associates were condemned for ignoring traditional values,
making them symbolic deviants emblematic of society's decline.
Amongst their many transgressions the Family were said to have filmed
their sex orgies and ritual murders, and after the sensational reporting
of the Tate murders anything seemed possible.

The crimes were brutal and bizarre. Newspapers gravitated to the
story because of the sensational violence as well as the fact that the
victims were a beautiful movie star (Sharon Tate), the heiress to a coffee
fortune (Abigail Folger), a jet-set playboy (Voytek Frykowski), and an
internationally known hair stylist (Jay Sebring). As the wire services
carried the news of the murders in Benedict Canyon Sharon Tate's
husband, Roman Polanski, was in a London discotheque accompanied
by, amongst others, *Playboy* publisher Hugh Hefner.[4]

In her film roles Sharon Tate was often characterized as a naïve
innocent, and that is the way the media represented her after the
murders, contrasting these depictions with vivid and shocking reports
of the killings and detailed descriptions of the crime scenes. Tate was
found wearing a bra and panties with a rope around her neck, which
was slung over a beam, the other end wrapped around the neck of
Sebring (dressed in a blue shirt and black and white striped trousers).[5]
According to the coroner's report Tate was stabbed sixteen times,
penetrating the heart, lungs and liver, and causing massive internal
haemorrhaging.[6]

3   Paul O'Neill, "The Wreck of a Monstrous Family," *Life* (19 December 1969): 22.
4   Miller, *Bunny: The Real Story of Playboy*: 179.
5   Vincent Bugliosi and Curt Gentry, *The Manson Murders: An Investigation Into Motive*, Penguin,
    London, 1989: 8.
6   Ibid: 29.

Much unofficial information was released to the press at the start of the investigation and, consequently, the LAPD clamped down hard to stem the flow. In response, lacking factual information, reporters speculated on the events. Lurid claims circulated that Tate's unborn child had been "ripped from her womb," that alternatively one or both of her breasts had been cut off and that several victims had been sexually mutilated.[7] A report in *Time* (22 August 1969) exaggerated the already grisly facts and claimed that the body of Sharon Tate

> was found nude, not clad in bikini pants and a bra as had first been reported. Sebring was wearing only the torn remnants of a pair of boxer shorts. One of Miss Tate's breasts had been cut off, apparently as a result of indiscriminate slashing. She was nine months pregnant, and there was an X cut on her stomach. What appeared to be the bloody handle of a paring knife was found next to her leg, the blade broken off. Sebring had been sexually mutilated and his body also bore X marks.[8]

Vincent Bugliosi later attributed the *Time* report to the "imaginative embellishments" of a reporter,[9] but theories about sex, drugs and the occult spread quickly through Hollywood because Tate and Polanski were known to have mixed with such people,[10] and one of the investigating police officers even said the murders appeared to be "ritualistic."[11] Later, in *Satan's Assassins* (1971), Brad Steiger and Warren Smith embellished existing graphic reports and claimed that the bodies in the Tate house were left in "weird positions, suggestive of perverted sex practices."[12] In the climate of hysterical reporting anything seemed possible. When Polanski returned home to Ceilo Drive (17 August 1969) he was accompanied by a journalist, a photographer from *Life* magazine and Peter Hurkos, a well-known psychic. Hurkos later added to the confusion by telling the press that three men had been responsible for the Tate murders, and he knew who they were. Friends of Tate's, the men were allegedly turned into homicidal

---

7   Ibid: 21.
8   "The Night of Horror," *Time* (22 August 1969): 12–13.
9   Bugliosi and Gentry, *The Manson Murders*: 57–58.
10   "The Night of Horror," *Time* (22 August 1969): 12–13.
11   "Nothing But Bodies," *Time* (15 August 1969): 22.
12   Brad Steiger and Warren Smith, *Satan's Assassins*, Lancer Books, New York, 1971: 135.

maniacs by massive doses of LSD, according to Hurkos, and the killings had taken place during a black magic ceremony called 'goona, goona'.[13] He also warned that if the perpetrators were not stopped they would continue killing.

Numerous Hollywood celebrities were terrified in the wake of the Tate-LaBianca murders. Frank Sinatra was reported to have gone into hiding and Mia Farrow was so frightened she would be the next victim that she did not attend Sharon Tate's funeral. Tony Bennett moved into a suite at the Beverly Hills Hotel for greater security, Steve McQueen began carrying a gun in his car, Jerry Lewis had a CCTV security system and alarm installed in his home, and Connie Stevens turned her Beverly Hills home into a fortress.[14] Across Bel Air insecure residents became nervous and suspicious, fearing for their safety.

The Tate murders occasioned a clash of two apparently contrasting groups. However, there were some similarities between the victims of the crime, who were affluent, fashionable and successful, and the perpetrators, who were social misfits barely scraping out an existence for themselves: "Both groups were rootless, restless, unsure of their goals and values, determined to live freely and flout convention."[15] Shortly after the Tate-LaBianca murders, in an unrelated article, Newsweek reported that there were 10,000 hippies living on 500 communes across America,[16] magnifying the potential threat faced by mainstream American society from members of the counterculture.

Susan Atkins, one of those who participated in the murders at the Tate and LaBianca homes, and whose confessions implicated the Family in the murders, had dabbled in the occult for years. Before meeting Manson she appeared as part of Anton LaVey's 'Topless Witches Review' in a bar in North Beach, San Francisco, and her autobiography Child of Satan, Child of God (1977) identifies LaVey as the catalyst in her downfall.[17] Ironically, Anton LaVey, self-styled Black Pope and founder

13 Bugliosi and Gentry, The Manson Murders: 55–56.
14 Ibid: 42.
15 Roberts, "All the Twists Are Bizarre in the Case," New York Times (7 December 1969) section IV: 4.
16 "Year of the Commune," Newsweek (18 August 1969): 54–55.
17 Blanche Barton, The Secret Life of A Satanist, Mondo, London, 1992: 79. Family members were arrested after they destroyed a vehicle near the Spahn Ranch and were also found to be in possession of other stolen vehicles. When interviewed at Indio County jail Susan Atkins

of the Church of Satan, claimed that on 8 August 1969, the same night as the Tate murders, he conducted a "Hippie Ritual" in which he bitterly condemned the "psychedelic vermin" and placed a curse upon them. He also called for a beginning to a new age of Satanic awareness, and the following day newspapers reported the Tate murders.[18]

However, Charles Manson was quick to distance himself from the conventional idea of a 'hippie'. The term 'Family" was not used by Manson, or any of the people who lived at the Spahn Ranch, an old movie set; it was coined in the middle of 1968 by a journalist reporting on the youth culture and subsequently popularized around the world in the wake of the murders.[19] Cultural critic Tony Williams considered 'family' in American culture as an icon to be defended, and, "Above all, in time of war, patriotism is defined in terms of Family." Immersed in a military conflict abroad and a cultural conflict at home, 'family' had a particular resonance for Americans: "Defence of the country means defence of the family. Outside there are only monsters."[20] When the term was applied to Manson and his group, they became monsters, a parody of traditional family values and practices.

In sharp contrast to the political mainstream Manson and the Family belonged to a diverse counterculture that the media generically labelled as 'hippies'. Conservatives were quick to seize the opportunity to make sweeping generalisations and condemn the unorthodox lifestyles adopted by these youths who felt they had no political voice so were unable to defend themselves. Whilst Governor

---

made cryptic references to the Tate murders. Up to that time the Manson group were not suspects in the crimes. Transferred to LA Atkins confessed to her role in the murders and Linda Kasabian turned state's witness in return for immunity.

18 Ibid: 197.

19 Nuel Emmons, *Manson in His Own Words*, Grove, New York, 1986: 149. Use of the term probably originated with the 'Digger' communal movement in and around San Francisco in the mid-1960s who were sometimes called the 'Digger Family'. The Spahn Ranch, owned at the time by George Spahn, a semi-invalid eighty-year-old blind man, is located in the Simi Hills, northwest of Chatsworth. The Ranch was used for years as a location for shooting many B-movie Westerns. King Vidor's classic western *Duel in the Sun* (1946) was made there as well as *Robinson Crusoe on Mars* (Byron Haskin, 1964), a science fiction film, and low-budget nudie cuties such as *Linda and Abilene* (Herschell Gordon Lewis, 1969). Around the same time Al Adamson's *The Female Bunch* (1969) was shot on the Spahn Ranch and reportedly used female members of the Family as extras, and *Angels Wild Women* (Al Adamson, 1972) was one of the last films to be made on the Ranch. Two of Manson's associates, Bobby Beausoliel and Catherine 'Gypsy' Share, did appear as extras in *The Ramrodder* (Ed Forsythe and Van Guilder, 1969).

20 Tony Williams, "American Cinema in the 70s: The Family," *Movie* 27/28 (1981): 122.

of California, Ronald Reagan famously described a 'hippie' as someone who "dresses like Tarzan, has hair like Jane, and smells like Cheetah."[21] Hippies were seen as a threat because they were usually middle-class American children dropping out of society, turning their backs on traditional social values and shunning the affluent lifestyles that their parents strove to achieve.[22] In the rhetoric of Nixon's conservative ideology, family values were central to the stability and cohesion of American society. The creed of 'family, country and God' dominated his symbolic politics, with the emphasis placed firmly on the idealized nuclear family as the building block of the nation's values and democratic institutions. Based on Christian values and heterosexual procreative activity the traditional family was dominated by a male authority figure who was the provider, with women and children in inferior roles.

Steven Roberts identified a breakdown in the traditional family structure as one of the reasons why the Family came into being; all of them, even Manson, came from "disrupted" homes.[23] From birth Manson was an outsider to acceptable society. An illegitimate child to a young mother and an irresponsible father, his institutionalized upbringing only prepared him for a career in crime, and he drifted across America, finally winding up in Haight Ashbury. Manson's dysfunctional personal history made him an ideal target for conservatives endorsing family values and his case served as a warning about the consequences of pre-marital sex and weak family structures.

Dr David Smith, Lecturer at the University of California, acknowledged the importance of family institutions, but also pointed to issues such as the Vietnam War and environmental pollution as equally important to adolescents. One crucial social change was the "instant information environment" of the 1970s. Smith notes

> There were pollution, and graft and unpopular wars years ago, but people didn't find out about them right away. Today, youth gets an instant feedback about what is happening. It makes them question the

21   Martin A. Lee and Bruce Shlain, *Acid Dreams. The Complete Social History of LSD: The CIA, the Sixties, and Beyond*, Grove, New York, 1992: 163.
22   Ibid: 164.
23   Steven V. Roberts, "Charlie Manson: One Man's Family," *New York Times Magazine* (4 January 1970): 34.

quality of American life and institutions, and this questioning comes at a very vulnerable period.[24]

Perhaps the wealth of information available was undermining public faith in American society. Newspaper and TV reports during the 1960s brought social unrest and the Vietnam War into homes across the nation in a way that was not previously possible, undermining faith in the national creed and traditional values.

After 'Tex' Watson and Patricia Krenwinkel were arrested in conjunction with the Tate-LaBianca murders LAPD chief Edward Davis described them as members of a "roving band of hippies."[25] However, Manson specifically rejected the label 'hippie' and the Family lifestyle did not fit the conventional description of a 'hippie' commune. Steven Roberts quotes a psychiatrist who believed "Manson was really a mirror image of the hippie." Where hippies stressed the positive and creative aspects of human nature Manson was an embodiment of the demonic characteristics in human nature that rarely come out.[26]

According to *Newsweek* the story of the Manson Family seemed like a cross between Nathaniel West and *Easy Rider* (Dennis Hopper, 1969), and presented "an incredible yet compelling vision of the darker side of contemporary American life." *Time* and *Newsweek* compared Manson to Rasputin, and claimed the Tate-LaBianca murders were the logical culmination of his career in crime. Stories of "drugs, sadism and profligate sex" circulating in news reports about the behaviour of the Family made fictionalised accounts of hippie excess seem tame in comparison.[27]

Exaggerated accounts of the deviant lifestyle of Manson and his followers circulated in the press after their arrest and rumours about "wild sex, mind shattering drugs, and sadistic mutilations" swept through the LA area,[28] encouraging a belief that there was no end to their degeneracy. Within a month of Manson's arrest the LA *Herald*

---

24 Ibid.
25 Robert A. Wright, "Two Held, One Sought In Tate Murders; Grand Jury to Act," *New York Times* (2 December 1969): A1.
26 Steven V. Roberts, "The Hippie Mystique," *New York Times* (15 December 1969): A1.
27 "The Case of the Hypnotic Hippie," *Newsweek* (15 December 1969): 32; "The Demon of Death Valley," *Time* (2 December 1969): 20.
28 Roberts, "All the Twists Are Bizarre in the Case," *New York Times* (7 December 1969) section IV: 4.

Examiner ran a headline reading "Hippie Commune Witchcraft Blood Rites Told,"[29] and according to Morris Cerullo, by 1971 the LAPD were convinced that "hippie types" were mixing LSD with the blood of sacrificed animals to heighten the drug's effect.[30]

In the aftermath of the Tate-LaBianca murders many people in California became cautious around 'long-hairs' who aroused suspicion because the police and media repeatedly referred to Manson and the Family as 'hippies'.[31] In nearby Topanga, California, the ongoing "war against the long-hairs" increased with more police raids looking for marijuana, while the local Chamber of Commerce tried to prevent hippies from opening shops and restaurants by refusing them licenses.[32] In other parts of America the hostility was more blatant. Beginning in June 1969 the Atlanta police, with the approval of city officials, "waged war" on hippies in the city. Police stopped and threatened young people who they deemed to look like hippies, raided homes, and harassed anyone who looked unorthodox. Whilst using excessively aggressive tactics against the hippies police ignored attacks by vigilante gangs and in one instance six hippies were jailed for disturbing the peace after they were shot at from a passing car![33]

The pseudo-documentary Mondo films quickly exploited the notoriety of Manson and the hippies, incorporating familiar and exaggerated imagery into their even more sensational reportage. American rights to the Italian documentary *Angeli Bianchi ... Angeli Neri* (Luigi Scattini, 1969) were bought up by filmmaker R. Lee Frost who released an amended version which he re-titled *Witchcraft '70* (1970) in the aftermath of the Manson murders. Frost added footage of what he claimed was a secretly filmed Satanic rite conducted by hippies in Devil's Canyon, near the Spahn Ranch. The purpose of the scene is to justify a moralistic warning about drugs and the occult and condone the commentator's conclusion that the possibility of human sacrifice will always be a great threat facing society. Despite

29 Ellis, *Raising the Devil*: 178.
30 Morris Cerullo, *The Back Side of Satan*, Creation House, Carol Stream, Illinois, 1973: 92. Cerullo claimed to have met Charles Manson twice, once at a Satanic ritual where a chicken was sacrificed but Manson was supposedly unhappy and favoured sacrificing a person.
31 Roberts, "The Hippie Mystique," *New York Times* (15 December 1969): A1.
32 Ibid: 42.
33 "The Great Hippie Hunt," *Time* (10 October 1969): 26–27.

being obviously faked, the footage contributed to media stereotypes of hippies, reinforced existing suspicions and added to the climate of fear. *Naked and Violent* (Sergio Martino, 1970) had a scene that also connected hippies to ritual sacrifice. After a long-range establishing shot of Roman Polanski's home in the Hollywood Hills, the director (Sergio Martino) intercuts a shot of hippies making a blood sacrifice at the command of a Manson-style guru. After dripping candle wax onto the bare breasts of a young woman a chicken's head is cut off and the blood poured onto the victim while sitar music plays in the background. The mishmash of transgressive imagery bore no resemblance to practices at the Spahn Ranch, but did reinforce the media stereotype of Manson and his associates.

Considering the media reporting of the crimes a backlash against hippies was not surprising. However, when President Nixon, a trained lawyer, condemned Manson as guilty *during* his trial the political manipulation of the story became clear. At a press conference, just before Nixon attended a series of private meetings sponsored by the Law Enforcement Assistance Administration in Denver, Colorado (3 August 1970), he foolishly asserted that Manson was "guilty, directly or indirectly, of eight murders without reason."[34]

His comments were made in the midst of a statement on law and order issues and on the role of the media in helping to maintain public respect for the criminal justice system. In the press conference Nixon addressed the reporters live and without notes hoping to give the impression of competence and confidence, and in the course of his comments he touched on a number of issues relating to crime in order to emphasise his administration's commitment to law enforcement. While Nixon sought to make drastic cuts in federal budgets, law enforcement was singled out for substantial increases. In 1969 the law enforcement budget was $60 million, increased to $280 million the following year, and projected to be between $450 and $500 million for 1971. Nixon emphasised his law and order credentials, complaining that Congress was slow to debate thirteen pieces of legislation designed to fight crime, and that to date only one had been approved. Calling for a sense of urgency he wanted more legislation to fight threats such as

---

34 "Nixon's Remarks on Manson and Statement in Washington," *New York Times* (4 August 1970): 16.

organised crime, narcotics and pornography, amongst others.

During his statement Nixon digressed into making comments about media responsibility in reporting crime. Using the film *Chisum* (Andrew V. McLaglen, 1970), which he had seen recently, as an example of the generic Western, Nixon sought to endorse a situation where "the good guys come out ahead ... [and] the bad guys lose." He liked the simplistic good versus evil morality and contrasted that situation with contemporary America where, in his opinion, criminals were being glorified and made into heroes. Using Manson as an example he complained that the trial dominated the front page of newspapers and several minutes of the TV news each evening. Nixon alleged, "Here is a man who was guilty, directly or indirectly, of eight murders without reason ... yet who as far as the coverage was concerned, appeared to be rather a glamorous figure to the young people whom he had brought into his operations..." In contrast he felt that the media had made a villain out of the judge when he found two defence lawyers guilty of contempt and warned "unless we stand up for the system, unless we see that order in the courtroom is respected, unless we quit glorifying those who deliberately disrupt ... then the system will break down."[35] Seeking to exploit the situation to his advantage, Nixon wanted to use Manson to rally support for his conservative crusade for law and order issues and traditional values.

Speaking of the legal system in general, Nixon concluded, "We must come to its defence and we must not consider that those, the judges, the police and the others, who are simply doing their duty, that they are the villains and that those who are provoking them are always in the right."[36] Nixon's intent was to attack Democrats on the crime issue and present himself as a strong advocate of the legal system, but his comments showed him to be too enthusiastic about convicting criminals and not attentive enough to civil rights and due process of law.

In Los Angeles, as a consequence of Nixon's comments, Judge Older faced a petition for a mistrial in the Manson case, and Paul Fitzgerald, Patricia Krenwinkel's counsel, argued, "The president is a significant opinion maker, a significant leader, an attorney. He was campaigning for law and order. Subliminally, maybe unconsciously, this cannot help

35   Ibid.
36   Ibid.

but influence in an extraordinary fashion the minds of jurors."[37] When the Judge called the jury back into the courtroom the three female defendants (Susan Atkins, Patricia Krenwinkel and Leslie Van Houten) rose and began chanting, "If President Nixon thinks we're guilty, why go on with the trial?"[38] Also, in court Manson held up a copy of the Los Angeles *Times* (4 August 1970) which carried the headline "Manson Guilty, Nixon Declares" for the jury to see. The process of transforming Manson from a petty criminal into a national symbol of criminality and degeneracy was well underway; Manson had become a national warning of the threat posed by countercultural values.

An editorial in the *New York Times* pointed out that, despite his training as a lawyer, Nixon "approaches the discussion of most public questions, not with the sensitivity to the nuances of language and the habitual caution of an experienced lawyer, but rather with the breezy metaphors and attention-getting if inexact analogies of the politician."[39] Conservative representative Charles E. Wiggins (Republican, California) criticized the press for emphasising the "unimportant news" for two days, asserting that Nixon's exact words were *not* necessary to the story and that repeating them in "dramatic headlines" could "only be intended to sell newspapers or prejudice the defendant."[40] Representative Carl Albert (Democrat, Oklahoma) defended the press for reporting the story and Representative Hale Boggs (Democrat, Louisiana) described Nixon's statement as "indefensible," adding that representative Wiggins' comments were "the most amazing speech I've ever heard in the thirty years I've been in the House."[41] Satirists at the *East Village Other* were quick to pick up on the irony of the situation and responded by printing a picture of Manson on the cover with the headline "Manson Declares Nixon Guilty!" (11 August 1970).

Throughout his administration Nixon implemented the image of the hippie threat as a political tool. It was observed that when Nixon addressed a crowd there were always a number of boisterous longhaired youths present. At one meeting in the conservative

37 Douglas Kneeland, "Manson Mistrial Barred Again: Jurors Still Held Unprejudiced," *New York Times* (6 August 1970): 34.
38 Ibid.
39 "Mr. Nixon's Loose Talk," *New York Times* (5 August 1970): 34.
40 Robert Semple Jr., "Press Criticized On Nixon Remark," *New York Times* (6 August 1970): 34.
41 Ibid.

stronghold of Orange County, California, newspapermen watched the guardsman and state police admit what appeared to be a prearranged number of obvious protestors before enforcing directives to only admit individuals with short hair who were smartly dressed. Cartoons appeared in newspapers depicting Nixon standing on stage behind a microphone asking his audience for four volunteers, "two to holler obscenities and two to throw rocks."[42]

Writing in *American Opinion*, the magazine of the extreme right-wing John Birch Society, David Emerson Gumaer claimed the Manson murders were part of a new, but already well-established, underground movement which spanned the nation and "embraced drugs, Devil worship, wanton sex, mutilation for pleasure, and ritual murder" and was inhabited by "some of the most monstrous sadists and perverts imaginable."[43] In *Time*, Dr Lewis Yablonsky, author of *The Hippie Trip* (1968), claimed to have found after studying the hippie phenomenon closely, "Many hippies are socially almost dead inside. Some require massive emotions to feel anything at all. They need bizarre, intensive acts to feel alive — sexual acts, acts of violence, nudity, every kind of Dionysian thrill."[44] Yablonsky's was an ideological statement rather than an objective and balanced judgement. According to Bill Ellis "Drug use, casual sex, and the threat of random violence" were the main features of the 1970s 'Satanic panic' in America, and of the rhetoric used to decry the behaviour of juvenile delinquents, the counterculture, and every other moral panic condemning teenage rebellion.[45] Dr David Smith of the Haight Ashbury Free Medical Centre recognized that the media usually focused on the worst aspects of the counterculture. Manson and the Family were made into symbols of that counterculture by the media and politicians, who chose not to acknowledge any of the positive developments such as the Free Clinic Movement, increased awareness of environmental issues, or rock concerts.[46]

In the wake of the Manson Family murders tabloid newspapers

---

42   Jerry Voorhis, *The Strange Case of Richard Milhous Nixon*, Paul S. Erikson, New York, 1972: 23.
43   David Emerson Gumaer, "Satanism: A Practical Guide to Witch Hunting," *American Opinion* (September 1970): 41.
44   Yablonsky quoted in "Hippies and Violence," *Time* (12 December 1969): 23.
45   Bill Ellis, *Raising the Devil: Satanism, New Religions, and the Media*, University Press Kentucky, Lexington, 2000: 67.
46   Smith in *Charles Manson: The Man Who Killed the 60s* documentary (Peter Bate, 1994).

published sensational stories claiming that some of the ritualistic killings had been filmed but similar stories had been circulating in California for some time. In Los Angeles Robert K. Dornan, a former actor and national CDL spokesman, reported on his talk show that in October 1968 the body of a young woman was found nude and decapitated on a Southern Californian beach. Her body was allegedly drained of blood and several 8mm film canisters were found nearby.[47] In retrospect the story appeared to give credibility to the rumours that Manson's acolytes had filmed the slaughter but the stories about the Tate-LaBianca murders being filmed were *not* substantiated and *no* films were presented at Manson's trial. The only mention of home movies during the investigation came when one of the witnesses, William Garretson, reported that there had been a party at the Tate house in June 1969 attended by about seventy-five guests. He testified that at the party he saw Voytek Frykowski making home movies of a nude woman in the swimming pool.[48] Those films were not produced in court.

Prosecuting attorney Vincent Bugliosi stated that during the first few days of the murder investigation, in a search of the loft above the living room, a "roll of videotape" was found and taken to the Police Academy for examination. It was a film of Sharon Tate and Roman Polanski engaged in sex. The film was not booked into evidence, instead it was returned to the loft where it had been found. A subsequent newspaper report claimed that a vast collection of pornography was discovered in the house, including films and photographs of famous Hollywood stars engaged in a variety of sexual acts, but the story was never substantiated. According to Bugliosi the Tate-Polanski sex film and a few unused rolls of film, along with a set of wedding photographs and a large quantity of Sharon Tate's publicity photographs, were all that was found in the house.[49] On 17 August Roman Polanski returned to Cielo Drive for the first time since the murders and during his visit took the sex film from the loft.[50]

47 Jay Lynch, "The Facts About the Snuff-Film Rumours," *Oui* (July 1976): 70.
48 Douglas Robinson, "Manson Counsel Objects to Key Witness," *New York Times* (28 July 1970): 15. Garretson, nineteen-years-old, lived in a guesthouse on the property and was employed by Tate to look after several dogs at her home. The police initially arrested him for the murders, but later the charges were dropped.
49 Bugliosi and Gentry, *The Manson Murders*: 21.
50 Ibid: 55.

One other piece of footage was acquired by the LAPD during the investigation. Jeffrey 'Pic' Pickett and Herb Wilson, early suspects in the Tate murders, claimed to have been in Jamaica making a film about marijuana from 8 July to 17 August, placing them out of the country when the murders occurred. However, in the course of the investigation Pickett gave the authorities a video made at the house on Cielo Drive while Polanski and Tate were away. The tape showed Abigail Folger, Voytek Frykowski, Witold Kaczanowski and another woman having dinner in front of the fire. The tape was generally uneventful, documenting a minor domestic argument, but at one point Frykowski, stoned, rushed to the fireplace with a camera trying to take a picture of a burning pig's head which he thought he saw.[51]

In 1976 Jay Lynch contacted Vincent Bugliosi to specifically ask about the Manson 'snuff' film rumours, and whilst Bugliosi had heard the stories he knew of *no* evidence that the films existed.[52] He acknowledged, "They used to have sex orgies all the time, and maybe some of them were on film. I don't know. But the sacrificial rites and all that — I didn't get one speck of corroborating evidence. That doesn't mean it didn't happen."[53] The 'snuff' rumours were an ideal opportunity for media speculation to further demonise the hippie counterculture and exploit public familiarity and fascination with the sensational Manson murders.

In the course of his investigation Ed Sanders heard a number of stories about 'snuff' films, and he reported a rumour that an LA drug dealer sold a film depicting the "ritual murder" of a young woman to a "famous New York artist," but he did not name the drug dealer or the artist.[54] Sanders was sent a note by 'Chuck', a friend of Gary Hinman, who claimed to own films of axe murders in San Francisco and Malibu, but the films never materialized. The majority of Sanders' claims about 'snuff' films are derived from an interview with an unnamed source who, it is claimed, spent two years on the periphery of Manson's Family. According to Sanders' information the Family had three Super 8 cameras to make "home movies" that were processed

51 Ibid: 63–64.
52 Lynch, "The Facts About the Snuff-Film Rumours," *Oui* (July 1976): 86.
53 Bugliosi quoted in ibid.
54 Ed Sanders, *The Family*, EP Dutton, and Co., New York, 1971: 211.

by their friends.[55]

An orgy that took place in July 1969 on the Spahn Ranch was one of those reported to Sanders as having been filmed. At the centre of the orgy was a fifteen-year-old girl called 'Simi Valley Sherri' (Sherri Ann Cooper) who usually tended horses on the Ranch, and more than twenty others. She was not a willing participant and, after being stripped down to her underwear, was punched in the face and threatened. She then reluctantly allowed Bobby Beausoleil to have sex with her, thereby beginning the orgy.[56] Sanders' informant claimed that the Manson Family made their 8mm films in 1969 and the summer of 1970, subject matter of which could be divided into three categories: Films of the Family (dancing and sex), animal sacrifices, and human sacrifices.[57] But by the summer of 1970 the Manson Family had been identified and arrested for the Tate-LaBianca murders, so they could not have been making home movies.

Almost exactly four months after the Tate-LaBianca murders the Rolling Stones concert at the Altamont speedway in Livermore, California (8 December 1969), twenty-three miles east of San Francisco, took place and events that night contributed to the growing rumours of 'snuff' films. Intended to be the West Coast version of Woodstock, the Altamont Free Music Festival, an impressive line-up of acts, played throughout the day. Because of their reputation Hell's Angels were used to providing security for bands like the Grateful Dead in exchange for free beer, and they were hired to keep the Altamont Festival under control. After a long delay the Rolling Stones appeared on stage and began their set. However when they played 'Under My Thumb' the Hell's Angels attacked Meredith Hunter, an eighteen-year-old black man in a bright green jacket who had leaned against one of their bikes. As the Angels surrounded Hunter he produced a gun; three Angels jumped on him, and Hunter was stabbed in the back, neck and face. The events of the show were captured in the theatrically released

---

55 Ibid: 210.
56 Ibid: 205–206. *The Manson Family Movies* (John Aes-Nihil, 1984), a series of disjointed set pieces, was supposed to be set in the summer of 1969 and depict the films the Family made themselves. The lack of evidence did not stop Aes-Nihil attempting to recreate what he *thought* the films would have looked like, even dramatizing Sharon Tate dancing topless to entertain her houseguests while Voytek Frykowski scores drugs.
57 Lynch, "The Facts About the Snuff-Film Rumours," *Oui* (July 1976): 70.

documentary *Gimme Shelter* (Albert and David Maysles, 1970), in which the film editors concentrate on the violence in the crowd, not the performances onstage, contributing to suspicion.[58] It seems obvious that the show's main notoriety, hence its commercial value, was derived from the murder, so why not put it in the film? In the wake of Mondo films showing documentary footage of executions and murder, *Gimme Shelter* was neither particularly graphic nor shocking.

In his continuing quest to find out more about the Manson films of which he had heard, Ed Sanders went to New York in 1970 posing as a pornographer with outtakes from Andy Warhol films for sale. He claimed to have been given the opportunity to purchase seven hours of assorted porn films, amongst which were sex films allegedly made by the Family that were purported to have been collected during pretrial investigations, but the asking price of $250,000 was too much for him.[59] While researching *The Family* two animal sacrifice films were described to Sanders by his informant, one featuring a dog and the other a cat; in the dog film the animal's body was already cut up and the participants smeared blood over two girls who had been stripped, then everyone had sex with the two girls. The informant recognized eight or ten of the people who appeared in the film as visitors to the Spahn ranch. In the other film a cat was blown up by an M-80 firecracker and the blood smeared over the spectators.[60]

The informant also remembered a short segment of film, lasting only five minutes, of a dead woman on a beach — described as a "snuff film" — but he believed it to be part of a larger film. The woman was estimated to be about twenty-seven-years-old with short red hair and she lay decapitated on a beach near a campfire, encircled by five people who wore black robes and hoods to cover their faces.[61] Questioning his informant Sanders asked:

Q. What was the scenario? Was she tied up. Did she look willing?

A. She was dead. She was just lying there.

Q. She was already dead?

58 A Hell's Angel, Alan David Passaro, was charged with Hunter's murder, but he was acquitted on the grounds of self-defence.
59 Sanders, *The Family*: 211.
60 Ibid: 213–214.
61 Ibid: 214–215. He also noted that there were a few other people in the background.

A. Yeah. Legs spread, uh. She was nude but nobody was fucking her. They said her head was chopped off and she was just lying there.

Q. That's when the movie started? They didn't show the actual sacrifice?

A. (Shakes head no) They showed people throwing blood all over, all around the circle.[62]

Importantly the informant acknowledged he had not been there, nor had he seen the film, he was simply recounting a story he had heard. The woman was already dead, her murder and decapitation were not shown, and no one had sex with her. The informant did not see the rest of the film but Sanders claimed it sounded like one he knew about.[63]

The informant described the human sacrifice film as "an interesting kind of flick;" however, the descriptions given are vague and stereotypical, and during the interview Sanders had to coax out most of the information. Despite the obviously leading questions which he used to elicit responses, Sanders melodramatically warned "If this information is true, there is no girl, no woman, no bather at the beach, no hitchhiker at the Freeway ramp who is safe in southern California till these people are taken off the streets."[64] By uncritically repeating the accusations that he had prompted from his informant in *The Family* (1971), Sanders further popularized the idea that the Family had filmed some of their killings, and that Manson himself had described them as 'snuff' films. But the films, allegedly buried in Death Valley, were never found.[65]

---

62   Ibid: 215.
63   Ibid.
64   Ibid: 215–216. In later editions of *The Family* Sanders acknowledges that no films depicting murder or murder victims were ever found.
65   This idea itself sounds like a distortion of another contemporary story. In the late 1960s Kenneth Anger began filming, but never completed, the first version of *Lucifer Rising*. It was purported to show actual Satanic rituals designed to raise Lucifer. Bobby Beausoliel, star of the film, stole Anger's van and the negatives for the film after an argument. In response Anger allegedly cursed Beausoliel, and tried to turn him into a toad, but the spell failed and the van broke down outside the Spahn Ranch. Anger remade the film but by that time Beausoliel had become associated with Charles Manson and was in jail serving a life sentence for the murder of Gary Hinman. A few fragments of footage from the original *Lucifer Rising* were used in *Invocation of My Demon Brother* (1969), but Anger's original concept of Lucifer as an angel of love had changed in the meantime and by the time he made *Invocation of My Demon Brother* Lucifer was a violent spirit. Bobby Beausoliel and Anton LaVey appeared in *Invocation of My Demon Brother*, and the music was by Mick Jagger.

As a colloquial term for death, 'snuff' has been in usage throughout the twentieth century and occurred in popular films in the early 1970s such as *A Clockwork Orange* (Stanley Kubrick, 1971), when the central character Alex (Malcolm McDowell), who is only interested in sex, violence and Beethoven becomes, like Manson, a pawn in a political game. Trapped between liberals and conservatives who are in conflict over the criminal justice issue, Alex tries to commit suicide and the word 'snuff' is used as a euphemism for death. In *The Dynamite Brothers* (Al Adamson, 1974) a ruthless drug boss is advised to "snuff out" his adversaries, with no mention of Charles Manson or the actual murder of an actress for the viewer's entertainment.

Shortly after the Manson murders Roy Stanley published *The Hippie Cult Murders* (1970), a fictional story based on the crimes. Fact based books quickly followed with Lawrence Schiller's *The Killing of Sharon Tate*, Jerry LeBlanc and Ivor Davis' *5 to Die* and J. D. Russell's *The Beautiful People* all being published in 1970. Responding to public interest the following year J. D. Russell's *Chronicle of Death*, John Gilmore and Roy Kenner's *The Garbage People*, and George Bishop's *Witness To Evil*, along with Brad Steiger and Warren Smith's *Satan's Assassins* were all published, but the most important of the early commentaries on Manson was Ed Sanders' book *The Family* (1971), which popularized the notion that the Family had made films of ritual orgies and sacrifices.

As a major international news story the Tate-LaBianca murders were a prime subject for exploitation filmmakers. Al Adamson made use of contemporary newspaper reports to promote *Satan's Sadists* (1969), enticing the audience by promising "Now: See on the screen the Shocking Stories you are reading about in the newspapers Today!" (even though the film is completely unconnected to Manson). *The Helter Skelter Murders* (Frank Howard, 1969), a rare documentary style film featuring Manson on the soundtrack performing songs that later appeared on the *LIE* album, was the first attempt to recount the events in any factual, albeit sensational, way. *Gabrielle* (Arlo Shiffen, 1970) is usually acknowledged as the first film released which exploited the notoriety of the Manson murders. In it a character called Dr Matson leads a group called 'the Family' whose lifestyle amounts to sexual degeneracy and murder. The film project was probably already in production, or just about to go into production, when the Manson murders were publicized, and minor alterations to the existing story were utilised to make it appear more topical. Likewise, *Angel, Angel Down We Go* (Robert Thom, 1969) was re-titled *Cult of the Damned* to exploit the public interest in Manson. Another early film exploiting the Manson myth, *Slaughter*, was shot in South America by husband and wife team Michael and Roberta Findlay but not released until 1976. Re-titled *Snuff*, and containing an extra scene, it became the focus of the 'snuff' film rumours and the basis of the backlash against 'porno chic'.

The murder orgy at the end of Russ Meyer's *Beyond the Valley of the Dolls* (1970) was specifically included to exploit the notoriety of the Tate murders. In *I Drink Your Blood* (David Durston, 1970) a band of Devil worshipping hippies spike an old man's drink with LSD, setting off a chain of sensational events. To get revenge his grandson sells the hippies meat pies injected with blood from a rabid dog, turning them into psychotic cannibals who infect everyone that they bite. The following year *The Love-Thrill Murders* (aka *Sweet Saviour*) (Robert L. Roberts, 1971), the first fictionalized account of the events surrounding the Manson murders, was released. Other films such as *The Omega Man* (Boris Sagal, 1971) made derogatory and sarcastic reference to hippies at the Woodstock festival and the Family. In *Deathmaster* (Ray Danton, 1972) the hippie cult leader turns out to be Dracula, and *The Night God Screamed* (Lee Madden, 1973) makes superficial connections to Manson and his followers as a way to build tension before the film's final twist. *Macbeth* (1971) was the first film Roman Polanski made after his wife's murder and while most critics found it excessively gory and violent, understandably a number of them also made connections between the film's imagery and the murders in Benedict Canyon: "It was as if Polanski was using the movie to exorcise his memories."[66] Receiving mixed reviews, *Macbeth* was credited with having the first convincing decapitation scene in film history.

---

66   Miller, *Bunny: The Real Story of Playboy*: 266. Throughout the seventies and beyond, the Manson case continued to be exploited by low-budget filmmakers in movies such as *The Commune* (Monroe Beeler, 1970), *Multiple Maniacs* (John Waters, 1970), *Night of the Witches* (Keith Erik Burt, 1970), *Cannibal Girls* (Ivan Reitman, 1972), *Hitchhikers* (Ferdy and Beverly Sebastian, 1972), *Blue Sunshine* (Jeff Lieberman, 1977), *The Manson Family Movies* (John Aes-Nihil, 1984), *Igor and the Lunatics* (Billy Parloni, 1986), *Thou Shall Not Kill ... Except* (Josh Becker, 1987) and *The Manson Family* (Jim Van Bebber, 2005).

According to Bill Ellis the main influences on the mainstream understanding of Satanism in America during the later 1960s and early 1970s were Ed Sanders and evangelists Michael Warnke and John Todd. Sanders collected rumours and speculation circulating in California after the Manson murders and reported them as fact. He spent a year in the LA area collecting information and visiting the places Manson was said to have frequented, and Sanders also hired a private investigator and advertised for information in underground newspapers. As a consequence, *The Family* recycled existing ideas about sex rituals and black magic and "tells less about Manson and his followers than about the wealth of rumours and beliefs about Satanism that were then current in the California subculture."[67] Subsequently Warnke and Todd further embellished the rumours that Sanders had gathered and linked them to existing conspiracy theories.[68]

Coinciding with jury selection for the Manson trial in June 1970, the shocking murder of schoolteacher Florence Nancy Brown in California was headline news and contributed to existing concerns about ritual murder. Brown, a mother of five, was attacked when her car stopped at an intersection. She was stabbed repeatedly and taken to Riverside County where her body was buried in a shallow grave before the offenders drove her car to Santa Cruz where it was later found abandoned and burned out.[69] In a gruesome twist Brown's heart, lungs and one arm were removed.[70] Steven Hurd was identified as the main suspect in the Brown case along with two associates who were also implicated in the murder of an individual by the name of Jerry Wayne Carlin. The trio were described as "drug-oriented transients" drifting around California, although it was acknowledged by authorities that they were not as cohesive as the Manson family.[71]

After being arrested and charged Hurd sought an insanity plea,

67 Ellis, *Raising the Devil: Satanism*: 181.
68 Ibid: 168.
69 Craig Turner, "Drifter's Life in Orange County Described," LA *Times* (2 July 1970) Section 2: 1.
70 Robert M. Getteny, "Satan Worship Tale Unfolds In Slaying Cases," LA *Times* (10 July 1970) Section 1: 3.
71 Ibid: 19. Besides Steven Hurd (twenty) two other people Herman Brown (seventeen) and Christopher Gibboney (seventeen) were also implicated in the murders, and it was they who were supposed to have made the sacrifice even though Hurd claimed he was the only true Satanist among them. Carlin was a twenty-one-year-old gas station attendant, murdered with a hatchet and robbed of $73 the night before Florence Brown was killed.

claiming to be a member of a Satanic group. Asserting his innocence in the murders of Carlin and Brown, Hurd described himself as a Satanist but according to his solicitor the murders were not Satanically motivated.[72] Explaining why the body had been decapitated he asserted that it was permissible to "'snuff people out' providing a part of the body is used in a sacrifice." Hence why her arm was removed.[73] Investigators however did not suspect any Satanic elements in the crimes until William Gamble, Hurd's attorney, disclosed that his client was a Satanist;[74] to stress the point he also reported that Hurd was frightened of being in a cell with a Bible — "he is afraid the devil won't like the Bible being there and he tells me the devil is telling him to snuff himself out." Hurd admitted to being present at both murders but maintained that he did not take part in the killings, claiming that he was pressurized into confessing because of threats against his family. His involvement with Satanism was not clearly established and according to attorney Gamble, Hurd claimed to have consulted with a 'chief devil' in San Francisco who gave advice,[75] but his attorney made it clear that Anton LaVey was not the 'chief devil' in question.[76]

Exacerbating public concerns, on 16 August 1971 *Newsweek* published an article listing several murders attributed to Satanism, but referring primarily to the Florence Brown case. A number of other crimes were described as being ritualistic; for example in June 1971 two youths from Vineland (New Jersey) killed their friend at his request. The following month Kim Brown, aged twenty-two, stabbed a sixty-two-year-old man to death in Miami and was later convicted of manslaughter and sentenced to seven years. The article dismissed assertions by the police and psychiatrists that the Satanic aspect of the crime was a manifestation of a mental disorder, adding that most of the offenders had some sort of involvement with the Church of Satan.[77]

Further shocking crimes contributed to the Satanic panic and the backlash against hippies. In a contentious case Dr Jeffrey MacDonald

---

72 Getteny, "Satan Worship Tale Unfolds In Slaying Cases," LA *Times* (10 July 1970) Section 1: 3.
73 Ellis, *Raising the Devil*: 178.
74 Bill Hazlett, "Cannibalism Possibility Probed in Satan-Cult Slaying of a Woman," LA *Times* (11 July 1970) section 2: 1.
75 Getteny, "Satan Worship Tale Unfolds In Slaying Cases," LA *Times* (10 July 1970) Section 1: 3.
76 Dave Smith, "'Head Satan' Speaks — to Set the Record Straight," LA *Times* (17 July 1970) Section 1: 1.
77 "Evil, Anyone?" *Newsweek* (16 August 1971): 34.

claimed that on 17 February 1970 hippies had attacked his home and, after knocking him unconscious, killed his wife and children. Initially suspected of committing the murders himself McDonald maintained his story and the charges against him were dropped. David Emerson Gumaer cited the gory murder of a young social worker in Montana in July 1970 and the case of Stanley Baker the same month as examples of Satanic crimes.[78] On 19 October 1970 John Linley Frazier killed Dr Victor Ohta at his home near Santa Cruz escalating tensions between hippies and local residents and quickly becoming an international news story. In the following years more high profile cases contributed to the Satanic panic and demonisation of the counterculture. Between 12 October 1972 and 13 February 1973 Herb Mullin killed thirteen people in California whom he later claimed were willing human sacrifices to prevent massive earthquakes on the San Andreas Fault. Contributing to conservative rhetoric about social decay was the case of Ed Kemper, who had shot and killed his grandparents in 1964 and was sent to Atascadero State Hospital for five years. After his release, between May 1972 and April 1973, Kemper murdered eight, keeping body parts as souvenirs.

The Reverend Billy James Hargis, a prominent evangelist from Tulsa's Christian Crusade, warned, "Devil worship is mushrooming. It ultimately will become the religion of the militants and the revolutionaries." He also preached that communism was Satan's handiwork.[79] However, the Church of Satan was *not* politically radical and LaVey himself admitted:

> We utilized a formula of nine parts social respectability to one part outrage. We established a Church of Satan — something that would smash all concepts of what a 'church' was supposed to be. This was a temple of indulgence instead of the temples of abstinence that had been

---

78 David Emerson Gumaer, "Satanism: A Practical Guide to Witch Hunting," *American Opinion* (September 1970): 72. Stanley Baker and Harry A. Stroup were arrested on the Pacific Coast Highway, south of Big Sur, as they left the scene of an accident. They were driving a stolen car belonging to a man who had been found shot and dismembered a few days earlier, notably his heart had been cut out. Both men were unkempt with long hair and beards superficially identifying them with media stereotypes of the counterculture. While no information linked either man with a cult, media speculation made the connection. Baker later claimed to be a cannibal.

79 Hargis quoted in "Evil, Anyone?" *Newsweek* (16 August 1971): 35.

built up until then. We didn't want it to be an unforgiving, unwelcoming place, but a place where you could go to have fun.[80]

LaVey condemned Manson as a "mad-dog killer," and acknowledged that the Church of Satan was an elitist organisation, which had turned many prospective members away, and was unlikely to accept amateurish Satanists. In a revealing interview with the LA *Times* LaVey acknowledged the Church of Satan ideology was "just Ayn Rand's philosophy with ceremony and ritual added." He also looked forward to a benign police state where "civility, good manners and courtesy will return, and emphasis will be placed on achievement and worth rather than on sanctimonious lip service."[81]

Whilst used by Charles Manson and numerous others, the term 'snuff' was used to describe death or killing, but when used by the tabloid media it referred to ritualistic murders that had been filmed. It was only in the aftermath of the Manson trial that 'snuff' took on another meaning, one that was more twisted and perverse than anyone could have imagined. While Richard Nixon's administration sought to promote a reactionary conservative ideology, CDL sought to expand their crusade using sensational rhetoric, culminating in the accusation that moral decay had reached such a peak that pornographic films which culminated in the actress being murdered were being made as entertainment. CDL appropriated the already sensationalized term 'snuff movies' and used it to describe these films and advance their own fundamentalist agenda.

---

80   LaVey quoted in Barton, *The Secret Life of A Satanist*: 79.
81   Smith, "'Head Satan' Speaks — to Set the Record Straight," LA *Times* (17 July 1970) Section 1: 24–25.

Charles Keating (right)

Chapter Four

THE SPEECHES OF THE PRESIDENT ARE THE RAVINGS OF A CLOWN

Nixon and the Commission on Pornography

IN *LIFE* MAGAZINE (28 AUGUST 1970) JOHN NEARY BOASTED SARCASTICALLY "We've done it at last! We have succeeded in supersaturating our frazzled poor selves in sex of every variety."[1] This was a message sure to arouse concern in Middle America. In the course of a decade the Supreme Court made a number of rulings extending the application of the First Amendment to cover adult materials. Beginning with the precedent set in *Roth v. United States* (1957) and continuing with *Jacobellis v. Ohio* (1964), *Mishkin v. New York* (1966), *Ralph Ginzburg v. United States* (1966), *Memoires v. Massachusetts* (1966), *Redrup v. State of New York* (1967) and *Stanley v. Georgia* (1969), the Supreme Court eased restrictions to reflect the changing values and standards of contemporary society. All of the decisions directly opposed the reactionary CDL crusade and, as a consequence, CDL pledged to appear on the side of the prosecution in every obscenity case that came before the Supreme Court.[2]

In *Jacobellis v. Ohio* (1964) the Supreme Court reversed a lower court ruling convicting a theatre owner who had been arrested for exhibiting *Les Amants* (Louis Malle, 1958). Writing the majority opinion, Justice Brennan articulated an important principle, that "material dealing with sex in a manner that advocates ideas, or that has literary or scientific or artistic value or any other form of social importance may not be branded as obscenity," nor banned. Justice Potter Stewart concurred with the idea that a work had to be "utterly without social

1   John Neary, "Pornography Goes Public," *Life* (28 August 1970): 19.
2   "Sex as a Spectator Sport," *Time* (11 July 1969): 51. This was a pledge that CDL representatives had been making for several years. See also "Obscene Material Becoming Bolder, Opponent Contends," *New York Times* (23 October 1965): 33.

importance" and acknowledged that Supreme Court decisions in relation to what could be banned as obscene realistically meant only hardcore pornography would be considered, and added, "I shall not today attempt further to define the kinds of materials I understand to be embraced within that shorthand definition; perhaps I could never succeed in intelligibly doing so. But I know it when I see it, and the motion picture involved in this case is not that."[3]

A few years later the Supreme Court decision in *Stanley v. Georgia* (1969) was another blow to anti-obscenity campaigners. Three reels of 8mm film were found by the police whilst conducting a search of the defendant's home, but the warrant being executed was granted on the basis of alleged illegal bookmaking activities, therefore the search was not related to an obscenity investigation and the seizure of the films was unwarranted. Thurgood Marshall wrote the majority decision for the Court in *Stanley* which agreed that the "private possession of obscene matter cannot constitutionally be made a crime," and asserted that the "right to receive information and ideas, regardless of their social worth is fundamental to our free society." Emphasising the individual right to privacy, Marshall wrote:

> If the First Amendment means anything, it means that a State has no business telling a man, sitting alone in his own house, what books he may read or what films he may watch. Our whole constitutional heritage rebels at the thought of giving government the power to control men's minds.

Referring to the Court's decision in *Kingsley International Pictures Corp. v. Regents* (1959), Marshall pointed out that constitutional protections were "not confined to the expression of ideas that are conventional or shared by a majority ... And in the realm of ideas it protects expression which is eloquent no less than that which is unconvincing." The majority decision in *Stanley* asserted:

> Nor is it relevant that obscene materials in general, or the particular films before the Court, are arguably devoid of any ideological content.

3   Jacobellis believed that it was the activities of CDL that caused his arrest and prosecution.

The line between the transmission of ideas and mere entertainment is much too elusive for this Court to draw, if indeed such a line can be drawn at all.

Openly sceptical of anti-obscenity rhetoric, Marshall also wrote, "the State may no more prohibit mere possession of obscene matter on the ground that it may lead to antisocial conduct than it may prohibit possession of chemistry books on the ground that they may lead to the manufacture of homemade spirits." The exaggerated and sensational claims of obscenity crusaders could not sway the Court.

While *Stanley v. Georgia* defended the right of an individual to possess pornography in their own homes, defence lawyers expanded on the logic of the decision, arguing that if there was a right to own pornography, then individuals had a right to buy it, and if the right to buy it existed then businessmen had a right to distribute it. Continuing this line of thought, if it was acceptable to own, buy and distribute pornography then it must be permissible to film, photograph or write about sexually explicit material.[4] In theory this established the basis for a legitimate industry to produce sexually orientated materials for an adult audience.

Two years before, in 1967, Post Office general counsel Timothy J. May noted a significant change in attitude when testifying before the Senate Special Subcommittee on Juvenile Delinquency when he disclosed that people who wanted to could receive erotic literature through the mail, but not hardcore porn. The Subcommittee was interested in the grey legal area of contentious material that was obviously not hardcore pornography and therefore did not violate obscenity laws. In May's opinion, "In a free society there is very little that we can and should do to restrict what a free citizen can read. We [the Post Office] don't want to be censors. We have a very difficult time just getting the mail delivered." He added that the public also had the right to privacy whereby they would not be targeted by businesses trying to sell smut to them or their children.[5]

Like Keating, Richard Nixon was prone to make exaggerated, and outright false, accusations about the pornography business. At a rally in California (9 October 1968) Nixon claimed that pornographers were

---

4   Bob Woodward and Scott Armstrong, *The Brethren,* Simon and Schuster, New York, 1979: 195.
5   Roy Reed, "Erotic Material in Mail Defended," *New York Times* (10 February 1967): 23.

buying the mailing lists of Cub Scouts in order to target obscene material at young people.[6] Alden G. Barber, chief Scout executive, was quick to reply to Nixon's accusation, pointing out that Boy Scouts of America did not sell mailing lists to anyone, especially not pornographers, and that no national mailing list for Cub Scouts existed anyway.[7]

Lyndon Johnson set up an advisory Presidential Commission of Obscenity and Pornography after a unanimous vote by Congress (21 September 1967). Originating from a Bill sponsored by Karl Mundt (Republican, S. Dakota) and Dominick V. Daniels (Republican, New Jersey), the Commission was intended to investigate primarily photographic and cinematic hardcore pornography that showed "sexual perversion" that was being legally distributed due to confusion about the obscenity law. It was also intended to set standards which would enable girlie magazine producers to self-regulate. The Commission was to firstly define pornography, then to study and determine its effects.[8] Congress assigned the Commission four main duties:

(1) with the aid of leading constitutional law authorities, to analyse the laws pertaining to the control of obscenity and pornography; and to evaluate and recommend definitions of obscenity and pornography;

(2) to ascertain the methods employed in the distribution of obscene and pornographic materials and to explore the nature and volume of traffic in such materials;

(3) of obscenity and pornography upon the public, and particularly minors, and its relationship to crime and other antisocial behaviour; and

(4) to recommend such legislative, administrative, or other advisable and appropriate action as the Commission deems necessary to regulate effectively the flow of such traffic without in any way interfering with constitutional rights.[9]

---

6   "Nixon Promises to Seek a Law Banning Lewd Mail to Children," *New York Times* (10 October 1968): 50.
7   "Chief Scout Executives Says Mailing Lists Are Not Sold," *New York Times* (11 October 1968): 53.
8   "Johnson to Set Up Pornography Study Under New Law," *New York Times* (5 October 1967): 25.
9   Weldon T. Johnson, "The Pornography Report," *Duquesne Law Review* 10 (1970): 195–196. The Commission members were Winfred C. Link (Methodist minister from Tennessee),

When the first official meeting of the President's Commission was held at the Kinsey Institute (Indiana) members were shown the erotica collection, briefed on the latest national statistics, and shown examples of early and contemporary stag films. Reflecting sharp differences in values amongst the committee members, Father Morton Hill was concerned that Barbara Scott, a lawyer, had to watch the stag films, but when Scott told him she was not horrified by the experience Hill was dismayed and said he would pray for the redemption of her soul.[10]

Chairman William B. Lockhart sensibly instructed the members of the Commission that they were free to discuss their work, findings, and opinions in private, but urged them not to reveal personal opinions to the public, press or politicians. He warned that premature disclosure could prejudice the study and generate enough controversy to undermine the final *Report of the Commission on Obscenity and Pornography*.[11] The *Report* was a political hot potato, something that a political system frequently has to deal with

> Whatever the particular 'potato', its temperature is presumably lowered through the prescribed two years of discussion by prominent persons, carefully organized public hearings, and an interim report and the final report. By the time the report is filed, the 'potato' is presumed to be cold.[12]

But the final report of the President's Commission on Obscenity and Pornography was, if anything, at its hottest by the time it was presented in 1970.

Rabbi Irving Lehrman, Morton A. Hill (Catholic priest and anti-obscenity activist), G. William Jones (clergyman and teacher from Southern Methodist University), Cathryn Spelts (English instructor from South Dakota), Barbara Scott (New York Attorney with the Motion Picture Association), Morris A. Lipton (Professor of Psychology at the University of North Carolina Medical School), Otto N, Larsen (Professor of Sociology at University of Washington), Edward D. Greenwood (Child Psychiatrist with the Menninger Foundation), Joseph T. Klapper (research sociologist with CBS), Thomas D. Gill (Chief judge of the juvenile court in Connecticut), Freeman Lewis (president of the Washington Square Press in New York), Edward E. Elson (president of the Atlanta News Agency), Marvin E. Wolfgang (Professor of Sociology at the University of Pennsylvania), Frederick H. Wagman (Director of the University of Michigan library), and the chairman was William B. Lockhart (Dean of the University of Minnesota Law School).

10   Talese, *Thy Neighbor's Wife*: 374.
11   Ibid.
12   Johnson, "The Pornography Report," *Duquesne Law Review* 10 (1970): 191.

Charles Keating was not a member of the initial President's Commission panel; he replaced judge Kenneth B. Keating of the New York Court of Appeals who was appointed US Ambassador to India in 1969. When Nixon appointed the head of CDL, a nationally known fanatical opponent of pornography,[13] to the President's Commission it was obviously a politically motivated move. Before Charles Keating was appointed to the Commission the White House asked the FBI to carry out a Special Presidential Inquiry into the old espionage charges from the 1950s. Even though John Ehrlichman, White House Chief of Staff, was informed that the charge was dropped due to "insufficient evidence" he let the appointment go through.[14] Keating wasted no time in making his intentions clear, in obvious conflict with the rest of the members, saying "I shall serve on the commission with the objective of seeing these criminals jailed."[15]

True to his word, in 1969, just before joining the Commission, Keating acted as a private attorney bringing a prosecution against Russ Meyer's *Vixen*. Arguing that *Vixen* was obscene, the film was confiscated the day it opened in Cincinnati and the subsequent court action cost Meyer $250,000. Memorably, Keating claimed Meyer "has done more to undermine the morals in these United States than anyone else," to which Meyer sarcastically responded, "I was glad to do it."[16] In his dissent from the *Report*, Keating criticized Twentieth Century Fox for employing a "pornographer" like Meyer to direct *Beyond the Valley of the Dolls* (1970).[17] But realistically it was nothing more than a shrewd economic move by the Hollywood studio looking to cut budget costs while increasing box office takings.

Ironically, while Keating's nemesis Meyer enjoyed making adult orientated films, he had reservations about developments in contemporary cinema that presented more graphic depictions of sex. *I Am Curious (Yellow)* (Vilgot Sojman, 1966) was one film that Meyer identified:

13 Talese, *Thy Neighbor's Wife*: 366.
14 Binstein and Bowden, *Trust Me*: 103.
15 Keating quoted in Strub, "Perversion for Profit," *Journal of the History of Sexuality* 15:2 (May 2006): 285.
16 Binstein and Bowden, *Trust Me*: 104.
17 "Report of Commissioner Charles H. Keating Jr.," in *The Report of the Commission on Obscenity and Pornography*: 612.

That film has put me at a crossroads. I have never shown genitalia in any of my films. Once you have to show that to get people into the theatre, how many people are going to do it with taste? I have always been against censorship in any form, but I have also maintained that you should leave something up to the imagination.[18]

When the judge delivered his twenty-two-page verdict against Meyer, Keating alerted local and national newspapers, television stations and influential publications such as *Time*, *Life* and *Newsweek*, but only local reporters covered the story. Furious, Keating wrote to vice president Spiro Agnew complaining, "In this case in spite of the fact that the news release went out on a CDL letterhead — which is impressive enough to say the least — that it came from a member of the Presidential Commission, and that a decent judge, properly outraged, really 'laid down the law,' the amount of coverage wasn't worth mentioning."[19]

When Meyer appealed the decision to the Ohio Supreme Court it produced an unusual ruling *against* the filmmaker. The decision of the Court in *State ex rel Keating v. A Motion Picture Film Entitled Vixen* (1971), which prevented the exhibition of *Vixen*, was interesting because it did not distinguish between the depiction of simulated sexual acts in the film and the performance of sexual acts in public places, declaring them both to be "conduct, not free speech." It is a judgement that might at first seem like a pedantic legal point, but one that is crucial to the theory of free speech as it is applied to literature and film. A film or book will be protected as free speech because it is a filmed or written depiction of conduct, a simulation, but *not* the depicted conduct. This is the line that later CDL allegations about the making of pornographic films culminating in real murder, and the advertising campaign for *Snuff*, claimed had been crossed. Films frequently depict conduct that would be criminal if actually performed, but where an actual murder should be prosecuted as a crime, a film presenting a dramatised portrayal of a murder should not.[20] The Ohio

---

18 Meyer quoted in "Glandscape Artist," *Time* (13 June 1969): 70.
19 Letter from Keating to Spiro Agnew quoted in Binstein and Bowden, *Trust Me*: 105.
20 Edward de Grazia and Roger K. Newman, *Banned Films: Movies, Censors and the First Amendment*, R. R. Bowker, New York and London, 1982: 332.

Supreme Court applied the "redeeming social value" test but found that despite issues such as racism, anti-militarism, communism and aeroplane hijacking, the film's social commentary was not related to the dominant theme which was the presentation of sexual intercourse for commercial exploitation.

Appointed to the President's Commission, Keating attacked the other members of the panel and even requested that Nixon should dismiss William B. Lockhart, but his plans were hindered when his counsel, James J. Clancy, was not permitted to observe the sessions of the Commission.[21] To differentiate himself from the other members, and distance himself from the work of the Commission, Keating constantly referred to himself as "Nixon's appointee." Because the other commissioners were appointed by Lyndon Johnson and drawn from the publishing and film business, Keating accused them of having an interest in protecting obscene materials.[22] Keating warned Nixon for almost a year before the final report was published that as a consequence of the Commission's findings "not only [is] the pornographer winning the war but your administration will receive the blame."[23] He again voiced his dissent from the Commission's *Report* in a *Reader's Digest* (January 1970) article, "The Report that Shocks the Nation." After stalling the publication of the report with a restraining order Keating encouraged CDL members to write to their congressmen calling for a full investigation into the Commission.[24] In 1970 he travelled more than 200,000 miles giving speeches attacking the Commission,[25] and the same year he also raised the necessary money and plotted tactics for his brother Bill's successful election campaign for the House of Representatives.[26]

Nixon urged a 'Citizen's Crusade' against smut[27] and began to distance himself from the Committee's findings before the *Report* was officially submitted. In the summer of 1969, a year before

21 Talese, *Thy Neighbor's Wife*: 375.
22 Binstein and Bowden, *Trust Me*: 105.
23 Keating quoted in Herbert L. Packer, "The Pornography Caper," *Commentary* (February 1971): 73. See also "Senate Leaders in Both Parties Denounce Findings of Pornography Panel," *New York Times* (2 October 1970): 50.
24 Talese, *Thy Neighbor's Wife*: 377.
25 Schlosser, *Reefer Madness and Other Tales from the American Underground*: 135.
26 Binstein and Bowden, *Trust Me*: 106.
27 Neary, "Pornography Goes Public," *Life* (28 August 1970): 19.

the final report was due to be released, Nixon's adviser John D. Ehrlichman acknowledged that the Commission's findings could hurt the administration, so he assigned Patrick Buchanan (a Nixon speechwriter) to help Spiro Agnew write the dissenting opinions to the majority report. In the fall of 1969 Morton A. Hill and Winfrey C. Link began holding their own public hearings with an emphasis on tightening legal controls.[28] Three Commission members, Hill, Link and Keating, wrote a dissenting minority opinion that began by condemning the majority report as a "Magna Carta for the pornographer." Alleging it was "slanted and biased in favour of protecting the business of obscenity and pornography, which the Commission was mandated by Congress to regulate," they added that the majority recommendations would be found "deeply offensive" to Congress and "tens of millions" of Americans, and that the conclusions reached were based on "scanty and manipulated evidence" which was "wholly inadequate." The dissenting commissioners asserted that $2 million of taxpayer's money had been used to produce a "shoddy piece of scholarship that will be quoted ad nauseum by cultural polluters and their attorneys within society."[29] While Keating was in the spotlight with the President's Commission, Raymond Gauer testified before the Subcommittee on Postal Operations hearings on obscenity in the mails to a sympathetic audience.[30]

Whilst the nation was still waiting for the President's Commission findings to be published, Abe Fortas returned to the political spotlight. *Life* magazine (4 May 1970) reported that Fortas received improper payments from the Louis Wolfson Foundation, and as soon as the story

---

28 Packer, "The Pornography Caper," *Commentary* (February 1971): 72.
29 "Report of Commissioners Morton A. Hill, S.J., Winfrey C. Link, concurred by Charles H. Keating Jr.," in *The Report of the Commission on Obscenity and Pornography*: 456–457.
30 *Obscenity in the Mails*, Hearings before the Subcommittee on Post Office and Civil Service, US Government Printing Office, Washington, 1969: 252–266. Gauer had previously submitted statements to the Postal Committee but this was the first time he had been called to testify. William Pfender, assistant national director of CDL, also submitted a statement to the committee. One member of the Committee, Glenn Cunningham (Republic, Nebraska) claimed to have worked closely with Charles Keating and Cunningham, along with Richard C. White (Democrat, Texas), congratulated Gauer during the hearings for doing a tremendous job. Around the time of Gauer's appearance at the hearings he was given opportunities to impart his opinions to receptive and influential audiences in an interview in the magazine the *Liguorian* (1968) and via lectures to numerous conservative organisations and several appearances on 'Dean' Clarence Manion's right-wing radio show *The Manion Forum*.

broke Strom Thurmond was one of the first to call on Fortas to resign from the Supreme Court. The money had already been returned but Thurmond seized on the political opportunity and continued his attack, questioning Fortas' conduct and encouraging the Justice to "search his conscience to determine if the faith of the people in the integrity of the Supreme Court would be better served by his resignation."[31] On 15 May 1970 Abe Fortas resigned his seat in the Court, and Thurmond characteristically gloated in satisfaction. Nixon now had the opportunity to appoint another justice to the Supreme Court.

Away from the political drama the President's Commission continued to conduct the first detailed study of the pornography business in an effort to understand the scale of the industry and the social impact of the obscenity issue. The Commission estimated that in 1969 the market for sexually explicit material, an industry fuelled by public demand, was worth about $200 million (gross), considerably less than the multibillion dollar estimates being made by conservative anti-obscenity crusaders. During the investigation they also found the market for pornography to be complicated and chaotic, not a monolithic industry as the crusaders claimed,[32] findings that raised questions about the rhetoric of anti-obscenity organisations. The majority opinion recommended that a "massive" sex education campaign should be launched to promote healthy attitudes toward sex that would provide "sound foundations for our society's basic institutions of marriage and family." The campaign, to work in conjunction with family, school and church, was not intended to establish orthodoxy, but allow for a plurality of values.[33]

Keating insisted that his forty-six-page dissent, largely written by Patrick J. Buchanan, was included with the published report.[34] Claiming that in 1967 the Supreme Court began forcing immorality upon the states, a situation that continued for several years, he added more optimistically that the appointment of conservative justices Burger and Blackmun were "hopeful indications that this disgusting

31 Thurmond quoted in Cohodas, *Strom Thurmond and the Politics of Southern Change*: 403. Wolfson was a wealthy industrialist who had been convicted of violating federal securities laws.
32 Binstein and Bowden, *Trust Me*: 105.
33 "Excerpts From Panel's Majority Report, Dissenting Opinions and Other Views," *New York Times* (1 October 1970): 20.
34 Schlosser, *Reefer Madness and Other Tales from the American Underground*: 135.

erosion of morality may be checked."[35] This was a blatantly ideological statement. Paradoxically asserting that Presidential Commissions do not work and never will, Keating did not explain why he agreed to participate in such a study although his conduct suggested it was simply to sabotage it. He also directed his criticism toward the staff hired to compile the *Report*, challenging their professionalism and describing them as being of "mediocre talent, hangers-on in government, or individuals not yet settled on a course in life who accept interim work on a Commission staff as a place to light and learn during the generally short life of a Commission."[36] Appealing to a populist sentiment he added, "it is too bad the majority of the Commission are not responsible to the voters. If they were, they would soon feel the brunt of national concern for decency."[37]

In his dissent Keating used several quotes from J. Edgar Hoover to support his claims about the harmful effects of pornography, but the comments were a matter of personal opinion rather than scientifically reasoned fact. Hoover claimed, "The circulation of periodicals containing salacious material and highly suggestive and offensive motion pictures and television, play an important part in the development of crime among our youth."[38] Building on this Keating asserted his belief that "pornography is a major cause of sex violence. I believe that if we can eliminate the distribution of such items among impressionable school-age children we shall greatly reduce our frightening sex crime rate."[39] Hoover also attributed the "increasing number of sex crimes" solely to "sex literature madly presented in certain magazines. Filthy literature is the great moron maker. It is creating criminals faster than jails can be built."[40] These were sweeping generalizations that magnified public fear but did not acknowledge the real causes of crime or offer any practical solution.

In contrast to the majority of members of the Commission, Keating pointed out that the issue of obscenity was a growing concern for

35 "Report of Commissioner Charles H. Keating Jr.," in *The Report of the Commission on Obscenity and Pornography*: 601.
36 Ibid: 583–584.
37 Ibid: 609.
38 Hoover quoted in ibid: 636.
39 Hoover quoted in ibid: 637.
40 Hoover quoted in ibid: 636.

"some of the finest people in our nation," and cited CDL members Ray Gauer and Jim Clancy (LA), Bill Pfender (Philadelphia), Dick Bertsch (Cleveland), and Al Johnston (Biloxi) as specific examples:

> These people take of their time and their fortunes to participate daily in the battle against the pornographers. They are representative of countless Americans who, awakening to the most serious threat to public decency in history are increasingly becoming aware and active.[41]

Presenting them as representative of the majority of Americans he therefore identified his own beliefs, and the CDL agenda, with grassroots America. However, Keating's dissent really reflected his own entrenched views on pornography, and predictably he made no attempt to be objective about the material contained in the report or to scientifically gather and analyse data to support his existing beliefs.

Before the *Report* was released Nixon's staff went on an offensive to distance it from the administration. On 22 August 1970 Attorney General John N. Mitchell spoke out against pornography, saying that it was time to "open a new front against filth peddlers." A few weeks later vice president Spiro Agnew stated that there was a need, nationwide, to "restrain bad taste and outrageous vulgarity."[42] When the *Report* was finally issued the US Postmaster General, the Republican and Democrat Senate leaders, and the head of the National Conference of Catholic Bishops joined Nixon in his sweeping condemnation.[43]

Speaking at a Republican fundraiser in Utah, Spiro Agnew publicly distanced the Nixon administration from the *Report*, stressing the erosion of decency in American society and claiming it "has been abetted by a political hedonism that permeates the philosophy of radical liberals." He went on to explain his comments by adding that "They may not openly condone indecency, but they help create the climate in which it flourishes by their inability to say no and their unwillingness to condemn." Agnew was only too willing to condemn and promised, "we are going to have strong laws against pornography

41   "Report of Commissioner Charles H. Keating Jr.," in *The Report of the Commission on Obscenity and Pornography*: 609.
42   Ibid: 608–609.
43   Talese, *Thy Neighbor's Wife*: 378.

and against obscenity."[44] Nixon's counsellor, Robert H. Finch, stated, "At least by implication the majority of the commission members recommend that permissiveness be sanctioned and even promoted as an official national policy," and added, "I reject this approach totally."[45]

Nixon's administration used the *Report* in their campaign against "radical-liberals" and the "permissive society"[46] which was condemned as the source of every social problem. Attorney General John Mitchell asserted, "If we want a society in which the noble side of man is encouraged and mankind is elevated, then I submit pornography is surely harmful."[47] Conservatives in the Republican and Democratic parties were quick to join the condemnation as soon as the *Report* was made public.[48] Senator Robert C. Byrd (Democrat, West Virginia) described the *Report* as "shameful" and the Commission as "outrageously permissive" and "malicious or misguided or both." He also used the *Report* as a yardstick to show "how far down the road of moral decadence" American society had travelled.[49] Evangelist Billy Graham went even further, condemning the *Report* as "one of the worst and most diabolical ever made by a Presidential Commission and one which no Christian or believing Jew could support."[50] Optimistically, William B. Lockhart announced that his "hope and expectation is that when the research papers are studied in a calm atmosphere uncomplicated by election appeals, the result will be a far more careful appraisal of public policy in this emotionally charged area."[51] Weldon T. Johnson also acknowledged public suspicion about the area of study, noting,

> the scientific study of human sexual behaviour is still often regarded as
> a kind of pseudo-scientific slum into which the responsible, or at least

---

44 James M. Naughton, "Epithets Greet Agnew in Salt Lake City," *New York Times* (1 October 1970): 22.
45 "Comments By Finch," *New York Times* (2 October 1970): 70.
46 "Senate Leaders in Both Parties Denounce Findings of Pornography Panel," *New York Times* (2 October 1970): 70.
47 Mitchell quoted in Talese, *Thy Neighbor's Wife*: 378.
48 "Senate Leaders in Both Parties Denounce Findings of Pornography Panel," *New York Times* (2 October 1970): 70.
49 Ibid.
50 Billy Graham's comment, printed in *Christian Century* (11 November 1970), quoted in Johnson, "The Pornography Report," *Duquesne Law Review* 10 (1970): 190–219.
51 Lockhart in the *Nation* (9 November 1970) quoted in ibid: 191.

respectable, scholar has no rightful entry. Despite serious efforts, sex researchers are regarded by many as harbouring something more than academic or professional scientific motivation.[52]

But neither could have predicted the dismissive and politicized response to the *Report*.

Just seventeen days after the *Report* was made public the Senate voted to reject its findings and recommendations. Furthermore, on 17 October the Senate passed a condemnatory resolution, introduced by Senator McClellan, by an overwhelming sixty votes to five.[53] Senator Robert P. Griffin (Republican, Michigan), who led the attack on Abe Fortas, echoed Nixon and advocated tightening existing anti-pornography laws rather than liberalising existing legislation.[54] A few days after the Senate rejected the *Report* Richard Nixon denounced it again, in rhetoric which echoed Keating's, warning, "if an attitude of permissiveness were to be adopted regarding pornography, this would contribute to an atmosphere condoning anarchy in every other field — and would increase the threat to our social order as well as to our moral principles."[55] The similarity is not surprising since Patrick Buchanan, one of Nixon's speechwriters, who was assigned by the White House to write Keating's dissenting opinion, probably wrote both.[56]

Nixon's dismissal of the findings of the Commission *Report* was sweeping and he firmly stated:

So long as I am in the White House, there will be no relaxation of the national effort to control and eliminate smut from our national life. The Commission contends that the proliferation of filthy books and plays has no lasting harmful effect on a man's character. If that were true, it must also be true that great books, great paintings, and great plays have no ennobling effect on a man's conduct. Centuries of civilization and ten minutes of commonsense tell us otherwise.

The Commission calls for the repeal of laws controlling smut for

52 Johnson, "The Pornography Report," *Duquesne Law Review* 10 (1970): 193.
53 Packer, "The Pornography Caper," *Commentary* (February 1971): 73.
54 "Senate Leaders in Both Parties Denounce Findings of Pornography Panel," *New York Times* (2 October 1970): 70.
55 Nixon quoted in Binstein and Bowden, *Trust Me*: 106.
56 Binstein and Bowden, *Trust Me*: 105.

adults, while recommending continued restrictions on smut for children. In an open society, this proposal is untenable. If the level of filth rises in the adult community, the young people in our society cannot help but also be inundated by the flood.

Pornography can corrupt a society and a civilization. The people's elected representatives have the right and obligation to prevent that corruption.

The warped and brutal portrayal of sex in books, plays, magazines, and movies, if not halted and reversed, could poison the wellsprings of American and Western culture and civilization.

The pollution of our culture, the pollution of our civilization with smut and filth is as serious a situation for the American people as the pollution of our once-pure air and water.

In sharp contrast to the recommendations of the *Report* Nixon asserted, "Smut should not be simply contained at its present level; it should be outlawed in every state in the union. And the legislatures and courts at every level of American government should act in unison to achieve that goal." Appealing to traditional conservative values he concluded by saying, "American morality is not to be trifled with. The Commission on Pornography and Obscenity has performed a disservice, and I totally reject its report." Condemnation of the *Report* was a symbolic gesture towards conservatives but the subsequent era of 'porno chic' showed that a significant proportion of the American population disagreed with the president.

By the time of the conservative national crusade on morality in the late 1960s, an editorial in the *New York Times* entitled "Mr. Nixon's Smutscreen" (26 October 1970) noted that Nixon had repeatedly identified the findings of the President's Commission on Obscenity and Pornography with his predecessor, Lyndon Johnson, to make the Democrats seem permissive and responsible for the undermining of American morals and values. Nixon dismissed the *Report* as "morally bankrupt,"[57] and his rhetoric encouraged other conservative commentators such as Walter Berns and Irving Kristol, who followed suit, arguing for censorship.[58] The editorial also added that the attack

57   "Mr. Nixon's Smutscreen," *New York Times* (26 October 1970): 36.
58   Walter Berns, "Pornography vs. Democracy: The Case for Censorship," *Public Interest* (Winter

on pornography and the 'war on crime' was an attempt to distort the political debate and distract from the real issues of the Vietnam War, inflation, unemployment and recession.[59] The lack of substance in Nixon's approach to political issues was apparent to some other commentators. In frustration, James Reston wrote in the *New York Times* (28 October 1970):

> No amount of public indifference to the dirty tricks of politics can remove the plain fact of this campaign: Mr. Nixon has not treated the American people in this election as they needed to be treated and deserve to be treated in this troubled time.

Instead of trying to put the contemporary moral and economic problems into perspective, and addressing them responsibly, Nixon chose to deal with them "narrowly and cleverly." In doing so he put political interest above the welfare of the nation. Reston continued,

> In short, [Nixon] is asking for the trust of the people, but he is not trusting them to deal seriously and responsibly with the staggering problems that affect their lives. Instead, he is using their anxieties for partisan gain, and arguing the preposterous proposition that the moral confusions of the age are somehow a party issue, and that human frailty, human violence, human selfishness, war, crime, drugs and smut are somehow the fault of the Democratic Party and can be minimized by the election of Republicans.[60]

The rhetoric was typical of Nixon's tactics because no one was going to defend crime, drugs or smut.

In the wake of the findings in the *Report* many conservatives, up to and including Nixon, were unhappy and wanted to challenge calls for a liberal pornography law. Even though the direction of the Supreme Court during the previous decade was generally liberal there was a constant conservative presence, often dissenting from precedents. In

---

1971): 3–24; Irving Kristol, "Pornography, Obscenity and the Case For Censorship," *New York Times Magazine* (28 March 1971): 24–25, 112–116.

59 "Mr. Nixon's Smutscreen," *New York Times* (26 October 1970): 36.

60 James Reston, "How To Lose Even If You Win," *New York Times* (28 October 1970): 47.

1970 the Supreme Court reversed the obscenity conviction of Donald Walker, an Ohio newsstand owner. Dissenting strongly in the case, Chief Justice Warren Burger objected to the ruling, stating,

> I can find no justification, constitutional or otherwise, for this court's assuming the role of a supreme and unreviewable board of censorship for the fifty states, subjectively judging each piece of material brought before it without regard to the findings or conclusions of other courts, state or federal.[61]

Burger did not think that was the purpose of the Supreme Court.

Journalist Herbert Packer suggested that, as a consequence of the *Report*, tougher laws would be passed against pornography, but he was not alarmed because a vigorous anti-obscenity campaign "would involve costs in money, manpower, and invasions of privacy that we as a society are unwilling to pay. Passing new laws costs a great deal. Given the dimensions of our present crime problem, rhetoric (passing tough laws) is the administration's only weapon."[62] In the contemporary climate the manpower and money could be used more productively in dealing with pressing social concerns.

In September 1971 Justices Hugo Black and John Marshall Harlan both retired from the Supreme Court for health reasons, and Nixon, as president, had the opportunity to appoint their replacements, who were conservative jurists Lewis F. Powell Jr. and William H. Rehnquist. This meant that Nixon had been given the opportunity to appoint four out of nine Supreme Court justices! Nixon's appointees to the Supreme Court created a difficult situation for publishers and filmmakers interested in sexual freedom. The Watergate scandal and other exposés related to his administration removed Nixon from office and undermined the conservative agenda he promoted, and Gay Talese recognized "it would be far worse if Nixon, Agnew, Mitchell and the rest were still in power. One of the chief aims of that administration was to eliminate pornography and sexual expression."[63]

Outside the social and political mainstream the 'white coater'

---

61   "Burger Criticizes Obscenity Ruling," *New York Times* (16 June 1970): 42.
62   Packer, "The Pornography Caper," *Commentary* (February 1971): 76.
63   "Porno Rama," *Oui* (February 1975): 115.

Red White and Blue (Ferd and Beverly Sebastian, 1970) was quickly produced by David Friedman's company to examine the findings of the *Report* and the political response it provoked. Claiming to be a visual study of censorship, the documentary also examined how the sex industry worked, interviewing filmmakers and performers and providing examples of nudity and softcore sex to illustrate different points. In November 1970, a pamphlet was distributed by Greenleaf Press to 55,000 recipients advertising an unauthorised edition of the *Report*. Promising not only the 352 pages of text from the official report, the new edition contained an additional 546 illustrations as examples of the material being discussed. While providing information on the contents of the forthcoming publication the pamphlet also denounced Richard Nixon:

> Thanks a lot Mr. President. A monumental work of research and investigation has now become a giant of a book. All the facts, all the statistics, presented in the best possible format [and] completely illustrated in black and white and full colour. Every facet of the most controversial report ever issued is covered in detail. This book is a *must* for the research shelves of any library, public or private, seriously concerned with full intellectual freedom and adult selection. Millions of dollars in public funds were expended to determine the *precise truth* about eroticism in the United States today, yet every possible attempt to suppress this information was made from the very highest levels. Even the president dismissed the facts, out of hand. The attempt to suppress this volume is an inexcusable insult directed at every adult in this country. Each individual must be allowed to make his own decision; the facts are inescapable. Many adults, many of them, will do just that after reading this report. In a truly free society, a book like this wouldn't even be necessary.[64]

FBI agents quickly acquired a copy of the illustrated report and sent it to J. Edgar Hoover, who brought it to the attention of Nixon. But the president was already aware of its existence because Raymond Gauer had bought several copies of the book in an LA sex shop and sent a

---

64   Pamphlet quoted in Talese, *Thy Neighbor's Wife*: 380.

copy to Charles Keating who, in turn, alerted the president. Nixon was furious and it was not long before legal strategies were discussed to prosecute the publisher.[65]

Faced with the sudden mainstream popularity of pornography after the success of *Deep Throat* (Gerard Damiano, 1972), conservative moralists increased their rhetoric, preaching an apocalyptic doctrine predicting the impending obliteration of traditional American values. Using the *Report* as a symbolic rallying point for his crusade, Keating's article for *Reader's Digest* restated his position on obscenity and introduced him to a huge audience of potential new recruits to CDL.[66]

Under Raymond Gauer's directorship in the 1970s CDL expanded its activities: a number of attorneys were trained and maintained by the organisation to fight obscenity cases, and a library of research materials including a collection of all case files and briefs filed in obscenity cases were assembled. Seminars were conducted and CDL representatives worked directly with civic officials to devise strategies and encourage prosecutions.[67] To raise the money necessary to pay for CDL's activities Gauer drastically enlarged the financial base of the organisation, expanding beyond the few anonymous wealthy patrons and private foundations that had supported the organisation's early activities. In addition Gauer instigated numerous nationwide aggressive direct-mail fundraising campaigns. A standard letter was sent to potential donors describing Charles Keating as an "active businessman" who, provoked by his faith and conscience, "decided some time ago that I owed it to my family and country to spend some money and time to try to preserve the moral decency of America."[68] The consequences were twofold: Supporters sent substantial donations to finance CDL, but the direct-mailing also provided Gauer with a list of potential activists who could be encouraged to write letters to elected officials and participate in other activities and campaigns.[69]

By 1972 CDL claimed 145,000 "Decent Citizens" were contributing

65   Ibid: 380–381.
66   Charles Keating, "The Report That Shocked the Nation," *Reader's Digest* (January 1971): 37–41.
67   See, *Blue Money*: 165.
68   The letter was signed by Charles Keating. Corn, "Dirty Bookkeeping," *New Republic* (2 April 1990): 14.
69   See, *Blue Money*: 165–166.

funds to the organisation[70] while around the same time Charles Keating was spending a lot of his energies lobbying for his anti-obscenity agenda in Washington, D.C. American Financial Corporation (AFC) began bankrolling politicians and Keating openly acknowledged that the contributions were ideologically inspired. Executives from AFC generously donated $259,969 to Richard Nixon's Committee to Re-Elect the President (CREEP) in 1972, but Nixon's campaign manager returned $107,000 to Keating after the election noting that, at that time, they had adequate funds but some of the money may be held in reserve for the 1974 election campaigns of Republican senators and congressmen.[71] CDL's national influence grew under the Nixon administration, as both emphasised traditional values and a moral majority within the nation who had remained silent for too long. Prompted by the sensational rhetoric of right-wing demagogues, however, this constituency was becoming more active against the deviant and degenerate minority, who reflected the social and political changes taking place in America after WWII.

70   Corn, "Dirty Bookkeeping," *New Republic* (2 April 1990): 14.
71   Binstein and Bowden, *Trust Me*: 106–107.

Chapter Five

DEEPER THAN DEEP

'Porno Chic' hits American Society

BECAUSE OF THE INCREASING POPULARITY OF TELEVISION IN THE 1950S AND 1960s, art-house cinemas began showing 'nudie cutie' films, offering something that television could not to draw in audiences. Soon they were joined by many small urban cinemas that were suffering because of the distribution policies being imposed by major studios favouring prestige cinemas for big budget releases.[1] The expansion of TV schedules also took audiences away from cinema and the Hollywood studios could only compete by narrowing the range of films being produced and emphasising blockbuster films aimed at a teenage audience. Whilst the plan provided a short-term solution for the studios the consequences were bad for small cinemas, especially those in run-down inner city areas. In response the small cinemas sought a new audience, and specialising in adult films was a niche market that TV and mainstream cinema could not tap into.[2] Because of pressure from politicians, policemen and religious leaders, about 100 producers, distributors and exhibitors joined together in 1968, establishing the Adult Filmmakers Association of America (AFAA) to protect and advance their economic interests. With the proliferation and growing acceptance of adult entertainment in America, Rabbi Jacob J. Hecht predicted in 1969, "The home of the future will consider pornography as commonplace and necessary as a colour TV or dishwasher."[3]

In 1968 the Motion Picture Association of America (MPAA) was established to classify films as G, PG, R or X. It was possible, if producers were willing to accept an X rating, to show virtually anything on screen. The following year *Midnight Cowboy* (John Schlesinger, 1969) became the only X-rated film to win an Oscar (for Best Film). Aside from formal

1   Hebditch and Anning, *Porn Gold*: 191.
2   Ibid: 216.
3   Desmond Smith, "Pop Sex Among The Squares," *Nation* (25 August 1969): 145.

classifications films could also be released unrated or with a self-appointed X. According to Joseph Slade the first hardcore pornographic feature film was shown at the original Avon Theatre (Sixth Avenue, New York) in 1968; prior to that it was illegal to show explicit sexual images.[4]

Whilst illegal and underground, pornography could exploit any social taboo. But the situation changed when the AFAA tried to make adult entertainment socially acceptable and develop legitimate business markets — now they had to appeal to more conventional social values. Matt Cimber's *Man and Wife* (1969) pseudo-documentary is acknowledged as the first theatrical hardcore film and, responding to its success, Cimber quickly made *Black is Beautiful* (aka *Africanus Sexualis*) (1970), *He and She* (1970) and *The Sensuous Female* (1970). However, *Variety* acknowledged *Mona, the Teenage Nymph* (Bill Osco, 1970) as the "long awaited link between the stag loops and conventional theatrical fare."[5] It was one of *Variety's* top fifty grossing films of 1971.[6]

The emergence of adult material into mainstream culture took decades and reflected social and economic changes taking place in America after WWII. By 1969 it was clear that a substantial audience existed for adult material and, according to Desmond Smith, 'pop pornography' was just a slick version of what had earlier been called 'smut'. It was a growth industry, and very competitive, but the potential profits attracted many competitors. "Pop pornography," wrote Smith,

is the new white-collar obsession. Lingerie manufacturers and Sunday newspapers revel in it. The *Ladies Home Journal* abandons faithful Princess Grace and the Duchess of Windsor in favour of serializing Jacqueline Susann. Kenneth Tynan approves. *Time* profiles it. Broadway musicals exploit it. Suburban housewives pant and lust for it. And, since the United States is a consumer society that thrives on satisfying wants and desires, what is pop pornography if not the ingenious one-handed icing on the manufacturers cake? In short, sex has become a very big business indeed.[7]

4   Joseph Slade, "Violence in the Hard-Core Pornographic Film," *Journal of Communication* (Summer 1984): 150.
5   "Mona," *Variety* (24 February 1971).
6   John Heidenry, *What Wild Ecstasy: The Rise and Fall of the Sexual Revolution*, Simon and Schuster, New York, 1997: 209.
7   Smith, "Pop Sex Among The Squares," *Nation* (25 August 1969): 142.

Smith criticized the 'sexual revolution' of the late 1960s for having "the ring of the cash register about it" rather than being an erotic renaissance evolved from continuing social change.

In marketing, 'pop porn' merchandisers had to replace the Gospel of Work (production) with an ethos of self-gratification (consumption). To that end Hugh Hefner advocated hedonism, arguing that religion "has kept man from enjoying, without guilt, the fruits of his earthly labours and to that extent is incompatible with the free market enterprise system." He declared the 'sexual revolution' to be "a liberalization of sexual morality within prescribed institutional limits"; for the most part the 'revolution' was simply a commercial opportunity "like Father's Day or National Shoe Week." The ambiguous decision in *Roth v. United States* (1957) was the primary impetus behind 'pop pornography', and uncertainty about the exact meaning of the legal ruling was exploited by numerous commercial enterprises.[8] Smith thought it a "grotesque notion" that publisher Sam Roth could pose as a "champion of literary freedom," but that he was a crusader was important, and many others followed his lead.[9]

Roth had its biggest impact on middle-class America and its disposable income; the subsequent commercial exploitation of adult material was aimed here. Smith astutely noted, "The mentality of pop pornographers can be studied by examining the kind of movies they produce, the magazines they edit, the newspapers they print, the advertisements they write."[10] According to Bill Ogersby, from its inception in 1954, "In its obsession with style and ostentatious display, *Playboy* embodied the rise of a new American middle-class for whom consumption, individuality and stylistic self-expression were becoming a way of life." *Playboy* painted its readership as "young, successful, adventurous and stylish — a young blade with a zest for living who showed expertise in the fields of fashion, furnishing conspicuous consumption, yet was also

---

8   Samuel Roth (1893–1974) was a notable publisher of adult literature and writer. His career ran from the 1920s to the 1960s, during which time he was responsible for numerous magazines, most importantly *Beau*, probably the first men's magazine. After 1940, he conducted most of his business through mail order. Roth's historic significance rests primarily on his role as the plaintiff in *Roth v. United States* (1957). While his appeal was unsuccessful the minority decision of the Court redefined the Constitutional test for determining 'obscene' material unprotected under the First Amendment and introduced the criteria of 'redeeming social value' for consideration in future prosecutions.

9   Hefner quote in Smith, "Pop Sex Among The Squares," *Nation* (25 August 1969): 143–145.

10 Smith, "Pop Sex Among The Squares," *Nation* (25 August 1969): 144.

confident and assured in heterosexual masculine identity." Male readers were directed "through the provinces of visual pleasure and consumer practice" to avoid "any suggestion of unmanliness or effeminacy." *Playboy* taught them how and what to consume through the fifties and sixties as masculine consumerism came into its own.[11]

'Pop porn', aimed at "the groin of suburbia," was epitomised by the bestselling novels of Irving Wallace, Jacqueline Susann and Harold Robbins, and in magazines such as *Cosmopolitan* and *Mademoiselle* that catered for a female readership, while *Playboy* addressed a male audience. When Jackie Kennedy was photographed leaving a cinema after seeing *I Am Curious (Yellow)*, the film's box office takings doubled because the story generated public interest which translated into increased attendances for the film.[12] Popular films such as *The Fox* (Mark Rydell, 1967), *Prudence and the Pill* (Fielder Cook and Ronald Neame, 1968) and *Three Into Two Won't Go* (Peter Hall, 1969) provided further titillation.[13] "Sex sells," noted Desmond Smith. "And by my yardstick this commercial takeover of the middle-class subconscious must be reckoned a prodigious financial success."[14] The same middle-class that CDL fundraisers looked to for donations was also being targeted by the producers of 'pop porn'.

In 1968, Alex de Renzy went to Copenhagen, filmed Denmark's first sex fair and made the documentary *Censorship in Denmark* (1969), the first full-length film to show explicit sexual intercourse, and the first to be reviewed in the *New York Times*. Costing only $15,000 to produce, it took $25,000 in its first week and eventually made more than $2 million. Responding to a critic in the San Francisco *Chronicle* who declared that *Censorship in Denmark* "boggles the mind," Vincent Canby noted,

> It may boggle the mind, but only after it boggles, shakes up and threatens a lot of other things that are more difficult — and less fashionable — to talk about, including the Puritan conscience and our traditional sexual taboos, which we all have (whether we admit it or not) and which have

11 Bill Ogersby, *Playboys in Paradise: Masculinity, Youth and Leisure-style in Modern America*, Berg, Oxford and New York, 2001: 4–5.
12 John Waters in *Inside Deep Throat* documentary (Fenton Bailey and Randy Barbato, 2005).
13 Smith, "Pop Sex Among The Squares," *Nation* (25 August 1969): 144.
14 Ibid.

nothing to do with the mind, but with emotions.[15]

As with previous generations of sexploitation filmmakers, the new films exploited the loneliness of their male audience. "I've exploited the basest human emotions" Dave Friedman reflected years later on his career in film, "But the one I exploited most was loneliness. That's who was paying my way, a lot of very lonely men."[16]

Vincent Canby continued his review of Censorship in Denmark saying, "My own experience is that some of the sequences in these new films [the pseudo documentaries] are erotic, but that it's a fleeting, certainly harmless kind of eroticism that depends largely on shock and curiosity, and then dwindles off in a sort of arrogant boredom."[17] This led him to conclude, "Pornography is, by definition, a limited and limiting art form."[18] He was also prompted to ask,

Can the American courts that permit us to see blue movies enclosed within a documentary frame legally deny an adult the right to see the same blue movie unencumbered by that frame? I really don't know, but it does seem that the entire subject should be re-examined if hypocrisy and double-think, which dominate so many other areas of our current political and social life, are not to chalk up another bleak victory.[19]

Canby suggested that pseudo-documentaries such as Censorship in Denmark were "really a new approach to the distribution of pornographic films in the United States,"[20] one that was brought about by Supreme Court obscenity verdicts that stressed 'redeeming social value'. Seeing the success of Censorship in Denmark others sought to cash in and a series of pseudo-documentaries ushered in the 'golden era' of porn cinema. While most Mondo films contained a sexual component, ones that focused exclusively on sex were known as "white coaters" or "fuckumentaries," and were the predecessors of full-length porn films

---

15 Vincent Canby, "The Screen: 'Censorship In Denmark' Begins Run," New York Times (17 June 1970): 41.
16 Eddie Muller and Daniel Faris, Grindhouse: The Forbidden World of Adults Only Cinema, St. Martins, New York, 1996: 136.
17 Vincent Canby, "Have You Tried The Danish Blue?" New York Times (21 June 1970): B29.
18 Ibid.
19 Canby, "Have You Tried The Danish Blue?" New York Times (21 June 1970): B1.
20 Canby, "The Screen: 'Censorship In Denmark' Begins Run," New York Times (17 June 1970): 41.

in the 1970s. In 'white coaters' the narrator or presenter was often falsely claimed to be a doctor or professor to justify the subsequent sexually explicit material. Films such as *Man and Wife* (Matt Cimber, 1969), *He and She* (Matt Cimber, 1970), *Black is Beautiful* (Matt Cimber, 1970), *Marital Relations* (European Institute of Marital Relations, 1970), *The Art of Marriage* (Nevada Institute of Families, 1970) and *Sexual Understanding* (European Institute of Marital Relations, 1971) were presented as instructional and educational to justify their public display, and *Pornography in Denmark: A New Approach* (Alex de Renzy, 1970) highlighted the difference between the conservative attitudes to sex in America and the more liberal Danish laws. Other films, such as *The History of Pornography* (Hans Wegmunsen, 1970) and *Erotography* (1971), made reference to historical examples of pornography as a valuable cultural product from earlier civilizations and, in documenting changes in society, *American Sexual Revolution* (John William Abbott, 1971) mixed footage of the contemporary United States, including interviews and documentary footage, with hardcore sex scenes.

As of August 1970, the President's Commission *Report* asserted, the majority of theatres exhibiting adult films showed silent 16mm colour films that were accompanied by prerecorded music. The theatres were located in metropolitan areas, the films being shown were easy to produce, inexpensive to duplicate, and the equipment required was portable so films could be made outside or indoors. The *Report* noted that in this small but expanding market, "As yet there are no recognizable film titles moving from city to city, and there is almost no nationwide distribution."[21] A concise summary of the state of the industry.

The speed of social change during the late 1960s was significant and in 1969 Vincent Canby posed the question 'Is Russ Meyer Archaic?' Despite being hailed for the watershed *The Immoral Mr. Teas* (1959) Meyer was seen to be falling behind the times.[22] Canby believed "Meyer's sole preoccupation with extraordinarily well-developed female breasts, usually photographed from a low angle while they're in some sort of motion, is no longer particularly erotic."[23] Developments in American society meant "rapidly changing patterns of sexual

---

21 *The Report of the Commission on Obscenity and Pornography*: 100.
22 Vincent Canby, "Screen: By Russ Meyer," *New York Times* (6 September 1969): 21.
23 Canby, "Screen: By Russ Meyer," *New York Times* (6 September 1969): 21.

behaviour in conventional films are making decently intended, softcore pornographic films increasingly difficult to achieve with any amount of success."[24] Some sort of novelty or gimmick was required to create a commercial success.

Impressed by Meyer's ability to make low-budget independent films that were financially successful at the box office, Twentieth Century Fox hired him to direct three films hoping that he could do the same for a major studio. Meyer planned to film adaptations of Irving Wallace's novel *The Seven Minutes* (1969), Peter George's *The Final Steal* (1966) and Edward Albee's *Everything in the Garden* (1967). The first of the films, *The Seven Minutes* (Russ Meyer, 1971), was intended as an anti-censorship statement.[25] In the film, the censorship organisation the Strength Through Decency League (STDL) is an obvious parody of CDL, and Meyer had high hopes for *The Seven Minutes*, wanting to get revenge on his old adversary; "I decided to take a great slap at Charles Keating, of the Citizens for Decent Literature, and that was stupid. I said 'I'll do it, I'll do it and I'll really make the common man understand the problems he's faced with as far as free speech." But he only realized afterwards that his audience did not like being lectured, and furthermore that the public would only be concerned about censorship after R-rated films had been banned.[26] A flop at the box office, he described *The Seven Minutes* as his "biggest disappointment" and felt he had let his fans down.[27]

Paradoxically, despite the campaigns of CDL and the rhetoric of Nixon's administration, the climate of economic decline and social decay fostered a "kind of porno chic" which was primarily generated by the media attention devoted to Gerard Damiano's *Deep Throat* after it opened in New York in June 1972.[28] 'Porno chic' was to some degree

---

24 Ibid.
25 According to Jimmy McDonough *The Seven Minutes* was a project Meyer inherited when the previous director associated with it, Richard Fleischer, left. Initially Meyer had no interest in taking on the script — however, under pressure from the studio, he accepted. Seeing an opportunity to get back at Charles Keating, Meyer introduced the anti-obscenity activists Strength Through Decency League, and told reporters he wanted to premiere the film in Cincinnati, Ohio. Told by the studio executives he had to get an R rating Meyer even sent a copy of the script to the MPAA in advance for approval. Jimmy McDonough, *Big Bosoms and Square Jaws: The Biography of Russ Meyer*, Vintage, London, 2006: 278–279.
26 Meyer quoted in Kenneth Turan and Stephen F. Zito, *Sinema*, Praeger, New York, 1974:33–34.
27 Ibid: 33.
28 Ralph Blumenthal, "Porno Chic," *New York Times Magazine* (21 January 1973): 28. In the early

legitimised by a succession of mainstream films addressing changing social values and conflicting ideas about sex and relationships such as *The Graduate* (Mike Nichols, 1970), *The Owl and the Pussycat* (Herbert Ross, 1970), and *Carnal Knowledge* (Mike Nichols, 1971). Woody Allen's *Everything You Always Wanted to Know About Sex But Were Afraid to Ask* (1972) went further and, taking the question and answer format of Dr David Reuben's bestseller of the same name (1969), it explored subjects such as premature ejaculation, cross-dressing and bestiality. Because of the mainstream success of *Deep Throat*, pornography was no longer relegated to "flea-pit peep shows or stag nights."[29]

Curiosity was such that in the months following its release, screenings of *Deep Throat* were attended by Warren Beatty, Nora Ephron, Bob Woodward, Johnny Carson, Ben Gazzara, and Jack Nicholson. French delegates to the United Nations paid by traveller's cheques when they viewed the film and, embarrassingly, when off-duty policemen went to see it they were searched in theatres by on-duty cops. Employees of the *New York Times* went in a group, followed later by the staff from the *New York Times Book Review*.[30] Mike Nichols, director of *Carnal Knowledge*, allegedly saw *Deep Throat* three times and recommended it to Truman Capote, while LA *Free Press* claimed that Frank Sinatra showed *Deep Throat* to Spiro Agnew.[31] Addison Veril, reporter and film critic for *Variety* noted, "Once it [*Deep Throat*] broke in the society columns, it was OK to go."[32] For better or worse pornography had been embraced by popular culture.

However, it was not only anti-obscenity groups who were unhappy at the emergence of hardcore pornography in the mainstream. Even

---

1970s photographers Guy Bordin and Helmut Newton gained notoriety for mixing images of sex and death in their fashion pictures for *Vogue* magazine. In his autobiography Helmut Newton claims that his book *White Women* (1976) was the first of its kind and that the term 'porno chic' was coined because of it. Helmut Newton, *Autobiography*, Gerald Duckworth and Co., London, 2003: 205. In actuality, most of the pictures in the book were shot between 1973 and 1976 when pornography had already broken into the mainstream, and Ralph Blumenthal coined the phrase 'porno chic' in a *New York Times* article in January 1973.

29 Kerekes and Slater, *Killing for Culture*: 28.
30 Blumenthal, "Porno Chic," *New York Times Magazine* (21 January 1973): 30; Luke Ford, *A History of X: 100 Years of Sex in Film*, Prometheus, New York, 1999: 49. Because of the publicity the Russian basketball team tried to see *Deep Throat* in Albuquerque, New Mexico. Turan and Zito, *Sinema*: 143.
31 Turan and Zito, *Sinema*: 143.
32 Blumenthal, "Porno Chic," *New York Times Magazine* (21 January 1973): 30.

notable civil libertarians such as lawyer Morris Ernst, a long-time opponent of censorship, were unhappy about the contemporary graphic depictions of sex and sadism. Ernst objected to the pandering for profit which he saw but, refusing to adopt the role of censor, was "not saying where to draw the line... I'm not as wise as people who say they'll draw it here or there. I think we should draw it [from time to time] as society constantly changes."[33]

Dave Friedman believed that for sexploitation filmmakers "The old con was working just fine until a few assholes decided to go hardcore and show the last act right up front," violating every principle of good showmanship.[34] He was also sceptical about the long-term future of hardcore films, viewing them as a fad that would last another year or so and then fade away; "They see it all in the first four minutes, and its over ... Simulated sex is much more erotic."[35] A few years earlier, amidst the public controversy surrounding *I Am Curious (Yellow)*, Russ Meyer made clear his opposition to censorship. However, he also added "you should leave something to the imagination," and warned "I have never shown genitalia in any of my films. Once you have to show that to get people into the theatre, how many people are going to do it with taste?"[36]

When Bill Osco made *Mona, the Teenage Nymph* (1970), the first feature length non-documentary adult film with graphic depictions of sex, he tried to present it like a legitimate film with titles and cast credits. Similar to *Deep Throat*, the film focuses on depictions of oral sex, but the main character, Mona (Fifi Watson), is a teenager who has pledged her fiancé that she will remain a virgin until they marry. That does not stop her giving blow jobs to a variety of men.

Porn performer Bill Margold viewed oral sex as a "good image" on camera and also the most important sex scene in a film because the male audience can go home and have sex but they may not be able to get a blow job.[37] Similarly, the final *Report* of the President's Commission noted in their findings that men were much more aroused by depictions

33 Irving Spiegel, "Censor's foe sees need for limits to freedom," *New York Times* (5 January 1970): 46.
34 Muller and Faris, *Grindhouse*: 136.
35 "Sexploitation: Sin's Wages," *Newsweek* (12 February 1973): 45.
36 "Even 'Teas' Prod. Upset By 'Curious'," *Variety* (18 June 1969): 5.
37 Maggie Paley, *The Book of the Penis*, Fusion, London, 1999: 177.

of oral sex than women.[38] America *not* being an "enlightened nation," stated Margold, is "obsessed with the blow job."[39] In the 1960s oral sex was classified as a form of sodomy, and it was illegal in most states even when practiced in private by married couples. Such were the cultural values at the time that for men to perform cunnilingus on women was seen as especially degrading and unmanly, an activity only for perverts. Punishment for anyone convicted of performing oral sex varied by state but in Connecticut conviction meant a thirty year jail sentence, or twenty years in Ohio, and in Georgia a life sentence with hard labour.[40]

Bill Osco recognized that the social climate in America had changed in regard to adult films since his film was released in 1970 when pornography was still a taboo subculture. *Variety* also noted the significant changes in American film culture:

> Movie nostalgia buffs may well long for the old days when clothed couples dropped slowly out of frame while the Dimitri Tiomkin score soared and the director cut to lots of pounding surf. Not so any more, especially if the courts eventually give the national greenlight to hardcore pix. Then audiences may begin to demand more erotically imaginative material, but for now, 'Mona' and her sisters in sin are where the urban skin action and word-of-mouth is at.[41]

However, by 1972 there was a noticeable shift; "Now everybody says 'Did you see *Deep Throat* yet?'"[42] The media coverage and lure of potential profits attracted many opportunists into the adult film business, with varying degrees of success.

FBI agent Bill Kelly believed that part of the reason for the mainstream 'porno chic' engendered by *Deep Throat* was the death of

38 Heidenry, *What Wild Ecstasy*: 117.
39 Margold quoted in Hebditch and Anning, *Porn Gold*: 30.
40 Talese, *Thy Neighbor's Wife*: 239–240. In contrast, under Georgia state law the punishment for anyone convicted of having sex with animals was only five years. Federal Law 18 U.S.C.A. 2421 and 2422 states that "Whoever knowingly transports, or knowingly persuades, induces, entices, or coerces any individual to travel in interstate or foreign commerce, or in any territory or possession of the United States, with intent that such individual engage in any sexual activity for which any person can be charged with a criminal offense, shall be guilty of a felony."
41 "Mona," *Variety* (24 February 1971).
42 Turan and Zito, *Sinema*: 137.

America's moral watchdog J. Edgar Hoover:

> Had he lived and been in full possession of his faculties I think Hoover
> would've gone berserk with the success of *Deep Throat*. I mean
> he would've had us out kickin' tail in every jurisdiction where it was
> presented. J. Edgar Hoover would not have permitted *Deep Throat* to
> have gotten the jump on law enforcement that it did.[43]

But Hoover was dead, and once exposed to adult films by exploitation
entrepreneurs a large section of the American public embraced the
experience.

Louis and Joseph Peraino, a father-son business team, established
Bryanston Pictures in July 1971 and shortly after they created Damiano
Film Productions with Gerard Damiano. According to a joint company
prospectus prepared by Louis Peraino, the twin companies would be
"engaged in the financing, acquisition, production and distribution
of motion picture film products of every kind, nature and gauge."[44]
Where Bryanston made mainstream films, Damiano Film Productions
made porn.

Damiano, a hairdresser from New York, observed there was little
attempt at a story or production values in contemporary adult films
and felt they were just a series of sex scenes. He also aspired to put
humour into a sex film; "I realized the public was ready for something
else. In fact they'd been ready for years — it's just that nobody took the
time and the effort to do it before."[45] Assisted by Al Goldstein's "Gulp"
review in *Screw* magazine and a rating of 100 out of 100 on the Peter
Meter, Damiano's first film *Deep Throat* took $33,033 at the box office

---

43 Legs McNeil and Jennifer Osborne, *The Other Hollywood: The Uncensored Oral History of the Porn Film Industry*, Regan Books, New York, 2005: 77.
44 Ford, *A History of X*: 118.
45 Turan and Zito, *Sinema*: 154. After *Deep Throat* Gerard Damiano made *Legacy of Satan* (1972), his only non-porn effort. Prior to settling on *Deep Throat* as a title several other more traditional stag titles were considered, amongst them *The Doctor Makes a House Call* and *The Sword Swallower*. Damiano had made a number of films before *Deep Throat*: Aside from porn loops, he directed *We All Go Down* (1969), a softcore film, and *The Marriage Manual* (1970) a sex education film with softcore scenes. He also made the documentaries *Changes* (1971), *This Film is About ...* (1972), and *Sex USA* (1972), and two hardcore films *Doctor Love* (1971) and *Teenie Tulip* (1971). *Deep Throat* was followed by *Bottoms Up* (1973), *Meatball* (1973), *Memories Within Miss Aggie* (1974), and *Portrait* (1974).

in its first week at the New Mature World Theatre.[46] *Variety* reported that due the word-of-mouth advertising, the opening lunchtime show of *Deep Throat* at the World Theatre was packed.[47]

Deep Throat was different because it had more of a plot and characterization than would usually be found in a pornographic film, the script was humorous, and throughout the film there were references to contemporary popular culture such as the parody of the Coca-Cola 'I'd Like To Teach The World To Sing' advert, with lyrics rewritten for an adult audience:

I'd like to teach the world to screw
in perfect harmony
I'd like to see you all get laid
but leave a piece for me.

While only lasting sixty-two minutes, the film featured scenes of group sex, fellatio, cunnilingus, masturbation, conventional heterosexual and anal sex. Linda (Linda Lovelace) is a young woman who feels unfulfilled by her sex life and, along with her roommate Helen (Dolly Sharp), invites fourteen men to their apartment for a party and take it in turns to have sex until the men are too exhausted to continue. During the scene the director, Gerard Damiano, injects some humour by appearing in a camp cameo asking one of the male guests, "What's a nice joint like you doing in a dame like this?"

Still not satisfied after the party, Linda visits a psychiatrist, Dr Young (Harry Reems), who concludes that her problem is physical, not psychological, and upon examination discovers that her clitoris is in the back of her throat. For her to have an orgasm she must take a penis as far down her throat as possible. Once her problem has been identified, Dr Young hires Linda as a therapist making house calls to patients. Her therapy sessions are so popular that one enthusiastic patient wants two or three treatments a week and will charge it to his Blue Cross health insurance. Linda is also popular with her employer, Dr Young, who regularly enjoys her therapy as well as frequent sex with his nurse (Carol Conners).

46 Ibid: 143.
47 "Deep Throat," *Variety* (28 June 1972).

Linda's final client, Wilbur Wang (William Love), has a rape fantasy that she tries to help him with, but she does not act frightened enough for his liking, spoiling the effect. Wang wants to marry Linda, but she refuses, saying, "The man I marry has to have a nine-inch cock," and poor Wilbur laments that he falls four inches short of happiness. Encouraged by the possibility that Dr Young might be able to help with an operation or silicone injections, Linda and Wilbur have sex and, using her 'deep throat' technique, they find bliss together.

Variety declared *Deep Throat* "a superior piece which stands a head above the current competition," but it also noted that it was not the *Ben Hur* of pornography as had been claimed. Lovelace's performance was described as "spirited" and the film "put together with some style."[48] Notably, *Deep Throat* was given a glowing review in *Women's Wear Daily,* which also published an interview with Linda Lovelace. Arthur Knight, film critic for the *Saturday Review,* praised *Deep Throat* for its concern with female sexual gratification and its educational value in showing an audience that there were other ways to have sex than the missionary position.[49] In their book *Sinema,* Kenneth Turan and Stephen Zito complimented *Deep Throat,* describing it as "expertly made, funny, and most unique among sex films in its celebration of individual response."[50]

For many young men, going to see *Deep Throat* was a rite of passage. The effect was notable and for the one-hour duration of the film, critic and author Irv Slifkin and friends,

were fixated on a washed out, jumpy print of the most infamous movie in the world; a touching story of a woman who went very far to satisfy the tingle near her epiglottis. Men's magazines had nothing on the twenty-foot high images of the body parts we were witnessing, no matter how homely, ordinary or beautiful they were.[51]

Johnny Carson made jokes about *Deep Throat* on *The Tonight Show,*[52]

48 "Deep Throat," *Variety* (28 June 1972).
49 Knight cited in Willis, *Beginning to See the Light*: 72.
50 Turan and Zito, *Sinema*: 142.
51 Irv Slifkin, "The Summer of Deep Throat: Porky, Linda Lovelace and Me," *Something Weird Blue Book* (1997): 61.
52 Lang, "Happy Birthday, Baby!" *Cult Movies* (No.5, 1992): 36.

and Linda Lovelace was much in demand, appearing in *Playboy* (April 1973), on the cover of *Esquire* (May 1973), and being interviewed in *Oui* (February 1973), the *Bachelor* (August 1973), *Daily Girl* (September 1973) and *Venus* (November 1973). She was also a regular guest at *Playboy* parties during 1973, beginning with the visit for her photo-shoot, and Hugh Hefner frequently boasted that he had helped to create the social climate which enabled films like *Deep Throat* to be commercially exhibited.[53] It was not the script or the characterization which made the film notable.

Film critic Vincent Canby was baffled at the 'chic' surrounding *Deep Throat* and went to see it in the summer of 1972 because of Al Goldstein's superlative laden review in *Screw* magazine. Canby went away convinced it was junk and did not bother to write a review. In January 1973 he went to see it a second time and still thought it was "junk," and "much less erotic than technically amazing." He was more interested in learning how Lovelace discovered her skills, and believed the appeal of "The film has less to do with the manifold pleasures of sex than with physical engineering."[54] The media attention given to her special talents ensured that the ability to deep-throat became an industry standard for comparing porn actresses.[55]

Damiano claimed credit for creating the leading lady's performing name. The actress' real name was Linda Boreman but to Damiano 'Lovelace' was "like the American dream of putting love and old lace together and making it a sweet young thing." He wanted to present her as a sweet innocent girl-next-door type,[56] and the alliteration of Linda Lovelace was supposed to be reminiscent of previous cinematic sex symbols such as Marilyn Monroe and Brigitte Bardot. Lovelace continued to be portrayed as an all-American girl, until 1973 when Al Goldstein publicized the existence of porn loops which showed Lovelace having sex with dogs.

Coverage of the film was not always positive. Writing in *Esquire* (February 1973) Nora Ephron called *Deep Throat* "one of the most

---

53   Miller, *Bunny*: 196.
54   Canby, "What Are We To Think of 'Deep Throat'?" *New York Times* (21 January 1973): B1.
55   For instance in Robert Rimmer's review of *The Private Afternoons of Pamela Mann* (Radley Metzger, 1974), Rimmer claimed that Barbara Bourbon could "out-'deep-throat'" Linda Lovelace. Rimmer, *The X-Rated Videotape Guide Volume 1*: 122–23.
56   Turan and Zito, *Sinema*: 146.

unpleasant, disturbing films I have ever seen — it is not just anti-female but anti-sex, as well ... I came out of the theatre a quivering fanatic. Give me the goriest Peckinpah film any day."[57] In the *New York Review of Books* Ellen Willis wrote that she thought *Deep Throat* was "witless, exploitative, and about as erotic as a tonsillectomy." She was not shocked by graphic images of sex and reminisced that when she saw *Un Chant d'Amour* (Jean Genet, 1950) in 1964 it had a strong effect on her. Aside from a few scenes of masturbation the majority of sex is in the minds of the characters (prisoners and guards), reflecting the director's point that sex is as much about imagination as anything else.[58] Ironically, *Un Chant d'Amour* was banned in Berkeley, California, for its vivid depictions of numerous sex acts. Brought to court, the film was judged to be obscene and the decision was upheld by the Supreme Court in 1966. However, Justices Black, Douglas, Stewart and Fortas dissented and noted they would have reversed the conviction.

Willis acknowledged that she found films like *Deep Throat* to be a "sexual depressant," partly because they objectify women's bodies, but also "because they deliberately and perversely destroy any semblance of atmosphere in which my sexual fantasies could flourish."[59] Surprisingly, Russ Meyer concurred and condemned *Deep Throat*, describing it as a "highly publicized movie on cocksucking, with a girl that has no finesse at all, she's like a piston motor,"[60] and reasserted he was not interested in making hardcore pornography because it left nothing to the imagination.[61]

While Damiano enjoyed making *Deep Throat*, he was also surprised by the attention being paid to the film; "I had enough experience to know when I had something unique, but I had no idea it would reach the proportion that it did. For it to be the main topic of discussion in the United States of America at any particular point is ludicrous."[62] Damiano was shocked at the success of *Deep Throat*; "It keeps knocking me on the head every time I turn around. Being recognized

57 Ibid: 144.
58 Ellen Willis, *Beginning to See the Light: Pieces of a Decade*, Alfred A. Knopf, New York, 1981: 73–74.
59 Ibid: 73.
60 Meyer quoted in Turan and Zito, *Sinema*: 34.
61 Ibid.
62 Ibid: 150.

in public places, my phone never stops ringing ... I'm the one who believes it least. It really hasn't caught up with me."[63] Attributing the popularity of *Deep Throat* to a public response to "some asshole idiots trying to legislate morality," Damiano believed the success was a snub to the rhetoric of conservative campaigners and politicians crusading against adult entertainment. Reflecting on the tactics of anti-obscenity campaigners, he added, "There's so much talk about trying to stamp out pornography. They don't have to stamp it out. All they have to do is leave it alone, and it will die a natural death in a very short time. It is only when they try and restrict it that, in effect, what they're doing is perpetuating it."[64] Their protests only piqued curiosity and provided free advertising.

In sharp contrast to conservative political rhetoric, Damiano saw *Deep Throat* as beneficial, helping people to understand their sexuality. He lamented the number of violent films that were *not* protested by moralists and viewed them as potentially *more* harmful. In his opinion avoiding the subject of sex, even though it is central in relationships, meant people were more afraid of sex than violence.[65] Calling himself a moralist, Damiano felt he was

changing the moral fibre, or the moral thinking, of the American people. I think there's so many people going around with guilt complexes who, after they see sex openly portrayed on film, can better cope with their own problems. I think I have opened a lot of doors for people. That is today the most rewarding thing that I have felt.[66]

Sammy Davis Jr. was one outspoken high-profile fan of pornography and in his autobiography, *Hollywood in a Suitcase* (1981), noted, "I make no bones about the fact that when they started making explicit sex films, I became an immediate and avid collector." Davis even organized premieres of *Deep Throat* in several countries.[67] Asserting that *Deep*

63 Damiano quoted in ibid: 149.
64 Ibid: 150.
65 Ibid: 150–151.
66 Ibid: 151.
67 Sammy Davis Jr., *Hollywood in a Suitcase*, Berkley, New York, 1981:174. Ironically Sammy Davis Jr., one time member of the Church of Satan, a closet bisexual and an outspoken porn enthusiast, campaigned for Richard Nixon and performed at an AFC Christmas banquet in the early 1970s. Company president Carl Henry Lindner liked Davis so much that besides the

Throat was significant in challenging cinematic and social taboos, taking X-rated films out of the stag movie house and putting them into local cinemas, Davis enthused, "It was wonderful in the sense that a guy could take his girlfriend and even his secretary without pulling up the coat collar."[68] Ned Tannen, vice president at Universal Studios, agreed, saying, "The thing that shocked me most about *Deep Throat* was that nobody in the audience was a dirty old man with a raincoat. They were all young couples."[69]

Hoping to emulate the success of *Deep Throat*, the following year *Screw* magazine produced its first adult film, a comedy entitled *It Happened in Hollywood* (Peter Locke, 1973). According to *Variety*, comedy porn such as *It Happened in Hollywood* and *Deep Throat* were the biggest sexploitation grosses at the box office "because couples and single women seem more comfortable viewing put-on sex than wallowing in the world of 'male chauvinist' fantasy which saturates the grittier porno dramas and stag loops."[70]

As a consequence of the media attention, *Deep Throat* was investigated by the Public Morals Department of the NYPD, which seized a copy of the film. A legal technicality meant the film had to be returned, but twelve days later it was confiscated again and charges filed.[71] The prosecution of *Deep Throat* began in August 1972, when a print was seized at the New Mature World and the exhibitor charged with obscenity. The trial took place in December 1972, and the verdict was delivered in March the following year.

Whilst law-enforcement officials viewed the Peraino brothers' company Bryanston Pictures as a money laundering operation, the Hollywood film industry saw it as good money and accepted the Peraino investments.[72] Bryanston functioned as an accounting dodge, to hide the illegal profits made from distributing *Deep Throat*, but the plan backfired when the legitimate films the company chose to distribute, such as *Andy Warhol's Flesh For Frankenstein* (Paul Morrissey, 1974),

agreed fee he gave him five shares of stock and a $35,000 black Stutz Bearcat. Binstein and Bowden, *Trust Me*: 114. Davis campaigned for Richard Nixon's re-election campaign in 1972 and was best man when Chuck Traynor married Marilyn Chambers in 1974.

68   Davis Jr., *Hollywood in a Suitcase*: 174–75.
69   Tannen quoted in Turan and Zito, *Sinema*: 158.
70   "It Happened in Hollywood," *Variety* (24 January 1973).
71   Turan and Zito, *Sinema*: 144.
72   Ford, *A History of X*: 120–121.

Return of the Dragon [aka *Way of the Dragon*] (Bruce Lee, 1973), *Blood* (Andy Milligan, 1974), and *Texas Chain Saw Massacre* (Tobe Hooper, 1974) proved unexpected box office hits and attracted the attention of the Inland Revenue Service and other government agencies.[73] Ironically, one of the first films financed by Bryanston was *The Last Porno Flick* (Ray Marsh, 1974), about two Italian-American cab drivers who raise $22,000 to make a porn film but tell their friends and family they are making a religious film. Their situation becomes impossible when the porn film becomes a box office hit.[74]

Outside of New York *Deep Throat* met with resistance and the first showing of the film in Cincinnati, Charles Keating's hometown, was attended by a judge and a police officer. There was no second showing.[75] In the climate of 'porno chic' Senator William E. Schulter acknowledged, "It should be clear that if 'Deep Throat' cannot be prosecuted, then nothing can."[76] Vincent Canby added that the censorship laws used against *Deep Throat* were "academically" wrong but that the film was *not* worth fighting for. He went on to say, "The necessity to prove a film totally without redeeming social value in order to get an obscenity conviction is, to my way of thinking, absurd." Everything, he believed, has some social interest.[77] Canby was not convinced of the film's value but was sure that if *Deep Throat* had not caught the public's attention "at this point in history, some other porno film, no better and maybe no worse, would have."[78] Because of changes in legal standards it was inevitable that porn would cross over into the mainstream, but ironically it was the media coverage of the film and subsequent trial that ensured *Deep Throat's* success.[79] Exploitation filmmaker David Friedman thought *Deep Throat* "was an ordinary X-rater, no better,

73 Bill Landis and Michelle Clifford, *Sleazoid Express*, Simon and Schuster, New York, 2002: 73.
74 *The Last Porno Flick* is also known as *The Mad Movie Makers*.
75 Richard Koenig, "Success of Crusade to Rid City of Smut Has Made Cincinnati a Model for Anti-Pornography Forces," *Wall Street Journal* (1 December 1986): 1.
76 Paul L. Montgomery, "State Loses a Round In Pornography Fight," *New York Times* (26 November 1972): 97, 111.
77 Canby, "What Are We To Think of 'Deep Throat'?," *New York Times* (21 January 1973): B1. Canby also noted that by defending *Deep Throat* in court the defence was co-opted into acknowledging the validity of the obscenity laws. The argument presented, that *Deep Throat* was better written and made than other contemporary pornography, still identified the film as pornography.
78 Ibid.
79 Turan and Zito, *Sinema*: 143.

or worse than several of the time, but it became a media event and because of all the media attention, the greatest grosser of all time."[80] The success of *Deep Throat* ensured a number of sequels and offshoots, and the phrase 'Deep Throat' entered the popular vocabulary during the Watergate scandal when Bob Woodward and Carl Bernstein used it to identify their secret informant. In the wake of *Deep Throat*, *Variety* noted, "Porno, perish the thought, is gradually getting respectable."[81]

Across America other aspiring filmmakers recognized the opportunities being created by the success of *Deep Throat*. In California, prior to making *Behind the Green Door* (Artie Mitchell, 1972), Jim and Artie Mitchell realised a lot of sex films were being made badly, and they wanted to make them properly.[82] Spending $50,000 on *Behind the Green Door*, they used visual effects to make the sex scenes more interesting. Most of the film was shot in one day while the brothers were on trial in San Francisco because of an earlier film, *Reckless Claudia* (1971), but when the judge and jury took a day off the brothers decided to make constructive use of the time.[83]

Based on a long established urban legend, Gloria (Marilyn Chambers), a woman travelling alone, is abducted as she arrives at a café and is taken to a strange sex club where she is the centre of attention and her ravishment is the main attraction. In the film's favour *Variety* acknowledged that Marilyn Chambers was attractive, unlike the "crones" who usually populated porn films.[84] *Behind the Green Door* also starred Jonny Keyes, a former middleweight boxer who had appeared in stage productions of *Hair*, and an appearance by Ben Davidson, a football player for the Oakland Raiders.[85] The film fuelled the arguments of both sides in the obscenity debate; advocates of explicit adult entertainment saw it as the story of a woman finding herself through sex, whereas anti-obscenity campaigners argued that the experience of the sex club humiliated and degraded Gloria, turning her into an automaton.

---

80 Friedman quoted in David Flint, *Babylon Blue*: 28.
81 "Behind the Green Door," *Variety* (16 August 1972).
82 Turan and Zito, *Sinema*: 175.
83 "Behind the Green Door," *Variety* (16 August 1972).
84 Ibid. Earlier Chambers had starred in *Together* (Sean Cunningham, 1971) a film produced by Wes Craven.
85 Ibid.

Noting the change in the social climate which had taken place over the previous few years, Ellen Willis wrote,

> Like all popular culture, pornography is shaped by its social setting, and the relaxation of the obscenity laws has not only brought it out in the open but inspired new genres, chief of which is the X-rated movie. Partly because of the logistics of moviegoing, which is communal rather than a private experience, and partly because the movie industry has only recently thrown off censorship of the crudest and most anachronistic sort, porn movies have retained an air of semi-respectability, fuzzing the line between liberated art and out-and-out smut.

Embraced by the mainstream of popular culture explicit sex films were defended as erotica and credited with redeeming social value when they turned up in art-house cinemas.[86] The prominence and popularity of pornography was noticed by mainstream filmmakers, and when Clint Eastwood's *Magnum Force* (Ted Post, 1973) began shooting in San Francisco Marilyn Chambers was offered a small part. She turned it down because she felt the role was demeaning and the violence in the film repulsive.[87]

The media attention given to the topic of sex generated more public interest and opened up a new niche for mainstream film. *Last Tango in Paris* (Bernardo Bertolucci, 1972) was made after Marlon Brando's Oscar winning appearance in *The Godfather* (Francis Ford Coppola, 1972), arguably while he was at the height of his career. The plot of the film has similar ingredients to many 1940s melodramas, but "the frankness of the sexual treatment would have been unthinkable even three years ago."[88] Sammy Davis Jr. went further, speculating that without *Deep Throat*, *Last Tango in Paris* could not have been accepted by critics.[89]

While the film was not pornographic by contemporary standards the dialogue, female nudity and sodomy scene led to an X rating, and once

---

86 Willis, *Beginning to See the Light*: 70.
87 Turan and Zito, *Sinema*: 174. In a similar vein Joe Dante reported in an interview that porn star Annette Haven was considered for the role of Marsha, the nymphomaniac werewolf, in *The Howling* (1981), but she objected to the mixture of sex and violence in the script. George, *Eroticism in the Fantasy Cinema*: 29.
88 "Last Tango in Paris," *Variety* (18 October 1972).
89 Davis Jr., *Hollywood in a Suitcase*: 175.

released the film provoked critical and public controversy. According to William Rotsler, *Last Tango in Paris*,

> is a breakthrough precisely because it is not a porno film, but does put into graphic visual form an erotic relationship which includes anal rape. It is a milestone film not so much for its eroticism, which is debatable, but because an Oscar-winning major star [Marlon Brando] chose to make it, and make it at a time when he was in contention for another Oscar, which he won and rejected.[90]

After *Deep Throat* and the more explicit films made by major studios, such as *Last Tango in Paris*, Meyer was concerned about the future of cinema: "The idea of [Marlon] Brando, the Academy Award winner, in there putting butter up some broad's ass and jumping her and you see his ass twittering as he's on top of her, it's hard to compete with that."[91] In the aftermath he was left wondering, "I don't know if there are any more frontiers left. That's where I question, I really question, what is there left?"[92] CDL condemned *Time* and *Newsweek* for running cover stories on *Last Tango in Paris*, and in response to the permissive climate Charles Keating predicted "The decent people of America ... are going to wage a holy, yes, a *holy* war against the merchants of obscenity." The contemporary permissive attitude toward pornography only made him more determined in his crusade and he restated his commitment, saying, "From this day forward I will not rest, and no one connected with CDL will rest, until every pornographer in America is out of business, in jail, or both."[93] As an indication of his sincerity Simon Leis Jr., elected in Ohio in 1971 thanks to the support of Charles Keating, was named 'prosecutor of the month' by CDL for his attempts to ban *Last Tango in Paris*.[94]

As mainstream cinema attempted to capitalize on the new permissiveness *Deep Throat* continued to draw crowds, enough to

90 William Rotsler, *Contemporary Erotic Cinema*, Penthouse/Ballantine, New York, 1973: 39.
91 Meyer quoted in Turan and Zito, *Sinema*: 35.
92 Meyer quoted in ibid: 35.
93 Corn, "Dirty Bookkeeping," *New Republic* (2 April 1990): 14. Ironically, it was Keating's own incarceration in 1989 that brought his personal moral crusade to an end.
94 Flynt, *An Unseemly Man*: 135. Over the course of his career Leis Jr. tried to prosecute everyone from the Contemporary Art Centre, for a Robert Mapplethorpe exhibition, to Barnes and Noble, for selling *Libido* magazine.

make it the most financially successful pornographic film to play in New York, and between June 1972 and January 1973 it reportedly grossed more than $850,000 at the New World Mature Theatre.[95] *Variety* (10 January 1973) reported that even in its eighth month in New York *Deep Throat* was still drawing crowds and breaking box office records,

> but the real impact is measured not so much by the spinning turnstiles as by the types of folks being introduced to the theatrical hardcore fare. A visit to the World [Theater] on Friday revealed the house fully sold out for a mid-afternoon show and a line outside composed of elegant unaccompanied ladies, young couples, middle-aged couples, and at least three silver-haired matrons with shopping bags who looked like refugees from Schrafft's.[96]

By January 1973 *Deep Throat* had played in seventy cities and grossed $3.2 million. Linda Lovelace had been the topic of gossip columns, appeared on TV talk shows and when she attended the LA premiere it was covered by the local evening news.[97]

After *Deep Throat*'s financial success other companies began producing explicit adult films to exploit the public interest, but Damiano saw these as predominantly "garbage" hastily thrown together by people who did not know how to make films. Aware of the market trend, Damiano wanted to experiment; "With the success of *Throat*, everybody and his brother was running around to make a sexy, funny, camp picture. And I felt that if this is what everyone else was doing, it was time to do something different."[98] After treating sex humorously in *Deep Throat*, Damiano decided to treat it seriously in *The Devil in Miss Jones*.

Setting up his own company, Damiano quickly directed *Meatball* (1973) and used the profits to finance his next film, *The Devil in Miss Jones* (1973), which he made over two three-day weekends at a cost

95 Canby, "What Are We To Think of 'Deep Throat'?," *New York Times* (21 January 1973): B1. The World Theatre on 49th Street near 7th Avenue changed its name to the New Mature World Theatre.
96 *Variety* quoted in Ford, *A History of X*: 51.
97 Turan and Zito, *Sinema*: 145.
98 Ibid: 154–155.

of $50,000.[99] Damiano believed that *The Devil in Miss Jones* was a superior film to *Deep Throat* in every way: "There's no comparison. *Throat* is a joke, a well-put-together joke, but still a joke. But *Miss Jones*, I think, is a film. That's the difference."[100] Reflecting the changes in public perceptions of pornography, when *Variety* reviewed *The Devil in Miss Jones* it acknowledged that it was "shot and cut with great skill," but noted that the film was often more disturbing than arousing. While the star Georgina Spelvin was not a conventionally beautiful woman, and she did not have a gimmick like Linda Lovelace, "her performance is so naked it seems like a massive invasion of privacy." Furthermore, because of the superior acting and production values, porn was approaching an "art form," and in future film critics would have difficulty ignoring it.[101]

The quality of the film, *Variety* speculated, could prove to be a problem for Damiano because "Booking a film of this technical quality into a standard sex house is tantamount to throwing it on the trash heap of most current hardcore fare. On the other hand, more prestigious houses may shy away because of the explicit nature of the material."[102] But the critical response to the film unsettled some commentators. In the *New York Times* Vincent Canby joked that since *Last Tango in Paris*, for film critics "finding breakthrough movies has virtually become an epidemic," and until he read the reviews for *The Devil in Miss Jones* he was prepared to accept that pornographic films were probably harmless for adults. "Now I'm not so sure," he added. "They seem to be warping the minds of some critics. Maybe they've seen too many. After a while the tendency is to seize on any slight variation, usually a variation that contradicts the erotic intent, to deny essential junkiness."[103]

After the seizure of a print of *Deep Throat* in August 1972 and the subsequent court case, on 1 March 1973 the New York court declared *Deep Throat* obscene. In his decision Judge Joel E. Tyler ruled that the

---

99   Ibid: 154.
100 Damiano quoted in ibid: 155.
101 "The Devil in Miss Jones," *Variety* (21 February 1973). Georgina Spelvin had been an understudy to Shirley MacLaine and in *The Devil In Miss Jones* she emulates MacLaine's style. Hebditch and Anning, *Porn Gold: Inside the Pornography Business*: 102.
102 Ibid.
103 Vincent Canby, "About Miss Jones and Mr. Oscar," *New York Times* (8 April 1973) section II: 1.

experts had not shown fifty-one per cent of *Deep Throat* to have social value and he condemned the film as,

> a feast of carrion and squalor … a Sodom and Gomorrah gone wild before the fire … one throat that deserves to be cut … a nadir of decadence … It does in fact, demean and pervert the sexual experience, and insults it, shamelessly, without tenderness and without understanding of its role as a concomitant of the human condition.[104]

Despite the exorbitant fine of $3 million Bob Sumner, owner of the New World Theater, responded with a sense of humour to Judge Tyler by putting the message "Judge Cuts Throat, World Mourns" on the cinema marquee.[105] As a consequence of the decision, theatres in other cities were sold out due to people trying to see *Deep Throat* in case it should be banned in their area.[106]

After the court ruling Ellen Willis commented sarcastically, "pornography may well be the characteristic mass art form of this decade." She added that, "a fiftyish, balding businessman in suit and tie, briefcase on lap, hands chastely folded over briefcase" watching a "pair of larger-than-life genitals copulating close-up" accompanied by a soundtrack of 'Stars and Stripes Forever' would be a perfect icon of the Nixon era.[107] No doubt that is just how the president would have wanted to be remembered.

---

104 Tyler quoted in Ford, *A History of X*: 52–53.
105 Ibid: 53. Between 1972 and 1981 *Deep Throat* was banned in California, Colorado, Florida, Georgia, Illinois, Iowa, Kentucky, Louisiana, Maryland, Massachusetts, Michigan, Mississippi, Missouri, Nebraska, New Hampshire, New Jersey, New York, North Dakota, Ohio, Pennsylvania, South Dakota, Tennessee, and Texas. de Grazia, *Banned Films*: 355.
106 Jean Lang, "Happy Birthday, Baby!" *Cult Movies* (No.5, 1992): 36.
107 Willis, *Beginning to See the Light*: 68.

Chapter Six

REVERSAL OF FORTUNE

The Conservative Backlash Against Porn

The Supreme Court, headed by Warren Burger and reshaped by four Nixon appointees, presided over the case of *Miller v. California* (21 June 1973). The case established the concept of community standards, redefining the obscenity debate and reversing a fifteen-year trend in court decisions.[1] Marvin Miller, the defendant, owned a West Coast mail order business and was convicted of sending sexually orientated adverts through the mail. The *Miller* decision substantially revised the standard of obscenity and meant that in future a publication or film need only be found guilty in the community in which it was tried. When setting local standards, lawmakers had to ensure that material appealed to prurient interests and depicted sexual conduct in a 'patently offensive' way, but in light of *Miller* they would also have to judge if the work "taken as a whole, lacks serious literary, artistic, political or scientific value." The decision also established that prosecutions did not have to offer proof or expert testimony to establish a definition of what constituted obscenity, contravening the conventionally accepted jurisprudence presumption that juries were not experts in areas of legal complexity. The consequence of the *Miller* decision was simple; you had to avoid offending the most conservative community in the country.[2]

The Supreme Court decision in *Miller v. California* made pornography an even more important symbolic crusade for conservatives. Religious leaders greeted the decision enthusiastically; prosecutors and conservative legislators predicted tougher anti-pornography laws would follow. Ronald Reagan, right-wing governor of California, and

---

1   Nixon appointees Warren Burger, Harry H. Blackmun, Lewis F. Powell Jr., and William H. Rehnquist voted with White to make the majority. Douglas, Brennan, Stewart and Marshall all dissented. The Court announced five decisions pertaining to obscenity laws on 21 June: *Miller v. California, Paris Adult Theatre I v. Slaton, Kaplan v. California*, and *United States v. 12 200ft Reels of Super 8mm Film*.
2   Flynt, *An Unseemly Man*: 131.

Philadelphia Mayor Frank L. Rizzo were prominent supporters of the *Miller* decision.[3] One prosecutor in New York pointed out:

> Before this decision, it was virtually impossible to prove what the national standard was ... And it was, after all, always the local community anyway — the jury — that made the final determination. Now, in places like New York City, the application of local standards will make the defendant's case even easier.[4]

This raised questions about what would happen outside metropolitan areas. In towns of under 5,000 most cinemas would not touch X-rated films, and those who did usually came into conflict with the police, clergy and citizens groups. One Wisconsin cinema owner, Robert Hodd, acknowledged, "We play X films on a spotted basis, usually in the fall when things are slow." They attracted a different audience: "when we do run 'em we see people who seldom come to our theatres. Older people. I get customers who can't even drive a car, because they're too old. Farmers will patronize 'em, too, whereas we never see them for other shows." Hodd received petitions from church groups protesting about the X-rated films, but he refused to be pressured.[5]

However, civil libertarians and dealers of adult materials denounced the decision, seeing the ruling as an infringement of First Amendment freedoms.[6] Supreme Court justice William O. Douglas believed the *Miller* test "would make it possible to ban any paper or any journal or magazine in some benighted place." Furthermore, "To send men to jail for violating standards they cannot understand, construe and apply is a monstrous thing to do." Lawyers on both sides predicted a substantial increase in prosecutions as cases were brought to test the *Miller* standard and establish its limits precisely.[7] Frank Kelley, Michigan Attorney General, was critical of the ruling, saying "This really sets us back in the dark ages. Now prosecuting attorneys in every county and

3   Lesley Oelsner, "Experts Agree Prosecutions Will Rise, But Differ on the Over-all Impact," *New York Times* (23 June 1973): 1.
4   "Pornography: A Turn of the Tide," *Newsweek* (2 July 1973): 35.
5   "Mid-America Report: Wisconsin," *Variety* (27 October 1976): 34.
6   Oelsner, "Experts Agree Prosecutions Will Rise, But Differ on the Over-all Impact," *New York Times* (23 June 1973): 1.
7   "Pornography: A Turn of the Tide," *Newsweek* (2 July 1973): 34.

state will be grandstanding and every jury in every little community will have a crack at each new book, play and movie."[8]

The situation was ideal for CDL and the decision created a suitable climate in which to conduct the citizens' crusade that Nixon had called for. The state of Utah was regarded as having some of the toughest anti-obscenity laws in America and after *Miller* state officials announced that if the scheduled exhibition of *Last Tango in Paris* went ahead the film would be seized. Deputy attorney general Robert Hansen pledged, "It will never be shown here without undergoing lots of prosecution."[9] Other observers were curious about the reception William Friedkin's *The Exorcist* (1973) would receive — a horror film (with a R-rating) which did not feature explicit sex scenes.[10]

Barney Rosset, president of Grove Press, was critical of the decision and called *Miller* "a giant step backward that will create more contempt for the law than there already is."[11] Russ Meyer, one time nemesis of CDL, was disappointed by the *Miller* ruling and said, "I think I'll go fishing." Unwilling to jeopardize investors' money, he cancelled *Foxy*, the proposed sequel to *Vixen*, in the summer of 1973, even though filming had begun and advertisements for the film had been distributed.[12] Meyer lamented, "The schlock operations have brought the whole house down on us." He differentiated between his own films and 'schlock', claiming his were quality softcore as opposed to the cheap films made quickly by entrepreneurs "who don't care if they have a story, don't care if they have only two cameras instead of three covering the action, don't care if their cuts match and don't care if their heroine has pimples on her back."[13] For the remainder of his career Meyer refused to make hardcore films or show genital close-ups. Dave Friedman, who predicted hardcore to be a passing fad, ominously warned, "The hardcore industry is going to dry up" because the decision was further reaching than anyone had expected.[14]

---

8   Kelley quoted in Oelsner, "Experts Agree Prosecutions Will Rise, But Differ on the Over-all Impact," *New York Times* (23 June 1973): 14.
9   "Hard-Nosed About Hard-Core," *Time* (2 July 1973): 12.
10 Paul Gardner, "What the Court Has Done To Movies," *New York Times* (17 August 1973): 15.
11 "Pornography: A Turn of the Tide," *Newsweek* (2 July 1973): 35.
12 Lee Beaupre, "Can't Risk Investors Coin Anymore, Russ Meyer Cancels $400,000 'Foxy'; Raps 'Schlock' Films As Spoilsports," *Variety* (4 July 1973): 5.
13 Ibid.
14 "Hard-Nosed About Hard-Core," *Time* (2 July 1973): 12.

In the case of *Paris Adult Theatre v. Slaton* (1973), two adult films showing simulated sex — *Magic Mirror* (1970) and *It All Comes Out in the End* (1970) — were banned as obscene, and the Supreme Court decision announced the same day as the *Miller* verdict. In the *Paris* judgement the Court denied consenting adults were constitutionally permitted, outside of the privacy of their own homes, to read books or view films that were obscene, and Chief Justice Burger cited the minority opinion of the President's Commission *Report*, the dissent authored by Nixon speechwriter Pat Buchanan on Keating's behalf, as an example of an arguable correlation between obscene material and crime, even though it was a collection of anecdotes and accusations rather than a scientific study.

Justice Brennan, in his dissenting opinion, was quick to point out, "It is clear that as long as the [Burger] test remains in effect, one cannot say with certainty that material is obscene until at least five members of this court … have pronounced it so." Brennan acknowledged the concept of 'obscenity' but noted it,

> cannot be defined with sufficient specificity and clarity to provide fair notice to persons who create and distribute sexually-orientated materials, to protect substantial erosion of protected speech as a by-product of the attempt to suppress unprotected speech, and to avoid very costly institutional harms.

Frustrated by the situation in the Court, Brennan claimed that the five-man majority could uphold or overturn convictions without reviewing the material.

The Supreme Court ruling in *Miller* brushed aside existing precedents for obscenity prosecutions and left lawyers and prosecutors in a state of confusion, but they were able to agree on one thing; prosecutions of pornographers would increase.[15] Stanley Fleishman, a lawyer representing a number of adult film producers, conceded, "My clients which are the major ones, will comply with the law," but they would also continue to produce adult films with "serious literary, artistic, political

---

15   Oelsner, "Experts Agree Prosecutions Will Rise, But Differ on the Over-all Impact," *New York Times* (23 June 1973): 1.

or scientific value."[16] Noting the vague wording of the *Miller* guidelines Fleishman stated, "in my opinion the ruling does not outlaw sex-writing or pictorial representation of sexual matters" but he acknowledged that the previous court protection had been watered down.[17] After *Miller*, Linda Lovelace was quoted as saying, "The last person that started censorship was Adolf Hitler, and the next thing they'll be doing is knocking on your door and taking away your TV and radio."[18]

Faced with the uncertainty posed by *Miller*, publishers and film producers could choose one of two forms of self-censorship; either stay out of certain states, or direct films and books to cater to the most conservative tastes.[19] A sequel to *The Godfather* was planned, but until the *Miller* ruling by the Supreme Court was clarified there would be no more mainstream films like *Last Tango in Paris*.[20] In the *New York Times* Paul Gardner succinctly noted, "The X-rating (for adults only) has become a scarlet letter."[21]

After the *Miller* ruling, sex shop customers began stockpiling books, magazines and stag films, in case supplies ran out. With the increase in demand prices rose.[22] Lester K. Randolph, owner of an adult bookstore in Washington, D.C., told *Newsweek* that a lot of detectives had visited his store in the wake of *Miller*, but business was good because people were stocking up, expecting the worst.[23] John Weston, West Coast lawyer and spokesman for the adult film industry, was not panicked by the decision: "At first blush the opinion seems to be suggesting that ... we go back to sex scenes like the one between Deborah Kerr and Burt Lancaster in *From Here to Eternity*." But he was reassured by his belief that "creative people tend to be intrepid and the public has proved in dollars and cents that it wants explicit sexual materials — filmmakers won't let those dollars go to waste."[24]

Without *Miller*, according to Al Goldstein, there would have been nothing to stop major Hollywood studios from making explicit adult

16 "Smut Rakers Call Business Viable," *New York Times* (1 July 1973): 36.
17 Ibid.
18 Talese, *Thy Neighbor's Wife*: 414.
19 "Pornography: A Turn of the Tide," *Newsweek* (2 July 1973): 35.
20 Paul Gardner, "Crime In, Sex Out in New Film Season," *New York Times* (4 September 1973): 30.
21 Ibid.
22 "Porn: The Vice Goes on Ice," *Newsweek* (12 February 1973): 46.
23 "Pornography: A Turn of the Tide," *Newsweek* (2 July 1973): 35.
24 Ibid.

films. Wanting a share of the lucrative new market, the major studios could have produced higher quality films with better scripts and production values. As a consequence some of the small adult film producers were glad that the major studios had been dissuaded from entering the adult market, keeping porn on the periphery of popular culture and removing competitors from the marketplace.[25] Russ Meyer concurred, and criticized the MPAA for promoting X ratings as "the equivalent of a skull-and-crossbones on a bottle of poison." He believed that what happened as a response to the success of *Deep Throat* made a "financial mockery" of many big budget mainstream Hollywood films being produced by studios that belonged to the MPAA.[26]

Before *Miller*, producer Stephen Krantz was working on an adaptation of Hubert Selby's controversial novel *Last Exit to Brooklyn* but as a consequence of the court ruling the project was dropped and he lamented, "A climate of depression has settled over Hollywood."[27] He continued, "If people can't see adult stories, why go to the movies? The pabulum is on television."[28] Krantz acknowledged the climate of uncertainty, "We don't want to produce lawsuits, we want to produce pictures ... Nobody wants to make a picture today which is going to be rejected by thirty per cent of the communities in the United States."[29] For the same reason Russ Meyer predicted that the *Miller* ruling would be devastating for adult entertainment: "you can't jeopardize investors money." Uncertainty surrounding the boundaries for acceptable depictions of sex meant there was a great deal of uncertainty about exhibiting films.[30]

Al Goldstein, Jim Buckley and Peter Locke budgeted $134,000 to make a hardcore film with high artistic standards called *Kitty Can't Help It*. As a result of *Miller* Buckley and Locke wanted all the hardcore sex taken out, so the investors would have a chance to make a return on their money, but that meant *Kitty* would have to compete at the box office against mainstream films.[31] *Fourplay* (Robert McCarthy et

25 "Porn on the Run: A Mini-Interview with Al Goldstein," *Oui* (February 1975): 114.
26 Beaupre, "Can't Risk Investors Coin Anymore, Russ Meyer Cancels $400,000 'Foxy'; Raps 'Schlock' Films As Spoilsports," *Variety* (4 July 1973): 5.
27 Paul Gardner, "What the Court Has Done To Movies," *New York Times* (17 August 1973): 15.
28 Ibid.
29 "Porn: The Vice Goes on Ice," *Newsweek* (12 February 1973): 47.
30 "Smut Makers Call Business Viable," *New York Times* (1 July 1973): 36.
31 "Porn on the Run: A Mini-Interview with Al Goldstein," *Oui* (February 1975): 114.

al., 1975) was originally intended to be a four-part sex comedy co-written by Terry Southern, Dan Greenburg, Jack Richardson and David O'Dell, but after *Miller* the producers anticipated trouble so multiple versions of some scenes were shot to be used in different markets and protect the investment, with the European versions of the film having more nudity.[32] Robert Weiner was trying to attract financing for *Cruising* but several Hollywood companies decided it might face censorship problems, even though Weiner made it clear he had no intention of producing an X-rated film.[33] The project was dropped until William Friedkin eventually directed the screenplay in 1980. In some instances, after *Miller*, film producers were forced to cancel projects or seek financing from Europe.[34] Richard Shepherd, executive at Warner Brothers, made his company's position clear when he told the *New York Times*, "We're not interested in X-rated films. During this period of uncertainty, you just have to go on what you think is good taste. If you give it too much worry you can end up at Menninger's clinic."[35]

Miller did not stop the adult entertainment business because there was an enthusiastic audience and public demand could not be suppressed. "No matter what new weapons the anti-porn crusade develops," said Al Goldstein, "people still want to see hardcore films."[36] Jim and Artie Mitchell called the *Miller* decision "totally insane" but remained defiant; "They'll have to put us in jail ... we're prepared to go down fighting."[37] Jim Mitchell was not worried by potential legal changes and promised, "The young turks don't give a damn. They'll keep on making movies. They don't know any better. After all, we're only in it to have a good time and make money."[38]

Concessions were made, however, and after *Miller* Al Goldstein published two different versions of *Screw* in an effort to avoid prosecution. One edition was specifically for distribution in New York and to subscribers, and would contain graphic hardcore pictures, while an out-of-town edition was for sale on newsstands

32   Gardner, "What the Court Has Done To Movies," *New York Times* (17 August 1973): 15.
33   Ibid.
34   Ibid.
35   Gardner, "Crime In, Sex out in new film season," *New York Times* (4 September 1970): 30.
36   "Porn on the Run: A Mini-Interview with Al Goldstein," *Oui* (February 1975): 114.
37   "Smut Makers Call Business Viable," *New York Times* (1 July 1973): 36.
38   Ibid.

nationwide and did not have hardcore pictures.[39] The biggest effect of *Miller*, remarked Goldstein, was "to reduce the economic base that supports pornographers such as myself." The market for explicit adult entertainment, which had been rapidly expanding, began to shrink.[40] The number of cinemas willing to show adult films declined. At its peak there were 240 nationwide but, frightened by the implications of the case and the potential legal costs entailed by prosecution this quickly declined to about 100.[41] The implications of the Supreme Court ruling were quickly realised with Harry Reems' prosecution in Memphis in 1973 as a consequence of attorney Larry Parish's broad interpretation of the *Miller* decision.[42] Director Radley Metzger responded to the new interpretation of the law by adopting the pseudonym 'Henry Paris' to differentiate between his softcore and explicit hardcore sex films, but more importantly because he was afraid of prosecution.[43]

Despite the uncertainty prompted by the *Miller* decision, US Solicitor General Archibald Cox addressed a group of state judges at the American Bar Association convention (in Honolulu) and told them that the Supreme Court's tough anti-pornography decisions may make it possible to successfully prosecute "upper level girlie magazines" such as *Playboy* and *Penthouse*, enabling Charles Keating to achieve a long held goal. Cox was certain that it would enable successful prosecutions of cheaper pornographic magazines outside metropolitan centres.[44]

Miller did pave the way for the prosecution of porn producers, and coming in the wake of *Deep Throat*'s success it began the process that would end 'porno chic'. After the *Miller* decision Charles Keating wrote a triumphant editorial for the *National Decency Reporter* emphasising that a watershed had been reached and the tide in the fight against porn had turned. Marking the occasion, he wrote:

---

39 "Porn on the Run: A Mini-Interview with Al Goldstein," *Oui* (February 1975): 114.
40 Ibid: 82.
41 Ibid: 114.
42 Ibid: 142.
43 Muller and Faris, *Grindhouse*: 139. Under the pseudonym 'Henry Paris' Radley Metzger made *The Punishment of Anne* (1975), *The Private Afternoons of Pamela Mann* (1975), *Naked Came the Stranger* (1975), *The Opening of Misty Beethoven* (1976) and *Maraschino Cherry* (1978).
44 "Cox Sees Strong Porn Law Impact," *National Decency Reporter* (November–December 1974): 2. Cox was Special Prosecutor during the Watergate investigation and taught at Harvard Law School.

For more than fifteen years, since I started CDL, the pornographers have run roughshod over the American public, engulfing this nation in a tidal wave of filth and turning her along the path of moral corruption and decay. Their reason was money. Big Money. Billions of dollars. And for money they were willing to sell their country, their fellow-citizens, and our children into the bondage of sexual debauchery. These gutter merchants wrapped their merchandise in the flag of the United States, and cowered behind the Constitution. They tried to use that great document which freed men's minds and spirits as a device to enslave the men and debase the women of America. Those sordid years are now behind us. One day soon we will look back with shock and disbelief at the depths to which we allowed ourselves to be dragged in the name of 'freedom'.[45]

Using his familiar rhetoric and bravado he evoked the symbolic corruption of the Constitution, the exploitation of children, and the erosion of moral standards that he attributed primarily to liberalism and the Warren Court. Keating noted the change in judicial philosophy to rally his supporters,

now it is our turn. And your turn. The decent people of America, backed by the United States Supreme Court, are going to wage a holy, yes, *holy* war against the merchants of obscenity. From this day forward I will not rest, and no one connected with CDL will rest, until every pornographer in America is out of business, in jail, or both.[46]

Raymond Gauer, national spokesman for CDL, concurred: "Well, thank God for the new Supreme Court decision. We've finally got them where we want them, or at least a start on where we want them, but God knows things have gone so far now it's hard to tell how we'll ever roll them back."[47] Were it not for the Watergate scandal, in his second term Nixon might have waged "a holy rampage to purge the country of its sexual sinners," but the looming impeachment brought his early resignation. Gay Talese on the other hand believed "the jails would have been occupied not only by such hardcore people as Linda

45 Keating quoted in Talese, *Thy Neighbor's Wife*: 412.
46 Keating quoted in ibid: 412–413.
47 Gauer quoted in See, *Blue Money*: 162.

Lovelace, Gerard Damiano and Al Goldstein but also by the likes of Hugh Hefner, Bob Guccione and perhaps Alex Comfort and Masters and Johnson."[48] Perhaps even by Talese himself.

In the aftermath of *Miller* prosecutors were active, bringing numerous obscenity cases to the courts. However, when the cases came to trial the juries sometimes refused to convict, even when the materials were obviously obscene. Stanley Fleishman believed this was due to social changes that had taken place in the previous fifteen years and because seventy-five per cent of people felt it was not an offence to community standards for consenting adults to view explicit films, so long as they were not forced upon unwilling audiences and kept away from children. While the situation was frustrating for prosecutors who could not get convictions, defendants knew they could not be sure of acquittal nor could they assume that the Supreme Court would eventually overturn a conviction.[49] As a consequence of *Miller* and *Paris*, hardcore adult material was not available in small towns, but it could still be easily be found in large cities.

On its release in America *Emmanuelle* (Just Jaeckin, 1974) was promoted as "a classier breed of porn. It is as if being French somehow makes it fancier."[50] The film was a box office success in France, so David Begelman, president of Columbia Pictures, decided to distribute *Emmanuelle* and accompany it with a high-profile advertising campaign. Trying to justify his decision, Begelman claimed that he saw the film in a Parisian theatre and noticed that seventy-five to eighty per cent of the people waiting in line were women; "we would have had no interest in the film if its appeal was totally to men. Then it could be taken as pornographic."[51] This reflected the changing times and also mainstream film studios' attempts to cash in on 'porno chic'. *Emmanuelle* was the first X-rated film distributed by Columbia, and it was stressed that the film was not explicit hardcore pornography.[52] The film's promotional material emphasised that it was an X-rated film unlike any others, which were stereotypically attended by men in

48 "Porno Rama," *Oui* (February 1975): 116.
49 "Porn Before the Bench: Mini-Interviews With Stanley Fleishman," *Oui* (February 1975): 100.
50 Jay Cocks, "Queen Klong," *Time* (6 January 1975): 48.
51 Begelman quoted in "Analysing 'Emmanuelle's' B.O. Impact on the U.S. Market," *Variety* (7 May 1975): 56.
52 Ibid.

raincoats and which left the audience feeling guilty about their illicit pleasures. The marketing campaign was aimed at people who would not normally attend the New York grindhouses, and advertisements promised "X was never like this."[53] In *Time* Jay Cocks observed the cultural situation facing *Emmanuelle* upon its American release:

> It should be kept in mind, of course, that the well-lathered extremes of American porn are banned in France. Without knowledge of *Deep Throat*, *Emmanuelle* might seem like pretty hot stuff. This gives the film rather too much credit, however. *Emmanuelle* would have to go up against something like *The Greatest Story Ever Told* before it could begin to look titillating.[54]

Legal and social changes also took their toll on the market for established adult magazines like *Playboy*. At one point in 1971 *Playboy* corporate stock was selling at $23.50, but by 1975 it had dropped to a low of $2.25. The magazine's circulation fell to below six million while competitors *Penthouse* had monthly sales of four-and-a-half million and *Hustler*, begun in June 1974, was close to two million. Profits made by Hugh Hefner's corporation also declined from $11.3 million in 1973 to just $1.1 million in 1975.[55] While Hefner boasted that he had helped create the social climate that enabled films like *Deep Throat* to be publicly exhibited,[56] it seemed that subsequent developments had passed him by.

Tired of the novelty of pornography, Vincent Canby gave a cutting assessment of Gerard Damiano in the *New York Times*: "Damiano, I'm afraid is not Hitchcock, no Polanski, no Faulkner. He's just your ordinary run-of-the-mill movie goer and sometime reader who doesn't hesitate to lift the cast-offs, the remnants, of other people's ideas, which are evidently all he is capable of lifting."[57] Hoping he approached the subject with an open mind, Canby concluded that there was probably no such thing as "good pornography." While films such as *Behind the Green Door* might be slick to a degree, with good camerawork and

53 Ibid.
54 Cocks, "Queen Klong," *Time* (6 January 1975): 48.
55 Talese, *Thy Neighbor's Wife*: 491–493.
56 Miller, *Bunny*: 196.
57 Vincent Canby, "The King of Porn, ah — Corn," *New York Times* (23 June 1974) section II: 1.

an attractive cast, they were still not *serious* films[58] because their sole intention was to depict explicit sexual images. By 1974 *Time* was already reporting that the 'sexual frontier' was in retreat because swinging, open marriages and bisexuality was in decline. Gilbert Bartell, author of *Group Sex* (1971), attributed the reversal to the "depressed and unsettled times," believing "There's a more somber feeling among people, a retreat from sexual frivolity."[59] Claiming a retrenchment of the adult entertainment industry, *Time* also reported that adult bookstores in many cities saw sales drop by as much as fifty per cent and the number of sex clubs was also in decline.[60]

In 1975, Walter Goodman noted the arrival of five heavily promoted adult films, *Exhibition* (Jean-Francois Davy, 1975), *Sensations* (Alberto Ferro, 1975), *The Naughty Victorians* (Robert Kinger, 1975), *The Story of Joanna* (Gerard Damiano, 1975) and *The Story of O*, to cinemas on New York's East Side.[61] Acknowledging *Last Tango in Paris* and *Emmanuelle* as the "mild mannered advance scouts" for the current releases,[62] Goodman felt jaded after watching five porn films in one week and concluded,

> It's not exactly that if you've seen one dirty movie you've seen them all, but the progressions do become predictable, the movements mechanical, the episodes repetitive; unless one is an incurable buff, interest must flag. Whips and chains may serve as audience restoratives for a while, but my guess is that animals, vegetables and fruit will be putting in an appearance on the East Side any time now.[63]

An observation that was more accurate than he may have realised. Joseph Slade reported on the changes within pornographic films, observing that "Weird as these matters sound, there is about the loops a curious air of innocent experimentation, as if their producers were simply trying to assess the predilections of a heterogeneous audience."[64]

58 Ibid.
59 Bartell quoted in "Avant-Garde Retreat?" *Time* (25 November 1974): 49.
60 Ibid.
61 Walter Goodman, "The New Porno Movies: From X to Zzzzzzzzz," *New York Times* (23 November 1975) section II: 1.
62 Ibid.
63 Ibid.
64 Joseph P. Slade, "Recent Trends in Pornographic Films," *Society* (September–October 1975): 79.

But in exploring the spectrum of human sexuality the pornographic loops intentionally touched on taboo subjects that provoked outrage. Always looking for new taboos to challenge in order to maintain its position as transgressive, S+M themes became popular in mainstream films such as Just Jaeckin's softcore *The Story of O*, also made as an explicit hardcore film, *The Story of Joanna*, by Gerard Damiano the same year. In that climate Joseph Slade noted,

> The hardcore movie seems to be turning back in upon itself. When porno first began to be shown in theatres, the apology took a standard liberal form: sex is beautiful, sex is healthy, sex is less obscene than violence, there is nothing dirty about it and so on. Pornographers — and some of the rest of us — are beginning to sense that idyllic sex is simplistic and, from the standpoint of eroticism, simpleminded.[65]

As pornography moved beyond the limited boundaries of the eroticism permitted by mainstream opinion, accepted moral standards were challenged and transgressed. The resulting pornographic films questioned the basic premise that sex is healthy and beautiful, but Slade believed that was a good thing because,

> We probably need 'perverted' sexual metaphors and raw sexual fantasies as clues to these energies, some of which are decidedly unpretty. Putting aside the repugnance at least acquaints us with some of the faces; without the metaphors and the fantasies, we cannot even see.[66]

However, despite his articulate attempt to explain the existence of such films, the mixture of sex and violence made many liberals feel uncomfortable and gave more ammunition to anti-obscenity crusaders.

New York was not a squeamish city by any means and the popularity of films like *Dirty Harry* (Don Segal, 1971) and *Death Wish* (Michael Winner, 1974) made it clear that a substantial section of the movie going audience found violence a simple and acceptable solution to social problems. In *Death Wish* an ordinary citizen is prompted to

65   Ibid: 84.
66   Ibid.

become a vigilante after an attack on his wife and daughter, and the film brings together contemporary concerns about Charles Manson, porn, rape, and violent crime. Reactionary and exploitative, *Death Wish* depicts how Paul Kersey (Charles Bronson), a liberal-minded architect and conscientious objector during the Korean War, becomes a vigilante after his wife Joanna (Hope Lange) and daughter Carol (Kathleen Tolan) are attacked in their apartment by three criminals who follow them home from a neighbourhood store.

During the attack Spraycan (Gregory Rozakis) paints a swastika and other graffiti on the walls, reminiscent of vandalism found at the scenes of the Manson Family murders, while his two friends turn to the women. When one assailant (Jeff Goldblum) attacks Joanna he screams at her "God damn rich cunt. I hate rich cunts!" — words reminiscent of Manson's reported hatred of the affluent. The same assailant sexually assaults Carol and claims he is going to "paint her mouth," suggesting he is familiar with the film *Deep Throat*. The idea of forced oral sex is also a statement of morals and reinforces the idea that this is something that men want, but nice girls have to be forced into. Joanna Kersey is beaten so badly that she later dies from her injuries and Carol traumatized so severely that she is left hospitalized in a near vegetative state. Blatant cultural references to the contemporary 'porno chic' could also be found in the crime drama *Truck Turner* (Jonathan Kaplan, 1974). While looking for his adversary, the eponymous protagonist Truck Turner (Issac Hayes) threatens a prostitute and tells her pimp "this bitch is going to deep throat this six inch [gun] barrel" unless he gets the information he wants. Again this inverts the image of oral sex, making something healthy and pleasurable into something torturous and harmful.

It is the murder of his wife and rape of his daughter that sets Charles Bronson off on his revenge spree in *Death Wish*. According to the film's ideology, New York's mugging problem could be solved quickly and easily by murderous vigilantism. In the *New York Times* Vincent Canby noted that *Death Wish* exploited the audience's paranoia. It is "a bird-brained movie to cheer the hearts of the far-right wing," he wrote, "as well as the hearts of those who don't think much about politics but just like to see people get zapped, without regard to colour or creed." He also noted that he had no doubt that muggers would find *Death*

Wish "a great deal of fun," and while the film sometimes succeeded "in arousing the most primitive kind of anger" it remained a "despicable movie that raises complex questions in order to offer bigoted, frivolous, oversimplified answers."[67]

Blatantly exploitative, *Death Wish* pandered to conservative fears without addressing any of the issues raised. The same year it was parodied by the porn film *Sex Wish* (Victor Milk, 1974), in which Zebedy Colt plays a deranged pervert with sadistic tendencies who invades homes and sexually abuses the occupants. After forcing his way into the home of a black couple, he makes them perform a live sex show at gunpoint before killing them both and castrating the man. Harry Reems, star of *Deep Throat* and *The Devil in Miss Jones*, plays the fiancé of one of Colt's victims who becomes a vigilante and hunts down the sex maniac. Made quickly with a small cast and budget, here the adult film business showed it could satirize popular culture and respond to current events faster than TV or the Hollywood studios.

The potential legal difficulties created by *Miller* were quickly realised in the case of *Jenkins v. Georgia* (1974), where a cinema owner in Albany, Georgia, was convicted and fined $750 for exhibiting *Carnal Knowledge* (Mike Nichols, 1971), an R-rated film which had earned Ann Margaret an Oscar nomination. The prosecution case was based on a misinterpretation of *Miller* and focused on a simulated sex scene near the end of the film where Jonathan (Jack Nicholson) is fellated by a prostitute. To properly hear the case the Supreme Court Justices needed to watch *Carnal Knowledge* and form their own opinions about the film. Thurgood Marshall was not impressed and commented, "The only thing obscene about this movie is that it is obscenely boring." Chief Justice Burger left early but complemented the lighting and camerawork, and Rehnquist liked the music.[68]

All nine Justices agreed that *Carnal Knowledge* was not obscene. The four liberal members (Douglas, Brennan, Marshall, and Stewart) wanted the Court to acknowledge that the problem stemmed from the decision in *Roth* and *Paris*, but Chief Justice Burger, unwilling to criticise the precedent he had set, only wanted to send a message to the local jurisdictions. Rehnquist was assigned the responsibility of writing the

67   Vincent Canby, "Story of Gunman Takes Grim View of City," *New York Times* (25 July 1974): 27.
68   Woodward and Armstrong, *The Brethren*: 280–281.

majority decisions in *Jenkins v. Georgia* and *Hamling v. United States* (both 24 June 1974), in which he explained *Carnal Knowledge* was not obscene because it only showed scenes of simulated sex, where the *Illustrated Report* had explicit illustrations.

In *Jenkins* (1974), Rehnquist wrote, "it would be a serious misreading of *Miller* to conclude that juries have unbridled discretion in determining what is 'patently offensive'." Overruling the jury's guilty verdict, even though their opinion reflected 'local standards,' Rehnquist concluded that in the opinion of the Supreme Court *Carnal Knowledge* "could not, as a matter of constitutional law, be found to depict sexual conduct in a patently offensive way, and that it is therefore not outside the protection of the First and Fourteenth Amendments because it is obscene." Justice Brennan concurred with the reversal of the conviction in *Jenkins*, but reiterated the observation he had made in *Paris* (1973): "one cannot say with certainty that material is obscene until at least five members of this Court, applying inevitably obscure standards, have pronounced it so."

In *Miller* a state case and a state law were being challenged and the Supreme Court ruled that it was not necessary to use a national standard and that local communities would set the standards used for obscenity convictions, but in *Jenkins* the Supreme Court overruled a state conviction which allegedly reflected those same local standards. In *Hamling v. United States* (24 June 1974), a federal case, the Supreme Court ruled again that local standards must be used. This clarified *Miller* in so far as it established that thousands of different standards exist with regard to any magazine, book, or film. The consequences for national distribution were enormous. Federal prosecutors could bring cases in localities where a conservative community and favourable judge could be expected to bring prosecutions and convictions. The government could also force publishers to travel several thousand miles to stand trial, which could last weeks if not months, thereby imposing an additional economic burden.[69]

Lawyer Stanley Fleishman lamented that the Supreme Court, dominated by a conservative majority, began with the assumption that pornography was harmful, despite the findings of the *Report of the*

---

69 "Porn Before the Bench: Mini-Interviews With Stanley Fleishman," *Oui* (February 1975): 100–102.

President's Commission on Obscenity and Pornography (1970). They chose to ignore the findings of the best-qualified social scientists in favour of dogmatic advocates of censorship, such as Charles Keating and Father Hill.[70] Fleishman added,

> The minute you break new ground, you're running into trouble. Do something that everybody else has done before and you're on relatively safe ground. But if you do something a little different and it catches somebody's eye, you run a risk. Creativity, which is a scarce enough commodity at best, is the first casualty.[71]

When the Supreme Court upheld William Hamling's conviction in 1974, Fleishman organised several authors, editors, publishers and lawyers to join with family members in writing to the San Diego judge appealing for mercy. After the $87,000 fine was paid Hamling was told that the prison sentence could be reduced to less than a year in Terminal Island if he severed all business ties with erotic publishing and ceased writing, editing and distributing any material pertaining to sex. The five-year probationary period imposed by the judge meant that Hamling could not write any books or magazine articles pertaining to his own case or obscenity legislation because it might be construed as violating his probation.[72]

In a letter to Fleishman, Hamling expressed his shock and disappointment at the verdict. He knew that if Justice Hugo Black had still been on the bench he would probably have been acquitted, but Nixon appointee Lewis F. Powell Jr. had replaced Black, shifting the balance of the Supreme Court and, as a consequence, Hamling was convicted. The situation was perplexing, and Hamling wrote, "therefore I am a criminal, consigned to the limbo of convict life and brand. How does one adjust to this? A question of personal taste and legal ambiguity that swings the scales of justice five to four either way ... as capricious as the changing wind at sunset."[73] The *National Decency Reporter* celebrated the *Hamling* decision with a front-page story and

---

70   Ibid: 100.
71   Ibid: 102.
72   Talese, *Thy Neighbor's Wife*: 446–447.
73   Ibid: 446–447.

a picture of Justice Rehnquist under the headline "All Systems 'Go' for Obscenity Prosecutions."[74]

According to Harold P. Fahringer and Michael J. Brown,

> Once pornography is exposed to the strong sunlight of a completely free and uninhibited people its appeal will surely diminish. And if that assumption proves to be wrong, then we must live with the level and variety of tastes which the marketplace theory of the first amendment encourages and protects.[75]

They added that the prevalence of sexually orientated adult entertainment as a contemporary phenomenon "apparently proves that a nation gets the kind of art and entertainment it wants and is willing to pay for."[76] Minneapolis lawyer Robert J. Milavetz concurred, "You won't ever close out pornography as long as the majority are not really stirred up by it. Or as long as they are willing to pay for it."[77] To advance their crusade Raymond Gauer and Charles Keating needed to find a symbolic panic that would stir up the public and provide a focus for the CDL anti-obscenity crusade. To further their agenda they concocted an allegation so shocking and outrageous that there could be no moral or legal defence.

---

74 Ibid: 446.
75 Harold P. Fahringer and Michael J. Brown, "The Rise and Fall of Roth — A Critique of the Recent Supreme Court Obscenity Decisions," *Kentucky Law Journal* 62 (1973–74): 766.
76 Ibid: 766–767.
77 Seth King, "Pornographic Shows Spread In Midwest," *New York Times* (11 March 1973): 48.

Chapter Seven

COMING ATTRACTIONS
THE ULTIMATE ATROCITY

1975 Newspaper Reports and
Shackleton's Pre-Publicity

RAYMOND GAUER'S ANTI-OBSCENITY RHETORIC ESCALATED IN THE WAKE OF *Miller v. California* (1973). Sensing an opportunity he began making wild accusations to demonise liberals who defended pornography and gather more support for the CDL crusade. Gauer's allegations were just as exaggerated and apocalyptic as Charles Keating's had been in the 1960s, but Gauer incorporated even more shocking claims into his rhetoric. He developed the themes used in existing CDL accusations, adapting them to reflect social changes and technological developments in popular entertainment, and created a new symbolic threat, the pornographic 'snuff' film. In the early 1960s CDL distributed a film called *Pages of Death* (1962) about a young woman who is raped and murdered by a man who is corrupted by, and addicted to, pornography.[1] Since its production, legal and social developments — alongside the increasing popularity of 8mm cameras and projectors — brought new possibilities for pornographers and new threats to American morality.

In denial of the blatantly obvious, when delivering talks on behalf of CDL Gauer falsely assured his audience, "I don't do this just to make this talk sensational or to try to shock some of you people." Instead, he claimed, he wanted to educate people who were ignorant of the "serious nature" of the material. His disclaimer was a way to justify the graphic descriptions in his presentation. His desire to encourage public

---

1   Allegedly based on a real incident *Pages of Death* was produced by Karl Holtsnider of Franciscan Communications/St. Francis Productions in California. It was shot on 16mm colour film and lasted thirty minutes. The film recounts the story of an eleven-year-old girl who is sexually assaulted and murdered by a teenage boy. When the police search the boy's room they find girlie magazines and hardcore pornography, and this, it is indicated through numerous statements by the police, is the cause of the attack, but no other supporting evidence is offered.

outrage was obvious when he promised, "We will get public opinion aroused as we never have before."[2]

Gauer regularly condemned the liberal permissiveness of the 1960s, during which time he claimed the nation suffered badly, and as a consequence,

> Communities all over America are being flooded with *worse filth than ever*! Indescribable pornographic and depraved material! It has lowered the moral tone of the entire nation! What we said all along *would* happen *has* happened! Even the so-called *respectable* media, the best-selling novels, the major studio motion pictures, the TV programs on prime time are often vile! Our children are *deluged* with filth!

This situation was not unexpected and Gauer cast CDL as defenders of traditional values and prophetic authorities whose warnings had gone unheeded;

> This has brought on what we always *said* it would bring on, a terrible increase in divorce, a terrible increase in abortion, everything is so easy now! A terrible increase in illegitimacy, in contraceptives, in homosexuality, marital infidelity — you name it![3]

Amidst the lingering 'porno chic' engendered by *Deep Throat's* mainstream popularity and the general climate of permissiveness, Gauer's anti-obscenity allegations had to be extreme to attract attention and elicit support.

At the start of the 1970s CDL was at the peak of its power and influence after the Fortas hearing and Keating's participation in the President's Commission, but the organisation's decline was rapid, due ironically to the centralization of power and reliance on direct-mail fundraising rather than grassroots activism.[4] Early in 1971 the desire to expand CDL's financial powerbase was evident when Keating signed a contract with Richard A. Viguerie aimed at increasing membership. The

---

2   Gauer in "A Typical CDL Talk" quoted by Strub, "Perversion for Profit," *Journal of the History of Sexuality* 15:2 (May 2006): 280.

3   Gauer quoted in See, *Blue Money*: 162.

4   Strub, "Perversion for Profit," *Journal of the History of Sexuality* 15:2 (May 2006): 287.

arrangement undermined the organisation's national pre-eminence. Viguerie was considered the king of direct-mail fundraising and by the 1980s his list contained more than a million names. The organisation made money by charging clients a rental fee for each individual name that was solicited from his list.[5]

Under the terms of the contract CDL agreed to pay Viguerie Co. two-and-a-half cents for each fundraising letter sent on their behalf, and Richard Vigurie quickly set to work distributing millions. The letters were similar to earlier CDL literature, which made absurd but provocative allegations about the quantity and nature of obscene material, but they also asked for donations. Since Viguerie's business was based on the quantity of letters sent, he was relentless and Whitney Strub noted that people on the mailing list could receive several letters in a month![6]

Tax returns (dated 3 May 1974) document that CDL income increased from $140,000 in 1970 to $1.2 million in 1971 and continued rising, most likely as a consequence of the mass mail fundraising, to more than $2 million in 1972. But in the process of becoming a national organisation, grassroots activists had been marginalised and played only a minor role. Unlike CDL literature and rhetoric of the 1960s, in the 1970s the number of local chapters was not mentioned; instead the emphasis was placed on organisational activities such as providing seminars for law enforcement, assisting prosecutors, and developing "innovative and ingenious techniques" to alert citizens to the dangers posed by pornography. Local campaigns of the 1960s gave way to a centralized organisation operating at a national level where members showed support through donations rather than active participation. Consequently the number of local CDL chapters sharply decreased and by 1973 there were only thirty-two.[7]

5   John F. Berry, "'King of Direct Mail' Fights To Keep Clients Under Wraps; Virginia Co. in Court To Keep Direct-Mail Deals Private," Washington *Post* (15 March 1982) Business Section: 1.
6   Strub, "Perversion for Profit," *Journal of the History of Sexuality* 15:2 (May 2006): 287–288. Viguerie Co. clients were almost invariably right-wing conservative causes, amongst them senator Jesse Helms (Republican, North Carolina), representative Phillip Crane (Republican, Illinois) and Ronald Reagan (Republican, California). During the 1970s it also represented Bibles For the World, Christian Service Corp Inc., Leadership Foundation Inc., Americans Against Union Control of Government, Prospect House, Conservative Caucus, Citizens Committee for the Right to Keep and Bear Arms, National Conservative Political Action Committee, Committee for the Survival of a Free Congress, Gun Owners of America, National Health Federation, National Rifle Association and American Life Lobby.
7   Ibid: 288.

Under the contract signed by CDL and Viguerie, sixty-seven per cent of donations sent to CDL went straight to Viguerie, an improper financing arrangement that came to the attention of officials in a number of states who took action accordingly. In 1973 Pennsylvania capped fundraising for charities at thirty-five per cent and later the same year refused CDL permission to raise funds in the state, as did North Carolina and Florida.[8] In New York, after an investigation of CDL fundraising practices, attorney general Louis Lefkowtiz filed a suit against the organisation because it was spending more than two thirds of its donations on fundraising. The organisation had budgeted for nearly $1.5 million in *expected* donations to Viguerie's organisation.[9] Lefkowitz described the fundraising as "a fraud upon the public" for claiming that donations would be used to support anti-obscenity activities when it was apparent that the money was really being used for "self-perpetuating revenue building,"[10] and he sought to have CDL barred from soliciting funds in New York as a consequence of his findings. In 1973 the state court voided the contract between CDL and Viguerie Co. after an investigation found that ninety-three per cent of the funds raised went to Viguerie because CDL were trying to pay off the previous year's bill.[11] Mass mailing was a lucrative business for Viguerie and two years later he raised $1.5 million for the Korean Cultural and Freedom Foundation, but his corporation kept $900,000, the Foundation received $100,000 and the rest of the money went on expenses.[12]

Viguerie identified the political significance of his company when he described direct-mail as a "lighted candle," one that "revolutionized American politics. It levelled the playing field for conservatives. It

8   Ibid: 288–289. See also Corn, "Dirty Bookkeeping," *New Republic* (2 April 1990): 14.
9   "Antipornography Group Accused," *New York Times* (23 November 1973): 39. The case *State of New York v CDL* (1973) is notable because it reflects Keating's unorthodox and illegal financial dealings years before the Savings and Loan Scandal was exposed.
10   "Tables Turn on Antismut Group," *Wall Street Journal* (21 January 1974) cited in Strub, "Perversion for Profit," *Journal of the History of Sexuality* 15:2 (May 2006): 289.
11   John F. Berry, "'King of Direct Mail' Fights To Keep Clients Under Wraps; Virginia Co. in Court To Keep Direct-Mail Deals Private," Washington *Post* (15 March 1982) Business Section: 1.
12   Ibid. Viguerie Co. continued the practice and in 1980 the Second Amendment Foundation paid Viguerie Co. 60.3% of money raised and Help Hospital Veterans paid 40.6%. John F. Berry, "'King of Direct Mail' Fights To Keep Clients Under Wraps; Virginia Co. in Court To Keep Direct-Mail Deals Private," Washington *Post* (15 March 1982) Business Section: 1; See also Sylvia Porter, "Defrauding your own charity," Bangor *Daily News* (24 May 1974): 19; "Beware," *The Bulletin* (Bend, Or.) (29 January 1975): 5; Jack Anderson, "The wizard of fundraising," Sarasota *Herald-Tribune* (3 June 1978): 7A.

brought us to the table."[13] It also made him a very wealthy and influential man. Viguerie compiled a list of names of potential donors who would be solicited regularly for contributions, but he emphasised the "lifetime value of a donor," because for him it was more than just fundraising. Viguerie saw himself as building a movement "to identify our activists, pass legislation, defeat legislation." In his opinion the list was potentially a tool for governing,[14] and he contended that if he could identify an issue that was significant to an individual he could use that as a means to introduce them to a second and third issue. Peter Swire, a privacy expert, warned of a nightmare scenario which could develop because of Viguerie's practices where public debate is sidestepped, and the candidate knows everything about a voter but the voter does not know what the candidate really believes. The consequence would be a serious distortion of the political process.[15] By 2004 it was estimated that Viguerie Co. sent out 120 million letters annually on behalf of conservative causes.[16]

Ron Royhab, an investigative journalist, reported in 1974 that CDL had invested more than $230,000 in the American Financial Corporation (AFC), at a time when Keating was head of CDL and an executive vice president at AFC. Despite the obvious conflict of interest, Keating's economic and political influence in the state enabled him to negotiate a deal with the Ohio attorney general, allowing CDL to continue fundraising if the organisation submitted periodic financial statements.[17] Even with CDL's social and political influence a series of revelations about fundraising and financial practices crippled the organisation. In the social climate created by the Watergate scandal the suggestion of corruption or malpractice limited CDL access to

---

13 Jon Gertner, "The Very, Very Personal Is the Political," *New York Times Magazine* (15 February 2004): 46.
14 Ibid.
15 Ibid: 47.
16 Ibid: 46. In the early 1970s CDL attempted to extend their crusade into Oregon as they had done elsewhere, asking for donations and requesting that mass produced postcards be sent to elected officials. However CDL were not familiar with Oregon's revised criminal code which made the consumption of pornography by adults legal (only criminalising publicly offensive displays or the involvement of juveniles) and one journalist suggested that Keating would have better luck "in a state where the people and the laws are less mature." "The wrong place," Eugene (Oregon) *Register-Guard* (22 January 1972): 6.
17 Strub, "Perversion for Profit," *Journal of the History of Sexuality* 15:2 (May 2006): 289.

political figures and tarnished its reputation.[18] It was in 1973, in the midst of the legal and financial crisis facing CDL, that Raymond Gauer first claimed that 'snuff' movies existed.

A widely distributed CDL mailing in 1972 asked its readers "Did you know that in [whichever city was targeted by the mailing] there are theatres that show movies of men and women having sexual intercourse?" Not content with that observation the letter continued, describing the perversions depicted, of "women having sexual intercourse with animals and other sexual activities too unbelievable to mention."[19] Familiar CDL claims, but with repetition their impact and shock value declined sharply. Speaking to a Federated Women's Club in Redondo Beach in December 1973 Gauer introduced the idea of a new threat posed by new developments in the adult entertainment business when he condemned the proliferation of vending machines selling obscene material. The machines, he argued, could be used by anyone, even children. Convinced that children could not be protected from the machines, Gauer asserted, "We've got to get pornography out of the legitimate channels of distribution and back into the gutters of society — where it belongs."[20]

But the CDL practice of constantly escalating allegations had to be outdone, and when Gauer claimed that pornographic films existed where the actress was killed at the conclusion he referred to them as 'snuff' films, because her life was 'snuffed out',[21] he created an outrageous accusation that would be perpetuated by rumour and politically motivated lies for decades to come. His claims about 'snuff' films — pornographic excess that was completely unjustifiable — reinforced CDL claims that sex and violence as entertainment were inextricably connected, and that behind the wave of 'porno chic' lay a ruthless and inhuman industry. Selecting a sympathetic and naïve audience, Gauer played on their religious values and social concerns.

When Gauer addressed the thirty-eighth annual breakfast of the Holy Name Society at the Hollywood Palladium in January 1974

18 Ibid.
19 Mailing quoted in ibid: 281–282.
20 "Put Pornography Back Into Gutters of Society — Legally, Speaker Says," LA Times (23 December 1973): CS6.
21 Gauer quoted in Eithne Johnson and Eric Schaefer, "Soft Core/Hard Gore," Journal of Film and Video (Summer–Fall 1993): 41.

154

he suggested that the latest trend in pornography was a film where someone was actually murdered. "For many years there was simulated sex on the screen," reported Gauer, but that was insufficient for thrill-hungry consumers of obscene materials and "Today we have actual clinical sex. Traditionally there has been simulated violence. That, too, is not enough." To satisfy the demands of depraved viewers "There may very well be filmed an actual murder — for kicks."[22] According to Gauer, entrepreneurs in the adult film business were driven by a constant need to shock and therefore were always looking for a new novelty. A tactic that had been used successfully by a few pornographers, he contended, to make huge profits which they could use to hire capable lawyers to defend them in court under the guise of freedom of expression.[23] Cardinal Timothy Manning also addressed the breakfast meeting, adding his own theological commentary on obscene material. Identifying "his satanic majesty" as one source of pornography, Manning continued: "the conclusion from the Gospel is unmistakable: the devil does exist, he is a personal devil, and he is active."[24]

In another speech in January 1974, later summarized in the *National Decency Reporter*, Gauer embellished his earlier account and warned:

We have seen the progression from simulated sex in magazines and films to the most explicit, clinical hardcore sex in recent years. We have also seen a progression from simulated violence to sadomasochistic films in which participants are tortured with whips, cigarette burns, etc. It is not hard to believe a progression to the ultimate obscenity: the taking of human life for sexual kicks.[25]

His view contrasted sharply with the contemporary emphasis on sex as fun and liberating, and the findings of the *Report* of the President's Commission.

Gauer and exploitation filmmaker Dave Friedman met in debate

22 Dan L. Thrapp, "Real Murder May be Filmed, Catholics Told," LA *Times* (28 January 1974): C9. David Friedman also acknowledged that Gauer first made his allegations about murder in pornographic films in front of the Holy Name Society. Seeing the reaction it provoked, Gauer repeated the claim and began calling them 'snuff movies'. David Friedman, "A history of the AFAA," *Box Office* (March 1982): 20–26.

23 Thrapp, "Real Murder May be Filmed, Catholics Told," LA *Times* (28 January 1974): C9.

24 Ibid.

25 Gauer quoted in Lynch, "The Facts About the Snuff-Film Rumours," *Oui* (July 1976): 86.

at a Writer's Guild of America seminar held in California during the summer of 1974, and the CDL spokesman's suggestion that murder for entertainment *could* exist became a claim that it *did* exist. In the course of the discussion Gauer claimed to have evidence that 'snuff' films existed, and Friedman responded by advising him to turn whatever evidence he had over to the appropriate authorities or he would be considered an accessory to a crime. Gauer did not turn over any evidence.[26] However, he did continue to make the claims and a few months later published an article entitled "Perversion for Profit" in the *National Decency Reporter* (November–December 1974) which specifically referred to 'snuff' films. Repeating earlier, familiar CDL claims, Gauer began:

> Pornography has obviously increased in quantity in recent years — but has increased in depravity even more. That is the nature of the beast. It must continually seek new extremes in order to pique the interest of perverts who constitute its major market.
>
> Just as the liquor industry depends on alcoholics, the sexual pervert constitutes pornography's major market. Mature, healthy adults are repelled by pornography, recognizing it to be what it is — a corrupting influence in their own lives — and in the community in which their families must thrive. Some may be occasionally attracted, out of curiosity, to view a much publicized porno flick, but that only serves to reinforce their conviction that obscenity is harmful to the public morality.

This was an obvious reference to films such as *Deep Throat* that sought social respectability by emphasising their middle-class audiences, composed of couples. Consistent with their rhetoric, CDL considered all porn to be threatening to society, especially when viewed by impressionable minds:

> But there is a segment of society that is immature at any age — and who have a perverse and continuing interest in the pornographer's products. Like the alcoholic, their 'appetite' is not that of the normal healthy adult — for no doubt very complex psychological and/or physiological reasons.

26 Ibid.

This small segment of the total population comprises the major market for pornography — along with the curious and miscellaneous incidental purchasers. This fact is the basis for many serious problems in society created by the porno trade.

His assertion that a small segment of the population made up the majority of the audience for pornography was naïve considering the enormous figures being cited by CDL to estimate the value of the pornography business. For CDL statistics and economics did not reflect reality — instead, they were tools used by the organisation to deny widespread public curiosity about sex and pornography throughout America and reinforce the organisation's core assumptions:

One major problem is the obvious fact that an overabundance of porno outlets exist — in relation to the limited population interested in their products. This is frequently misinterpreted by writers who 'lament' declining porno business — evidenced by so few patrons in porno theatres and shops. What they fail to acknowledge is that there are few poor pornographers. Prices and admissions charged provide very very lucrative profits despite relatively few customers.

Competition forces pornographers to exploit their wares to attract patrons. Thus we see blatant and offensive marquees for porno outlets — and display advertisements in newspapers featuring the most suggestive and salacious copy. They can get away with it. This exploitation constitutes an intrusion by the pornographer into the lives of all citizens of the community — whether they are potential customers or not.

All this creates additional not-so-obvious problems. The very fact that porno emporiums proliferate and blatantly exploit their wares cloak them with an aura of social acceptance that is unwarranted and undeserved. This very omnipresence of pornography causes young people — and the immature not-so-young — to rationalize that pornography must not be so bad after all. They are thus virtually seduced into becoming porno addicts.

Rather than develop a rational argument against sexually explicit material Gauer resorted to rehashing the rhetoric of 1950s comic book paranoia and condemning the adult entertainment industry for engaging in the same sort of business practices as every other business in American society. His tirade culminated in the most outrageous claims yet made about the pornography industry:

> Another alarming aspect of the overabundance of porno outlets is that competition forces the pornographer to constantly seek ever more perverse material in order to keep customers coming back. The result is that much current pornography is literally indescribable — dealing as it does with human excrement, bondage and torture, sex with children and animals and other unthinkable perversities. Reliable informants report as many as twenty-five 'snuff' films in current circulation among certain selected pornophiles. These incredible films culminate in the actual murder of a human being during a sex orgy — thus providing the ultimate kick for sick porno voyeurs.
>
> Can it get any worse? We have thought it impossible for years — and yet the mercenarily motivated pornographer constantly manages to find new and more shocking depravities.

Gauer's claims about 'snuff' movies were a culmination of two decades of CDL rhetoric and a fulfilment of its dire warnings.

Encouraged by contemporary legal decisions, most obviously *Miller*, CDL sought to focus their supporters' actions and exploit the favourable political climate. Gauer's article concluded by offering a cure for the excess of pornography:

> The only solution is for an outraged citizenry to demand strict enforcement of obscenity laws. In recent decisions, the United States Supreme Court has reinforced the right — and the ability — of communities to protect public morality through obscenity law enforcement. The pornography problem will not go away until the producers, distributors, sellers, and exhibitors are either put out of business — or in jail — or both.[27]

27 Gauer, "Perversion for Profit," *National Decency Reporter* (November–December 1974): 1, 2. *Perversion for Profit* was also the title of a thirty-minute anti-obscenity documentary film that CDL produced (1964) along with others such as *Printed Poisons* in the early 1960s which they showed at their own meetings and when addressing other civic and religious groups. As a consequence of the proliferation of pornography *Perversion for Profit* links pornography to the Communist threat facing America and warns of the decline of Western civilization.

The CDL crusade, fuelled by distortion and exaggeration, with supporters in the White House and a sympathetic Supreme Court, continued to gather momentum.

CDL accusations about 'snuff' provoked a response from a sympathetic conservative audience so the organisation persisted.[28] On a number of occasions before and after the Perversion for Profit article, CDL mass-mailed a similar fundraising letter to potential supporters and early in 1975 one recipient was concerned enough about the accusations being made to contact the FBI and forward the letter (dated 1 December 1974) in an effort to discover if the claims were an alarmist threat or true. The CDL letter in this instance was shockingly direct:

They're producing 'snuff films' now.

They're called 'snuff' films because they show the torture, rape, and murder of a young girl. The torture is real. The rape is real. The murder is real.

The monsters who make these films and the perverted people who watch them, have taken one more giant step on the downward path of pornography.

Where once these men could satisfy lust with pinups, now they demand filmed scenes of multiple intercourse with an innocent girl — where once they could create sexual arousal with scenes of simulated sex, now they must make full-colour movies of every imaginable perversion, from sodomy to bestiality. Where once they needed sexual brutality, now they have actual murder.

Are they showing 'snuff' films in local theatres yet?

No, not yet. Impossible, you say? Well, think back ten years or even less. Suppose someone told you then that a theatre in your neighbourhood would be showing colour films of uninterrupted sexual activities — between men and women, men and men, women and animals, and even men and children. Would you have believed it then?

Pornography is taking a strangle hold on the very sensibilities of the people of this country. It deadens the mind, the senses, the soul — it shocks us briefly with every new and revolting plunge downward, and prepares us at the same time for the next, unthinkable step. From

28 Rotsler, "Down With Snuff!" *Adam Film World* (August 1976): 21.

pinups to actual rape-murder in less than one generation!

The pornographers are using the most powerful communications tools in the world to deaden the conscience and dull the moral standards that more than 2,000 years of Judeo-Christian culture and training have built.[29]

Technology, one of the cornerstones of American culture, was being used to undermine the traditional social values of that society. The outrageous accusations in the letter could *not* be substantiated but CDL targeted a naïve audience, one that was in the main unfamiliar with the workings or products of the porn industry. As a consequence of the 'snuff' allegations, CDL received a lot of publicity and cash contributions.[30]

Concerned by the allegations, Dave Friedman, as a representative of the Adult Filmmakers Association of America (AFAA), again called on CDL to hand over any evidence of 'snuff' films in their possession to the authorities so the claims could be investigated. After a few weeks Friedman contacted an FBI agent, with whom he was acquainted, to see if CDL had passed any information along, but they had not. Even though the CDL director had testified at Congressional hearings, the FBI agent told Friedman that he considered Gauer to be "flakey,"[31] and *not* a reliable source of information. Undeterred, Gauer continued making speeches alleging that the pornography industry was filming the torture and murder of performers, even repeating the charge on a TV show.[32]

Gauer used his accusations, which far exceeded any previous allegations made by anyone against pornographers, to generate positive publicity for CDL and draw attention to the anti-obscenity crusade, as well as to encourage donations from people who were outraged that such material could exist. Gauer acknowledged that he needed "the help of a citizenry which is truly aroused and justifiably irate" as well as funding from sympathetic donors to fight the "unchecked social plague."[33] He hoped that in a decade or two the *"vicious flood of mindless lust"* would be stamped out, but "in the long run it doesn't

29 Citizens for Decency through Law letter dated 1 December 1974.
30 William Rotsler, "Down With Snuff!" *Adam Film World* (August 1976): 21.
31 Hebditch and Anning, *Porn Gold*: 337.
32 Ibid.
33 See, *Blue Money*: 163.

matter whether we win or not, because it's the fight that counts!!"[34]

The FBI began an investigation into the 'snuff' rumours in January 1975. It was prompted by the aforementioned letter from a concerned citizen acting on a letter received from CDL, *not* because the Bureau had seen a 'snuff' film or were following up on the Charles Manson rumours. The inquiry was passed on to the Bureau Special Crimes Unit, which handled all Interstate Transportation of Material (ITOM) cases, but the unit had no information on 'snuff' films, nor did any FBI files. However, in a memo (dated 10 February 1975) FBI agents acknowledged that they were aware of a rumour reported by a West Coast police department that "a few" 'snuff' films, made somewhere in Mexico, were in limited circulation in America.[35] The Perversion for Profit article from the *National Decency Reporter* (November–December 1974) was referred to by the FBI because of its claims about 'snuff' films, and the memo concluded with CDL's assertion that 'snuff' was a type of pornography which was the basis for a subsequent investigation "initiated in an effort to verify the above information and determine if a violation within the FBI's jurisdiction has occurred."[36] The FBI Pornographic Files Unit (Laboratory Unit) had also heard of 'snuff' films from the LAPD and the *National Decency Reporter*.[37] Documents acquired from the LAPD vice squad acknowledged stories about 'snuff' movies that originated in Mexico were in circulation, but the reports were not verified and the origin of the stories never established.[38]

Initially the Cleveland FBI office was requested to contact the CDL and determine the sources for its claims, and the LA office was directed to contact the LAPD vice squad and ascertain what they knew about 'snuff'.[39] The Cleveland office was designated to lead the investigation until the existence of 'snuff' films was determined and their place of production identified.[40] A memo (dated 12 February 1975) from Clarence M. Kelley,

34 Ibid. Emphasis in original.
35 "Citizen Inquiry — Obscenity; Interstate Transportation of Obscene Matter (ITOM)," memo dated 10 February 1975 in FBI, *Snuff Films*, File Number 145–5568–x.
36 Ibid.
37 Response to the inquiry (dated 10 February 1975) in FBI, *Snuff Films*, File Number 145–5568–x.
38 Ibid.
39 "Citizen Inquiry — Obscenity; Interstate Transportation of Obscene Matter (ITOM)," memo dated 10 February 1975 in FBI, *Snuff Films*, File Number 145–5568–x.
40 Memo to Cleveland and LA (dated 6 February 1975) in FBI, *Snuff Films*, File Number 145–5568–xi.

FBI director, identified Raymond Gauer as the national director of CDL, the editor of the *National Decency Reporter*, and author of Perversion for Profit. In interview, Gauer acknowledged that he had contacted individuals in the LAPD vice squad and FBI field office in LA about 'snuff' films, and reported that he would disclose the names of his informants to the FBI. The memo went on to note that CDL was entirely dependent on public contributions and maintained a large mailing list of supporters.

According to Gauer's informants, 'snuff' films were said to have originated in California in 1969 when a murder, committed as part of a Satanic ritual, was allegedly filmed, evoking the rumours surrounding the Manson Family and subsequent stories of ritual murder. The FBI could not ascertain if this was the original 'snuff' film, or even if it was the only ritual murder that had been filmed. Sammy Davis Jr., a notable collector of pornography and at one time a member of the Church of Satan, was reported as having information on the ritual murder films,[41] and Robert Dornan, a national CDL spokesman, also made claims that the nude and decapitated body of a young woman found on a Southern Californian beach in October 1968 was the victim of a ritual murder that had been filmed.[42] It was a story that sounded very similar to those rumours Ed Sanders heard about the Manson Family films but it added no new information or evidence to support the claims.

The FBI received a second copy of the CDL letter about 'snuff' movies from Cleveland (Ohio) police,[43] and copies of the Perversion for Profit article were circulated to a number of FBI field offices along with a memo titled "Snuff Films" (dated 12 February 1975). In the course of a detailed discussion with the LAPD (Administrative Vice Detail, Pornography Unit) the FBI were informed that inquiries had already been made about 'snuff' films and the rumours that films of actual rape and murder, made in Mexico, were allegedly in "private collections of prominent individuals." Outside of the rumours there was no verifiable information. CDL was named by the LAPD as their source for the 'snuff' rumours, but they had *not* been provided with any factual information to support the claims. The LA County Sheriff's

41 Memo from the FBI director (12 February 1975) in FBI, *Snuff Films*, File Number 145–5568–x.
42 Lynch, "The Facts About the Snuff-Film Rumours," *Oui* (July 1976): 70.
43 "Production and Distribution of 'Snuff' Films Interstate Transportation of Obscene Matter" (20 February 1975) in FBI, *Snuff Films*, File Number 145–5568–1.

Office (Vice Detail, Pornographic Section) acknowledged that they had made inquiries about 'snuff' films, but made it clear that they had *not* seen a 'snuff' film, they were *not* aware of anyone who had done so, and were *not* aware of the production and distribution of such films if they did exist. The FBI office in LA reported the "sick rumours" that twelve 'snuff' films were circulating on 8mm in America,[44] but also asserted it was *not* aware of anyone who had seen a 'snuff' film.[45]

Hollywood celebrities such as Warren Beatty, Sammy Davis Jr. and Dennis Hopper were all alleged to have seen 'snuff' films. Despite his status as outspoken fan of pornography and self-acknowledged "avid collector,"[46] there was no evidence to connect Sammy Davis Jr. to 'snuff' movies. There were several versions of the story implicating Hopper on the other hand: one claimed he saw the 'snuff' film in Durango (Mexico) whilst making *Kid Blue* (James Frawley, 1973), while another identifies Peru as the location, a few years earlier, during the shooting of *The Last Movie* (Dennis Hopper, 1971). Hopper's agent of twenty-two years, Robert Raison, was at both locations with Hopper and asserted that neither of them had seen a 'snuff' film and had only heard of them in 1975.[47] Hugh Hefner, publisher of *Playboy* and prize target for CDL, was rumoured to own a print of a 'snuff' film, but the allegation was denied by Jay Lynch's sources at *Playboy*, who also claimed they had not heard of 'snuff' until 1975.[48] In all of the police investigations rumours about 'snuff' movies could usually be traced back to CDL but evidence to substantiate the existence of such films was never found. A memo (dated 3 March 1975) from the SAC in Los Angeles concluded that there was "no factual basis for the existence of 'snuff' films" and recommended no further investigation.[49] A subsequent memo from the Cleveland SAC (24 April 1975) concurred,[50] but the results of the investigation were not widely publicized.

---

44 "Snuff Films" memo (12 February 1975) in FBI, *Snuff Films*, File Number 145–5568–x2. The memo explicitly points out that the films were *not* on 16mm or 35mm.

45 "Snuff Films" memo (12 February 1975) in FBI, *Snuff Films*, File Number 145–5568–x2.

46 Davis Jr., *Hollywood in a Suitcase*: 174.

47 Lynch, "The Facts About the Snuff-Film Rumours," *Oui* (July 1976): 86.

48 Ibid.

49 Memo from Los Angeles SAC (3 March 1975) in FBI, *Snuff Films*, File Number 145–5568. SAC is an FBI acronym for 'Special Agent in Charge'. The FBI doesn't have ordinary agents in the field, it only has SA (Special Agent) and SAC.

50 Memo from Cleveland SAC (24 April 1975) in FBI, *Snuff Films*, File Number 145–5568.

Towards the end of 1975 the New Orleans Police Department informed the FBI field office about new rumours that a series of 8mm films called 'snuffers' were circulating. The unnamed informant reported to the police that a film production company approached a young woman to make several porn loops. After accepting she was sent to South America where a number of films showing conventional sexual acts were made, but "in the last movie in the series the female model is actually decapitated and various sexual organs are physically removed, culminat[ing] with an incision being made in the abdomen followed by disembowelment." Police did not find the film, but the informants accounts were chilling, alleging that the victim's screams were allegedly recorded as part of the soundtrack.[51] This was to be an ominous foreshadowing of the final scene of *Snuff* (1976), and led to speculation that the anonymous informant was film producer Allan Shackleton. The emergence of the rumour about 'snuffers' also coincided with one of the most important events in American media history.

More than a decade after the most famous murder in twentieth-century America, footage of the event was broadcast on TV for the first time to further contribute to the 'snuff' rumours. On 22 November 1963 the assassination of John F. Kennedy was accidentally captured on film, but remained largely unseen by the public for twelve years. Abraham Zapruder shot his twenty-two seconds of film recording Kennedy's assassination on Super 8 as he observed the President's motorcade moving through downtown Dallas. Richard Stolley of Time-Life Inc., along with the Texas Secret Service, were amongst the few who watched the footage on the day after the assassination, projected onto a sheet in a darkened office.[52]

Stolley negotiated with Zapruder to buy the film for his magazine and during their discussion Zapruder told Stolley of a dream he had which bothered him. In the dream, while walking through Times Square, Zapruder saw a movie marquee advertising "See The President Get Shot." He did not like that idea and wanted to make sure his film was not exploited. Stolley bought print rights to the film for $50,000, even though Zapruder had received higher bids, and later the deal was

---

51 SAC New Orleans to Director (18 August 1975) in FBI *Snuff Films*, File Number 145–5568–3xi.
52 *The Zapruder Footage: The World's Most Famous Home Movie* documentary (Tim Kirby, 1993)

renegotiated to $150,000 for all rights to the film.[53] *Life* (29 November 1963) published still pictures taken from the footage, but not frame 313 where Kennedy's brain is exposed. Rationalizing that still pictures were bad enough, Stolley did everything he could to make sure the film was not shown to the public. During the 1960s researchers only had access to a fuzzy copy of the footage, but rumours circulated about a clearer version of the film that existed, usually said to be in the vaults of Time-Life in New York. A few bootleg copies of the Zapruder footage also circulated in the 1960s, but they were of poor quality and only seen by small audiences. According to film director Michael Wadleigh, some people inter-cut the Zapruder footage with pornographic images to create a strange juxtaposition.[54]

On 6 March 1975 Geraldo Rivera devoted an entire episode of *Good Night America* to the Kennedy assassination and broadcast the Zapruder footage, allowing the American public the opportunity to see the film for the first time while risking lawsuits from Time-Life for copyright infringement. Robert Hennelley, journalist for the *Village Voice*, noted, "There is something about the human experience recorded that makes it something that sets the standard by which we judge all the recorded events in film. It's kind of like the gauge of brutality."[55] The existence of the Zapruder film made allegations of 'snuff' movies seem more plausible. The public presentation of the footage generated considerable debate and made a significant connection between film and murder in the public consciousness. If the murder of the president could be filmed then it seemed like any other murder should be easy to record.[56]

Footage of real deaths captured on film was not a new development in cinema. During the 1960s Mondo films, which presented authentic and fake footage in pseudo-documentary form, promised new thrills to entertain audiences, eventually presenting more extreme and graphic material that contributed to the 'snuff' panic. Where early Mondo films offered a colourful sort of ethnographic study that focused on exotic rituals, animal death and sexual rites, by the mid 1970s human

53   Ibid.
54   *The Zapruder Footage: The World's Most Famous Home Movie* documentary (Tim Kirby, 1993)
55   Hennelley in ibid.
56   After her suicide in 1972 it was rumoured that photographer Diane Arbus had set up a camera to record her own death, but the story was never substantiated. David J. Skal, *The Monster Show: A Cultural History of Horror,* Plexus, London, 1994: 22.

death was being incorporated. In *Savage Man ... Savage Beast* (Antonio Climati and Mario Morra, 1975) footage of a man identified as Pit Dernitz is included, showing him being attacked and eaten by lions after leaving the safety of his car to film a lioness feeding. When a second lion pounces, Dernitz is seen completely helpless and his wife, children, and other tourists can only look on in horror as he is mauled and eaten alive. Recorded by other tourists on Super 8 from an adjacent vehicle, the depiction of Dernitz's death is shocking, but obviously fake. Presented in an entertainment medium it reflected unpleasant aspects of American culture and human nature. Mondo movies and the Zapruder footage set a precedent, establishing that murder could be filmed and used as entertainment and prepared the wider public for a new series of 'snuff' allegations in the mainstream news media.

Whilst the FBI was still conducting a nationwide investigation of Gauer's allegations about 'snuff' movies, two unsubstantiated articles, both published in New York tabloids, thrust the concept of 'snuff' into the public eye and paved the way for the release of Allan Shackleton's *Snuff* (1976). The first, a report of a seizure of 'snuff' films in New York, by Dick Brass in the New York *Post* (1 October 1975), was sensationally entitled "'Snuff' Porn — The Actress Is Actually Killed," and it was followed a few days later by Edward Kirkman's "Last Picture Show: Sex and Real Murder" in the New York *Daily News* (3 October 1975). Both stories were based on the same unfounded allegations and speculation with no facts or evidence.

On 21 July 1975, several months before the publication of his article, Dick Brass made enquiries at the FBI's New York office about 'snuff' films, during which *he* informed the FBI that 'snuff' was a "new kind of pornographic film in which the leading female player is killed in the final scene." The journalist was unwilling to identify the source of his story but he did acknowledge that the existence of 'snuff' films was not yet confirmed.[57] By the time his article made it into print, almost three months later, the rumour was no closer to being substantiated.

With the title "'Snuff' Porn," Brass made the link between sex and violence clear. By attributing the origin of the word 'snuff' to Charles Manson he revived the unsubstantiated rumours that had circulated

---

57 "The Production and Distribution of 'Snuff' Films Interstate Transportation of Obscene Matters (12 November 1975)," in FBI, *Snuff Films*, File Number 145–5568–6x.

in California during 1969 and 1970, and that had been perpetuated by Ed Sanders. Brass noted the unconfirmed reports that had circulated around the time of Manson's arrest relating to allegations that the Family had made films of ritual murders that were never found.[58] Lionel Bascom, who eventually wrote an article for *Genesis* on 'snuff', immediately thought of Charles Manson when he heard the 'snuff' film rumours. Describing 'snuff' as "bizarre bloody porno films," Bascom acknowledged the possibility that the Family murders *could* have been filmed, that Manson *could* have given the order, but suggested information like that would have come out at the trial.[59] Even though Manson had been tried and convicted several years earlier he still remained a potent bogeyman.

For five years after the murders Manson was kept in the public eye as a criminal mastermind. Newspaper reports appeared throughout his trial and again in 1972 when the death sentences conferred upon him and other members of the Family were commuted to life sentences. Books and films based on the Manson crimes, fact and fiction, promoted and perpetuated the myth. Even documentaries such as *Manson* (Robert Hendrickson and Laurence Merrick, 1972) and *Helter Skelter* (Tom Gries, 1974), which retold the story of the Family from numerous viewpoints, added to the myth, and the continuing threat posed by the Family was highlighted after an attempt on President Ford's life in September 1975.

To give some authority to the unsubstantiated allegations in his newspaper article, Dick Brass quoted Detective Sergeant Joseph Horman (NYPD Organized Crime Control Bureau), stating that he had been told by reliable underworld sources that 'snuff' movies were available: "I am convinced that these films actually exist and that a person is actually murdered. I suppose you could say that they are the ultimate obscenity."[60] This was a significant statement considering the on-going debate concerning the legal definition of obscenity but it came from a man well known for his zealous anti-obscenity activities,

---

58 Dick Brass, "'Snuff' Porn — The Actress Is Actually Murdered," New York *Post* (2 October 1975): 23.
59 Lionel C. Bascom, "Tracking the Slashers: Murder On Film," *Genesis* (March 1976): 89. Bascom also refers to 'snuff' films as 'slasher' films and points out that the rumours drifted across America from the West Coast around the time of the Manson trial.
60 Brass, "'Snuff' Porn — The Actress Is Actually Murdered," New York *Post* (2 October 1975): 3.

which included shutting down numerous adult bookstores and massage parlours in New York.[61] Horman, a seasoned cop, was disgusted by the idea of 'snuff'. "The thing that is really astonishing is that there is such a market for these films." Horman continued, "That's the sickening part of it. That's almost as astonishing as the fact that somebody would actually commit murder for the purpose of making a film."[62]

Lionel Bascom first heard about 'snuff' films from Horman, but Horman in turn claimed he had only become aware of the rumours when journalist Pierre Salinger, former press secretary to President John F. Kennedy, inquired about the stories. Salinger was working for several French newspapers and gave Horman the initial detail about the films originating in Latin America and that the actress was actually murdered. Checking with what he considered to be reliable underworld sources Horman was told that the films probably came from Argentina, but following up on the information he was informed that there was only a tiny porn business in Argentina and it was highly unlikely that the films were made there.[63] However, the whole episode was a lie and when interviewed later by the FBI Horman admitted he had *not* heard of 'snuff' films until he had been contacted by Dick Brass.[64]

The 'snuff' scenarios reputedly started out as predictable porno loops and Bascom described one he heard about which began with a conventional cast of two men and a woman. However, "After a few turn ons things get really weird. One of the guys pulls out a dagger and stabs her. He repeatedly slashes her lovely body until she actually dies on camera. Then comes the climax, the most grizzly part of all — the body is dismantled limb by limb."[65] This was in shocking contrast to the 'sex as fun' emphasis of *Deep Throat* a few years earlier in the short lived era of 'porno chic'.

The article by Brass went on to claim that multiple 8mm 'snuff' films were in circulation and that they could be viewed at private screenings

61 Bascom, "Tracking the Slashers: Murder On Film," *Genesis* (March 1976): 90.
62 Ibid. Subsequently Joseph Horman became the source for numerous newspaper reports about 'snuff' movies'. See also "Porno movie climaxes with death," Lodi (California) *News-Sentinel* (3 October 1975): 6.
63 Ibid: 89.
64 "The Production and Distribution of 'Snuff' Films," in FBI, *Snuff Films*, File Number 145–5568–6x.
65 Bascom, "Tracking the Slashers: Murder On Film," *Genesis* (March 1976): 89.

for $200.[66] Bascom asserted that it cost $300 to see a screening of a 'snuff' film at "luxury apartments or on posh estates" and that there was a demand from "the well-heeled in the leather crowd" who were queuing up to see a 'snuff' film. According to Horman's sources at least eight 'snuffers' circulated, no doubt the same eight that the FBI had investigated, and they cost $1,500 per print.[67] However, despite two months of constant effort the NYPD had not been able to acquire any of the films because they were so closely guarded.[68] In one interview Horman said he had come close to confiscating a 'snuff' film in Miami: "I had a source who had access to it but apparently the FBI is putting quite a bit of pressure on Southern Florida and that killed it."[69] Brass tried to make his claims seem more plausible by referring to a survey of Times Square which showed an increasing number of films devoted to violent sex including rapes and disfigurement.[70] Horman emphasised the direction American culture was heading by pointing out, "The most popular film in the country is *Jaws* — that's the story of a fish that eats people." In such a society, where "People like violence, snuff films had to happen sooner or later."[71] To magnify the sense of urgency Brass reported that a few days prior to his article a 'snuff' film was allegedly shown at an undisclosed location in New York to a small, discrete audience. The purpose of the screening was to sell the film but $200 admission was charged to all who attended.[72] No verifiable information was ever offered by Horman, but his anecdote raised public awareness of the idea of 'snuff' films and contributed to the developing panic.

Sergeant Don Smyth (LAPD vice squad) was also interviewed by Brass, but he was more restrained in his comments:

---

66 Johnson and Schaefer, "Soft Core/Hard Gore," *Journal of Film and Video* (Summer–Fall 1993): 42. Beverly LaBelle noted the newspaper reports and claimed that the "underground" porn films that contained real murder footage were to cater for the jaded appetites of "a select pornography audience." LaBelle also claimed that when *Snuff* was first shown at the National Theatre in NYC it coincided with "considerable publicity being given to privately released pornographic films showing actual rape and murder." Private screenings of these films were allegedly organized, charging between $100 and $500 admission per person. LaBelle, "Snuff — The Ultimate in Woman Hating," in Radford and Russell (Ed.), *Femicide*: 189, 191. She does not name any of the films or state where they were being exhibited.
67 Bascom, "Tracking the Slashers: Murder On Film," *Genesis* (March 1976): 89, 90.
68 Brass, "'Snuff' Porn — The Actress Is Actually Murdered," New York *Post* (2 October 1975): 3.
69 Bascom, "Tracking the Slashers: Murder On Film," *Genesis* (March 1976): 90.
70 Brass, "'Snuff' Porn — The Actress Is Actually Murdered," New York *Post* (2 October 1975): 23.
71 Horman quoted in ibid.
72 Ibid.

Let's put it this way: There are many, many rumours circulating regarding snuff films ... So far, we don't know of any individual who possesses one. But then — even if there is such an item in circulation — there are probably a very small number of them and they are closely guarded.[73]

Lt. Lex Zabel of the LAPD vice squad was more direct in his comments, telling Bascom, "We're the centre of the porno industry and I've heard the rumours but so far that is all it amounts to. We haven't started an investigation because there is nothing to go on but talk." Since no substantive information could be found, Zabel concluded, "There is no evidence of such films except rumour. I've put the word out on the street but nothing has come down that would merit an investigation."[74] In October 1975 the LA *Times* reported that the FBI and New York Police department were investigating the 'snuff' rumours. A spokesman for the LAPD meanwhile confirmed that they had investigated the same rumours six months previously, but found no evidence to support any claim that the films existed.[75]

The underworld sources which had informed Brass of 'snuff' films in circulation pointed out that they were only offered to trusted customers. One of the films was reportedly made in South America, possibly in Argentina on colour 8mm film stock. The film was divided into eight sequences for "home viewing," at a cost of $1,500 for the set. Beginning with an assortment of conventional sex acts between several performers, the film culminated with the stabbing and dismemberment of the actress involved, who was "clearly unaware of the true nature of her role" until the killing began. It seemed obvious that this was the same story about 'snuffers' that the New Orleans FBI heard in August 1975 but was unable to substantiate. Reinforcing the link with the adult film business, Brass claimed that an informant, a "well-known porn-film director," remembered that a few months previously a film producer had been offering a large amount of money to someone who would be murdered on film.[76] Bascom also reported the rumour that producers recruited women who knew they would

73 Smyth quoted in ibid.
74 Bascom, "Tracking the Slashers: Murder On Film," *Genesis* (March 1976): 90.
75 "LA Police Discount Story: FBI Probes Reports of Mutilation, Death Films," LA *Times* (2 October 1975): 2.
76 Brass, "'Snuff' Porn — The Actress Is Actually Murdered," New York *Post* (2 October 1975): 3.

be killed and paid them in advance to appear in the 'snuff' films. This prompted Bascom to ask, "How much could you pay someone to be murdered?"[77] The absurdity of such an offer is obvious. Likewise, the act of advertising for a victim means that the killing would either be a premeditated murder or it undermines the idea that the woman in the South American 'snuff' film was "clearly unaware." The only thing it did clearly establish was that some people who worked in the adult film industry saw 'snuff' as viable mass entertainment.

Lionel Bascom ended his investigation into 'snuff' rumours after Horman told him that the authorities in New York City would only prosecute anyone possessing a 'snuff' film under obscenity laws and the FBI would only prosecute under the Interstate Transportation of Obscene Matter (ITOM). According to Horman neither would attempt to build a case against the murderer because it would be difficult to prove.[78] To further provoke the readers' sense of injustice and outrage, Brass also alleged that while an FBI ITOM prosecution would be the only available legal sanction against 'snuff' films, defendants could claim, when necessary, the murder was a theatrical fake, and not a real murder at all.[79] The articles by Dick Brass and Edward Kirkman repeated unfounded rumours and speculation, all of which paved the way for Allan Shackleton's marketing campaign for his film Snuff (1976).

Outraged by Brass' 'snuff' story Al Goldstein called the New York *Post* "the most gutless of all newspapers," and described their reporting of it as a clear example of parasitic journalism and an attempt to boost their declining circulation.[80] Being realistic, he acknowledged, "It's of course possible that somebody would film the murder of somebody,

77 Bascom, "Tracking the Slashers: Murder On Film," *Genesis* (March 1976): 89.
78 Ibid: 90.
79 Brass, "'Snuff' Porn — The Actress Is Actually Murdered," New York *Post* (2 October 1975): 23. The Interstate Transportation of Obscene Matter (ITOM) law of June 1955 criminalised the transportation of obscene materials across state lines. Two or more 'pornographic' items were considered evidence of intent to distribute and the crossing of state lines gave the Bureau jurisdiction. FBI spokesmen asserted that because of their training it would be easy for an FBI agent to identify items that were obscene and prosecuteable. Prosecuting pornographic films in this way made them an extension of earlier white slave traffic upon which the Bureau had built its reputation. Using its much publicized scientific expertise, the FBI confiscated films for fingerprints, subjected them to lab tests, searched for serial numbers and analysed film processing techniques to identify individuals involved in the production and distribution of pornography.
80 Al Goldstein, "The Stuff on Snuff," *Screw* (3 November 1975): 4.

but, to my knowledge, and my knowledge is monumental in the field of pornography, there simply is not any such film extant."[81] Goldstein confronted Dick Brass about the 'snuff' story, accusing him of "irresponsible journalism," but was even more incensed when he heard about the journalist's source. In defence of his story Brass explained that it came from an editor of the New York *Post* who had spent a drunken evening with Dennis Hopper. In the course of the conversation, it was alleged, Hopper claimed to have seen a 'snuff' film.[82] This was the same Dennis Hopper who was interviewed during the FBI investigation and denied all knowledge of 'snuff' films.

The inflammatory accusations made by Brass were reinforced two days later by Edward Kirkman's "Last Picture Show" article in the New York *Daily News*, which contained almost exactly the same allegations. Kirkman, like Brass, attributed 'snuff', as a synonym for murder, to Charles Manson, America's bogeyman, and also claimed that the films seized by the police were shot in Argentina. The previous year Jay Lynch had heard rumours about 'snuff' films from Mexico, traditionally a playground for decadent Americans, but the location for the story had now moved, conveniently for Allan Shackleton.[83] Despite the change of exotic locale the substance of the rumours remained the same. In a moment of clarity, however, CDL spokesman Raymond Gauer acknowledged that despite his claims about the existence of 'snuff' films, "We have no hard facts, just rumours." But then continued, "I am convinced that there is some substance to it. I have an informer in Hollywood who is close to the pornographers who told me about them. He told me he had heard that one snuff film was made in Mexico and involved a man stabbing a woman to death and mutilating the body."[84]

Brass and Kirkman's newspaper reports in New York became the basis for subsequent arguments presented by morality crusaders and anti-pornography feminists. New York was a centre of activity for the adult film business and Joseph Slade saw the subject matter of 8mm peepshow films being shown in Times Square as an indication of where 16mm and 35mm porn features were heading. What made the

---

81 Ibid. Goldstein was aware of the rumour circulating in *Variety*, and that no 'snuff' films had been acquired by any of the investigating agencies.
82 Ibid.
83 Lynch, "The Facts About the Snuff-Film Rumours," *Oui* (July 1976): 70.
84 Bascom, "Tracking the Slashers: Murder On Film," *Genesis* (March 1976): 90.

peepshow loops interesting was the diversity of subject matter, and as Slade observed, "whatever deviations prove popular in the arcades will show up within six months in New York movie houses"[85]— an ominous trend if 'snuff' loops were being made and shown covertly. Taking the moral high ground, Joseph Horman emphasised the moral decay of New York as circumstantial evidence to reinforce his claims about 'snuff' movies: "Have you seen Times Square porno stores lately? They feature sex with children, bestiality and sadomasochism. I guess this ['snuff'] is the ultimate sadomasochism."[86]

Expressing his own preference in the *Hollywood Press* (October 1975), actor/director Bill Margold claimed, "there is nothing more arousing than sexual terror. A helpless woman being strangled, stabbed, axed, suffocated or drowned is the most exciting thing I can watch. It unlocks my fantasies." But he was not endorsing 'snuff' movies or justifying the act of murder. Dramatizing his dark fantasy Margold specifically referred to *The Psycho Lover* (Robert Vincent O'Neill, 1970) as a particular favourite and noted that throughout the protagonist stabs and strangles his female victims. "A stylish dual electrocution/execution at the end of the film (with much writhing about)," determined Margold, "was particularly stimulating."[87] In their study of early seventies adult films, *Sinema*, Turan and Zito noted that

> the Roughies and Kinkies of the middle sixties generally represented the nadir of the sex exploitation film, ugly in spirit and appealing to the worst instincts of humankind. The death rattle of the woman with the severed leg replaces that unfettered cry of ecstasy, and the blood rather than semen becomes the symbolic fluid of erotic expression. Paradoxically, these grotesque films featuring neither complete nudity nor loving sexual contact, were largely exempt from the wrath of the censors, possibly because the United States has traditionally been a country that censors sex but tolerates violence.[88]

But the murders in *The Psycho Lover* and other 'roughies' were

85   Slade, "Recent Trends in Pornographic Films," *Society* (September–October 1975): 78.
86   Horman quoted in Edward Kirkman "Last Picture Show: Sex and Real Murder," New York *Daily News* (3 October 1975): 8.
87   Margold quoted in Ford, *A History of X*: 27.
88   Turan and Zito, *Sinema*: 25.

obviously staged with special effects.

Discussing 'snuff' films Horman was quoted in numerous reports stating confidently, "Our sources tell us the film is actually in existence in the city ... I know that the promise of a murder on film sounds wild, but I believe it actually happened. The film is now being sold to highly selected private dealers."[89] Other anecdotal reports emerged to sustain public curiosity and concern but provided no verifiable information. Edward Kirkman referred to an editor of the *Hollywood Reporter* who claimed to have spoken to unnamed porn producers who had gone so far as to purchase a "snuff script." Furthermore they were supposedly co-operating with Horman, and as a consequence the police were close to acquiring a copy of a real 8mm 'snuff' film.[90] John Charnay, news editor for the *Hollywood Reporter*, told Lionel Bascom that he first heard about 'snuff' while working in the story department of Four Star International Films. One of the stories offered to the company was called *Rough Cut*, and there was a rumour that the film had been made and shown at parties in Palm Springs. However Charnay only believed that 'snuff' films existed because he had talked to people who claimed to have seen them but he had not seen one himself. Pursuing this idea, there is no logic to the concept of a 'snuff' film script because the sexualised murder at the climax of the film would be all that mattered — story and character development are irrelevant. Raymond Gauer told Lionel Bascom that he had read at least one script for a 'snuff' film, and he believed it was authentic because "It had the ring of truth about it." Gauer also alluded to a Hollywood producer who claimed to have seen a 'snuff' film and been offered the 'snuff' script but when asked, as usual, could not reveal his name.[91] Despite the contradictions the vague and sensational reports spread outside New York City as other regional newspapers picked up the story.

The same day as Edward Kirkman's article appeared, a report in the Detroit *Free Press* (3 October 1975) quoted detective Horman, who recalled being told by an unnamed *Hollywood Reporter* journalist that eight 'snuff' films were being circulated for exclusive private screenings,

89 Horman quoted in Edward Kirkman "Last Picture Show: Sex and Real Murder," New York *Daily News* (3 October 1975): 8.
90 Ibid.
91 Bascom, "Tracking the Slashers: Murder On Film," *Genesis* (March 1976): 90.

and that $200 admission was being charged.[92] Some people believed the 'snuff' rumours were a ploy devised by organized crime to discredit small porn producers and drive them out of the industry, leaving the market as a virtual monopoly.[93] After the initial New York *Post* article about 'snuff' movies the story was picked up by newswire services, and the *Morning Advocate* (Baton Rouge, Louisiana) and Atlanta *Constitution* both ran articles about 'snuff' movies in early October 1975. Rumours also circulated that 'snuff' films had been shown in New Orleans and Miami, as well as New York and Los Angeles,[94] adding momentum to the developing panic.

On 6 October 1975 the Associated Press news service carried a story from Argentina concerning three prostitutes found murdered and mutilated in Mendoza, 650 miles west of Buenos Aires. All three died from knife wounds and the arms of one victim had also been cut off. Despite the limits of their evidence it was believed that the women had caused trouble for their pimps and were killed as punishment. In a bizarre twist it was also speculated that it was possible the killings were filmed and shown as a warning to other prostitutes *and* also as a product to sell into a specialist porn market. To be sure, the police needed to see copies of the alleged films for themselves, but none had been acquired.[95] There was no evidence that the murders had been filmed but for some unstated reason the police considered it a possibility. Since they only had second-hand accounts of 'snuff' films, however, they were unable to confirm the theory.

The Argentinean story was reported on the Associated Press news service and quickly picked up on by the conservative Chicago *Tribune,* which used it in an impassioned editorial that questioned America's moral fibre. Identifying with traditional values the editorial asserted, "The normal reaction is to say, 'This can't be true.' But a decade ago, we'd have said the same about what is being shown on the screen today. In a corner of society where the only goal is seeking new kicks, there is no telling where the kicks will lead." Shocked by the rapid changes in sexual values and the alleged excesses of the adult film

92 "Latin Sex Film Ends With Actual Killing," Detroit *Free Press* (3 October 1975): 6d.
93 Dirk Hammond, "Are Snuff Films For Real?" *Adam Film World* (April 1976): 84.
94 Lynch, "The Facts About the Snuff-Film Rumours," *Oui* (July 1976): 70.
95 Ibid.

industry the editorial continued:

> Remember when bare breasts in slick magazines were considered risqué? Then came softcore pornography, and then hardcore, and violent-core, and each in turn was acclaimed by a few slavish critics as the latest in art. Now, as the ultimate thrill, it seems, we are offered murder and dismemberment — live. Is the next step for some avant-garde critic to contend that this, too, is art?[96]

In charting the progression of sexual depictions in popular culture, 'snuff' became the next logical step for a section of society. For moral conservatives its emergence embodied the changes in American popular culture that led to a shocking decline in morality and humanity in the name of art or entertainment.

The 'snuff' reports coincided with publicity for the impending release of Susan Brownmiller's inflammatory *Against Our Will: Men, Women and Rape* (1975), which was heavily advertised in October and November 1975, being serialized in four national magazines and promoted with a nationwide tour. Previously, in *Sexual Politics* (1970), feminist Kate Millet had asserted that the system of patriarchy was not associated with violence because, "So perfect is its system of socialization, so complete the general assent to its values, so long and so universally has it prevailed in human society that it scarcely seems to require violent implementation."[97] However, the possibility of rape was ever present as an instrument of intimidation that could be called upon when patriarchy was being challenged, and used to reassert traditional authority and maintain the system of order. Susan Brownmiller, a right-wing conservative feminist, took that idea a few steps further. For feminists the concept of 'snuff' movies, rape and murder for entertainment, was a symbolic reflection of an exploitative patriarchy in crisis.

The rumours about 'snuff' movies came after several years of campaigns about obscenity and sex crime by some militant feminists. In 1974, Brownmiller, then joint head of the Manhattan Women's Political Caucus (MWPC), endorsed the candidacy of incumbent DA

---

96   Chicago *Tribune* quoted in ibid.
97   Kate Millet, *Sexual Politics*, Virago, London, 1993: 43.

Richard H. Kuh on the basis of his prosecution in 1964 of Lenny Bruce on obscenity charges. Other members of the caucus were not happy with her endorsement, and instead supported Kuh's main opponent Robert M. Morgenthau, a former US attorney.[98] A letter to MWPC members was drafted by Susan Brownmiller and Barbara Seaman and emphasised that "on the much debated obscenity issue, Dick Kuh's consciousness and concern is similar to our own, and we applaud many of the stands he has taken."[99] As far as Brownmiller and Seaman were concerned obscenity was the main issue in the campaign. In the letter, Brownmiller wrote,

> When Kuh was appointed all my liberal friends said 'That's the man who sent Lenny Bruce to his death.' What are they talking about? Lenny Bruce was a foul-mouthed comedian who died of his own addiction and paranoia. Should we, as feminists, think automatically that prosecutors are bad guys? Of course not. On this issue I can foresee a whole new alliance with conservative women.[100]

Barbara Keleman, a coordinator of the Candidates' Research and Development Committee for the MWPC, was offended when the issue was brought up and described Brownmiller's letter as "the most offensive thing I've ever seen as a feminist." She believed that the DA's position on the prosecution of sex crimes (rape) and the appointment of women candidates were the important issues for feminists.[101]

The following year, in her provocative book, Brownmiller depicted men as a class apart from women, unemotional and unable to relate to them, and asserted that rape is "nothing more or less than a conscious process of intimidation by which *all men* keep *all women* in a state of fear."[102] Declaring that modern society was built upon rape, "Man's discovery that his genitalia could serve as a weapon to generate fear must rank as one of the most important discoveries of prehistoric times,

---

98 Story is in *New York Times* (15 June 1974): 33, and in several subsequent articles.
99 Brownmiller and Seaman letter quoted in Steven R. Weisman, "Feminists Here Split Over An Endorsement of Kuh," *New York Times* (15 June 1974): 33.
100 Brownmiller quoted in ibid.
101 Ibid.
102 Susan Brownmiller, *Against Our Will*, Secker and Warburg, London, 1975: 15.

along with the use of fire and the first crude stone axe."[103] Emphasizing the 'battle of the sexes' Brownmiller claimed, "Rather than society's aberrants or 'spoilers of purity', men who commit rape have served in effect as front-line masculine shock troops, terrorist guerrillas in the longest sustained battle the world has ever known."[104] Her rhetoric was not representative and many other feminists disagreed with Brownmiller's agenda, seeing it as a threat to civil liberties and an argument for censorship[105] — but her inflammatory accusations were rivalled only by Allan Shackleton's outrageous promotional campaign for *Snuff*.

Concern about violent sex crimes had been building for some time and in 1973 Aljean Harmetz, writing in the *New York Times*, noted that there had been at least twenty films in the previous two years in which rape was used as a plot device.[106] She interviewed John Calley, head of production at Warner Brothers, who claimed it was a coincidence that the Warner studio had produced a number of films featuring incidents of rape, not a reflection of any conscious studio policy: "We mainly act as a financing and purchasing agent. We respond to what's submitted, and this is what has been submitted." Box office success ensured that more scripts featuring rape scenes would be submitted.[107] Harmetz concluded that the prevalence of 'rape' was another aspect of an "undeclared war between the men who make movies and their male allies shifting restlessly in the darkness on one side and, on the other, the women who see themselves as objects and victims." Whether the films were the "ripest garbage," "pedestrian but earnest," or "arrogantly brilliant," they all focused on female helplessness.[108]

---

103 Ibid: 14–15.
104 Brownmiller quoted in "Revolt Against Rape," *Time* (13 October 1975): 45–46.
105 Weisman, "Feminists Here Split Over An Endorsement of Kuh," *New York Times* (15 June 1974): 33.
106 Aljean Harmetz, "Rape — An Ugly Movie Trend," *New York Times* (30 September 1973) section II: 1. She mentions its use in films such as *Pat Garrett and Billy the Kid* (Sam Peckinpah, 1973), *Legend of Hell House* (John Hough, 1973), *The Exorcist* (William Friedkin, 1973), *The Damned* (Luchino Visconti, 1969), *Man of La Mancha* (Arthur Hiller, 1972), *Lolly Madonna XXX* (Richard Sarafian, 1973), *The Getaway* (Sam Peckinpah, 1972), *Blume in Love* (Paul Mazursky, 1971), *Straw Dogs* (Sam Peckinpah, 1971), *A Clockwork Orange* (Stanley Kubrick, 1971), *Billy Jack* (Tom Laughlin, 1971), *The Man Who Loved Cat Dancing* (Richard Sarafian, 1973), *Scarecrow* (Jerry Schatzberg, 1973), and *Deliverance* (John Boorman, 1972).
107 Calley quoted in ibid.
108 Ibid.

Brownmiller's conclusion emphasised her crusade, "My purpose in this book has been to give rape its history. Now we must deny it a future."[109] Determined to chronicle that 'history', even if she had to create it in her own distorted polemic, Brownmiller was aware that the rhetoric she used would divide men and women, but her allegations contributed to the social climate that made Allan Shackleton's *Snuff* a financial success.

Prompted by Brownmiller's work *Time* ran an article entitled "Revolt Against Rape" (13 October 1975), which mentioned 'snuff' films and defined them as "pornographic movies culminating in the actual murder of a woman." The article also noted that the New York police and FBI were investigating "persistent" reports that underworld figures were "renting out" 'snuff' films for $1,500,[110] giving credence to very dubious tabloid journalism and unsubstantiated allegations. Within a month of the article's publication a man approached a TV station in California claiming that he had seen a 'snuff' film in which a girl was raped, murdered and decapitated. From the visible terrain he believed the film was made on a beach in California. His claims led the police to re-investigate a number of multiple murders from the early 1970s, amongst them those committed by serial killer Ed Kemper. The claims also seemed plausible because in 1972 Santa Cruz was named murder capital of America, and subsequently there was "another rash of decapitation murders" near Santa Barbara and Oxnard, all of which had taken place on beaches and involved a "strange ritualistic pattern of decapitations, plus obvious acts of necrophilia."[111] The report to the TV station was very similar to CDL spokesman Robert Dornan's story from October 1968 about the decapitation of a young woman on a beach in southern California, as well as to the information passed to the FBI claiming that 'snuff' films originated when a Satanic ritual was filmed in California in 1969. However, considering it was such a sensational and shocking allegation there was notably no subsequent reporting of the story.

In the early years of the 1970s two low-budget horror films, noted for depicting shockingly realistic violence, were released. *The Last House on*

109 Brownmiller, *Against Our Will*: 404.
110 "Revolt Against Rape," *Time* (13 October 1975): 46.
111 Hammond, "Are Snuff Films For Real?" *Adam Film World* (April 1976): 43.

the Left (Wes Craven, 1972) and *The Texas Chain Saw Massacre* (Tobe Hooper, 1974) provoked outrage and challenged a stagnant cinematic mainstream. In 1972, before the release of *Last House on the Left*, *Texas Chain Saw Massacre*, or *Snuff*, Vincent Canby criticised contemporary films for being superficially realistic, but observed "They use up realistic actions so quickly that the actions become as unreal as the formula gestures of ritual." In the 1930s, the victims in gangster films and westerns doubled over when shot, no blood was shown and death was obvious and symbolic. However, with the passage of time, the audience became familiar with the theatrics and violence became more vivid and graphic. Canby concluded, "It may be about time for movies to realize that they aren't realistic. They are, for all the reality of their locales and of their actors and of their circumstances, only representations of reality and nothing more."[112] However, some aspiring filmmakers had other ideas, and eventually 'snuff', the depiction of real murder for entertainment, would be heralded as the final step in the evolution of cinematic violence.

Last House on the Left presented a menacing advertising campaign asking the audience "Can a movie go too far?" — to which it responded by advising viewers "To avoid fainting keep repeating, It's only a movie ... only a movie ... only a movie..." A gimmick that had been around for so long it was almost a tradition in exploitation films.[113] The ominous opening falsely claimed, "The events you are about to witness are true. Names and locations have been changed to protect those individuals still living." But set in contemporary America, not the distant past or an exotic foreign location, *Last House on the Left* was unsettlingly believable and the *vérité* film style and unfamiliar cast lent an authentic feel to the story.

Reworking Ingmar Bergman's *Virgin Spring* (1960), *Last House on the*

112 Vincent Canby, "Has Movie Violence Gone Too Far?" *New York Times* (16 January 1972) section II: 1.
113 Two decades earlier posters for *Strait-Jacket* (William Castle, 1964) promised vivid depictions of axe murders, warning "Just Keep Telling Yourself: It's Only A Movie ... It's Only A Movie ... It's Only A Movie..." and the following year *Color Me Blood Red* (Herschell Gordon Lewis, 1965) used a similar advertisement stating 'This Is Only A Movie, This Is Only A Movie...' *Night of Bloody Horror* (Joy N. Houck Jr., 1969), filmed in 'Violent Vision,' was a *Psycho* rip-off that promised sex and violence and also used the advertising line "keep telling yourself, it's only a movie." To emphasise the shocking nature of the film the producers pledged $1,000 to the family of anyone who died from a heart attack while watching the violent scenes.

Left depicted the misadventures of two young women who visit New York City. Mari Collingwood (Sue Cassell) and her friend Phyllis (Lucy Grantham) travel to New York on the night before Mari's seventeenth birthday to see Bloodlust, a rock band with a bad reputation because they once dismembered a live chicken on stage. In the city Mari and Phyllis try to buy drugs but find themselves taken hostage by a gang of wanted criminals. The gang, led by Krug Stillo (David Hess), is a kind of dysfunctional family of psychotically violent drug abusers: Sadie (Jeramie Rain) is a surrogate mother figure with Weasel (Fred Lincoln) and Junior (Marc Sheffler) their 'children'. The criminals are not alien monsters or supernatural creatures, yet together they are a serious Manson Family-like threat, representing a horrific parody of the idealized nuclear family. Director Wes Craven and producer Sean Cunningham had previously dabbled in the adult film industry, working on two 'white coaters', *Together* (Sean Cunningham, 1971) and *The Art of Marriage* (1971). *Together* posed as a serious study of sex to justify its social value, but was in fact "prurient peeking," and the review in *Variety* suggested that it was actually three different films edited together.[114]

When reviewing *Last House on the Left* for the *New York Times* Howard Thompson noted that he walked out of the film after fifty minutes, during the murder of the two girls. Thompson described the film as "sickening tripe" performed by "inept actors" and informed readers, "It's at the Penthouse Theatre, for anyone interested in paying to see repulsive people and human agony."[115] A reflection of the times, according to Fred Lincoln *Last House on the Left* was originally intended to feature disgusting hardcore sex scenes in which the murderers would rape the corpses of their victims. Wes Craven also acknowledged that the original script was "much more sexual" and the rape scenes explicit.[116] The psychological intensity of the film was compelling

114 "Together," *Variety* (12 January 1972). Producer Sean Cunningham directed *Case of the Smiling Stiffs* (1973) which featured porn stars Fred J. Lincoln, and Harry Reems. Wes Craven appeared in Howard Ziehm's *Hot Cookies* (1977) and directed the X-rated porn film *Angela the Fireworks Woman* (1975) under the pseudonym 'Abe Snake'.

115 Howard Thompson, "Last House On the Left," *New York Times* (22 December 1972): 21.

116 *The Celluloid Crime of the Century* documentary (David Gregory, 1972). In the aftermath of *Last House on the Left* other exploitation filmmakers sought to cash in on its success. *Don't Look In the Basement* (S. F. Brownrigg, 1973) was advertised as being "from the makers of *Last House on the Left*," *Bloodbath* (Mario Bava, 1971) was also released as *Twitch of the Death Nerve*, *New House on the Left* and the *Last House on the Left Part 2*. *Last Night Trains*

but the downbeat conclusion meant that even when the threat was vanquished there would be no happy ending. Financially an extremely successful meeting of low-budget sex and violence, *Last House on the Left* spawned a number of notable offshoots whose equally *vérité* style paved the way for films such as *Snuff*, the most notable of which was *The Texas Chain Saw Massacre* (Tobe Hooper, 1974).

Set in modern America *Texas Chain Saw Massacre* opens with a narrated on-screen message which reads:

> The film which you are about to see is an account of the tragedy which befell a group of five youths, in particular Sally Hardesty and her invalid brother Franklin. It is all the more tragic in that they were young. But, had they lived very, very long lives, they could not have expected nor would they have wished to see as much of the mad and macabre as they were to see that day. For them an idyllic summer afternoon drive became a nightmare. The events of that day were to lead to the discovery of one of the most bizarre crimes in the annals of American history, The Texas Chain Saw Massacre.

While the message is false the unknown cast and documentary style give the film a compelling realism, and *Texas Chain Saw Massacre* depicts a truly degenerate family, again evoking memories of the Manson Family. With no female members the traditional family structure is distorted and the murderers, three generations of them, are all former employees at a slaughterhouse. As times have changed they have continued to ply their trade on hitchhikers.[117] *Texas Chain Saw Massacre* and *Last House on the Left* are both disturbing

---

(Aldo Lado, 1974), a direct imitation of Wes Craven's film, was released as *New House on the Left* and the *Last House on the Left Part 2* and *Second House From the Left*. Other filmmakers exploited the 'house' as threatening and horrific in titles such as *The House That Vanished* (José Ramón Larraz, 1974), *Don't Go Into the House* (Joseph Ellison, 1979), *The House on the Edge of the Park* (Ruggero Deodato, 1980) that featured David Hess, and *The House by the Cemetery* (Lucio Fulci, 1981).

117 Kim Henkel, who co-wrote the script with Tobe Hooper, was familiar with the contemporary crimes of Elmer Wayne Henley and Dean Corll and incorporated some aspects of that sensational story into the screenplay. Henley lured young men to a house where they would be sexually molested and killed by Corll. There was a third man involved in the procurement of boys, and when he was killed by Corll, Henley feared for his own life and went to the police. After confessing Henley took the police around Houston showing them where the bodies had been dumped.

and psychologically intense with no happy ending or comfortable resolution. The popularity of the two films reflected social changes in American society where cinema audiences expected more realistic films and their financial success ensured that others would follow.

After more than five years without the restrictions imposed by the Production Code, film critic Pauline Kael speculated in the *New Yorker* on the future of film. She noted that in previous decades films relied on an "implied system of values which is gone now." Changes in American cinema in the aftermath of Vietnam and Watergate could not be accurately estimated but she observed that contemporary films tended to parody those earlier values. As a consequence of the changing value system, "Nobody understands what contemporary heroes or heroines should be, or how they should relate to each other, and it's safer not to risk the box office embarrassment of seriousness."[118]

Movie audiences had changed and "People no longer go to a picture just for itself, and ticket buyers certainly aren't looking for the movie equivalent of 'a good read.' They want to be battered, to be knocked out — they want to get wrecked." The main interest in cinema going, she speculated, was to see what everyone else was talking about. Kael also noted that "constant visceral excitement" in some films meant that audiences would not respond to the more nuanced work of serious artists and sensationalism would win out over subtlety. In her opinion, "People go for the obvious, the broad, the movies that don't ask them to feel anything. If a movie is a hit, that means practically guaranteed sensations — and sensations without feeling." These sensational films left Kael feeling "wiped out" and "desolate." Mainstream box office hits such as *The Exorcist* (William Friedkin, 1973) "give most of the audience just what it wants and expects, the way hardcore porn does." That is, blatantly, without any attempt at subtlety. As a consequence, "It's becoming tough for a movie that isn't a big media-created event to find an audience, no matter how good it is." Kael acknowledged the reality of a situation in which "businessmen have always been in control of film production" but "now advertising puts them, finally, on top of public reaction as well." Business ethics transcended quality and aggressive advertising and marketing played a major role in the

118 Pauline Kael, "Onward and Upward With the Arts: On the Future of Movies," *New Yorker* (5 August 1974): 43.

success of a film. In Kael's opinion "There are a few exceptions, but in general it can be said that the public no longer makes a picture a hit. If the advertising for a movie doesn't build up an overwhelming desire to be part of the event, people just don't go."[119] Even children yet to reach their teens wanted the 'events', "they were born into sixties cynicism and saturation advertising. They've never known anything but the noise and the frantic atmosphere; they think it's a cop-out if a movie cuts away from mayhem and doesn't show them gore."[120] Kael's insights defined the tone for the foreseeable future, but even she could not have predicted the arrival of *Snuff*.

Familiar with the rhetoric about sex crimes, pornography and 'snuff' the American public were ripe for exploitation by Allan Shackleton's marketing campaign. After the initial newspaper stories about 'snuff', to whet the public's appetite further Shackleton began sending out the first of several press releases for his movie on 1 December 1975. Word got back to Michael Findlay who was concerned about the film's content and warned Shackleton that he could face legal problems if he was exhibiting *Slaughter* under a new name. While *Slaughter* may have been shot by Michael Findlay, he received no credit on the posters or advertisements in Shackleton's extravagant remodel. Findlay had been told by a third party that this was the case and was waiting until *Snuff* opened in New York to see what legal action he should take.[121]

Prior to the film's release Shackleton visited David Friedman to show him *Snuff*, seeking his approval. "He had made this thing in response to all the publicity, figuring that he could make some money out of the deal," remembered Friedman. Rather than being impressed by Shackleton's opportunism Friedman was concerned, "I told him I thought the idea was crazy and it was the last thing that the industry needed to be associated with. I begged him not to release it."[122] After the success of *Deep Throat*, *Behind the Green Door* and *The Devil in Miss Jones* the AFAA saw the adult market as a lucrative niche which it wanted to develop, but *Snuff* threatened to undermine their plans.

Romanticizing the role of film entrepreneurs such as Shackleton,

---

119 Ibid: 43–45.
120 Ibid: 50.
121 "'Snuff' (Sex Murders) Film Now Thought Hoax From Argentina," *Variety* (17 December 1975): 4.
122 Friedman quoted in Hebditch, *Porn Gold*: 337.

Pauline Kael claimed they had no status: "Nobody respects the entrepreneur's dream of glory, and nobody respects his singular talent." In the tradition of P. T. Barnum the entrepreneur is a self-made man who has to raise and risk money, but stands to gain. He is more a gambler than a businessman; "a street fighter, his speciality is low cunning,"[123] and only goal the singleminded pursuit of financial success. To attract further attention to his film Shackleton organized interviews with an Indianapolis radio station and distributed fake newspaper clippings detailing the efforts of a fictional retired attorney, 'Vincent Sheehan' who, it claimed, used the Citizens for Decency organisation to crusade against *Snuff*.[124] Sheehan was possibly intended as a parody of Raymond Gauer, a retired accountant, or, more likely, Charles Keating, a former lawyer.

Boxoffice (8 December 1975) reported that Monarch Releasing was changing its image, moving away from softcore exploitation films to a more mainstream audience. The company did not release adult films with explicit hardcore sex because many theatres would not exhibit them,[125] reflecting the legal changes brought about by *Miller v. California* (1973), and in December 1975 Monarch's schedule offered a variety of G, PG and R-rated films. Two of the films, *Mrs. Barrington* (Chuck Vincent, 1974) and *The Young Divorcees* (Laurence E. Mascott, 1976), were originally X-rated sex comedies, but with appropriate cuts re-classified R. At that time Shackleton was optimistic about the company's future, saying that it was well financed and the schedule of upcoming releases promised an "extremely bright outlook."[126] At the same time Barry Glasser, a former film critic for *Playgirl*, *Motion Picture Weekly* and the *Independent Film Journal*, was appointed director of publicity and promotion at Monarch. As soon as he took up his position he worked with Shackleton organizing the promotional campaigns for *The Revenge of the Cheerleaders* (Richard Lerner, 1976), which featured

123 Kael, "Onward and Upward With the Arts," *New Yorker* (5 August 1974): 46.
124 Scott Stine, "The Snuff Film: The Making of an Urban Legend," *Skeptical Enquirer* (May/June 1999) online at http://www.csicop.org/si/9905/snuff.html
125 John Cocchi, "Monarch Releasing Is Changing Its Image," *Box Office* (8 December 1975): 12. In 1973 *Boxoffice* announced that the company formerly known as 'A. L. Shackleton Films Inc.' had changed its name to Monarch and in the forthcoming year expected to handle twenty-five exploitation films such as *The Farmer's Daughter*, *Alice in Fantasy Land* and *While the Cat's Away* (Chuck Vincent, 1972). "Shackleton Changes Name of Company to Monarch," *Box Office* (19 March 1973): 9.
126 Ibid. *Mrs Barrington* was remade by Chuck Vincent in 1988 as *Sexpot*.

David Hasselhoff in the nude, *Fantastic Invasion of Planet Earth* (Arch Oboler, 1966), a 3D sci-fi film in 'spacevision', and *Snuff*.[127]

Monarch began publishing provocative adverts for *Snuff* in *Boxoffice* in December 1975 that warned it would be, "The picture they said could never be shown ... The *bloodiest* thing that *ever* happened in front of a camera."[128] Howard Jacobson in *Variety* was aware of the rumours of 'snuff' films that had circulated a few months earlier and cautioned that *Snuff* could lead to a re-definition of the limits of screen violence if the murders were real. Also, Jacobson noted, if the killing in *Snuff* were real Shackleton was a material witness against the filmmakers who had committed, or paid others to commit, murder and could also face criminal charges himself.[129]

A month before the film was released, and several weeks before the climactic scene was even shot, *Variety* exposed *Snuff* as a hoax and Shackleton confessed to the "interesting bind" he found himself in with the film. He pointed out that if it were a real murder "I'd be in jail in two minutes ... I'd be a damn fool to admit it. If it isn't real, I'd be a damn fool to admit it."[130] Either way Shackleton claimed to have voluntarily rated the film X because he "thought young people might be damaged by seeing explicit violence."[131] When *Snuff* played in LA several months later Larry Gleason, an executive from Mann Theaters, was honest in pointing out, "The reason [Monarch] haven't submitted it to the rating board is because they thought it would only get an R. This isn't hardcore. We don't play hardcore. It's a self-imposed X."[132] Rumours reported in the newspapers claimed that the 'snuff' films being investigated by New York police were pornographic and Shackleton knew that an X rating implied hardcore sex, superficially adding to the authenticity of the film. However *Snuff* was not a porn film, it was a *very* cheap exploitation film with minor nudity. Word spread quickly about the film and before

127 "Barry Glasser Is Director of Monarch Publicity," *Box Office* (8 December 1975): 12. The *Fantastic Invasion of Planet Earth* was originally released as *The Bubble* in 1966.
128 Lynch, "The Facts About the Snuff-Film Rumours," *Oui* (July 1976): 70.
129 Harlan Jacobson, "If 'Snuff' Killings Are Real, — Film Violence Faces New Test," *Variety* (10 December 1975): 4. A sequel to *Snuff* called *The Slasher* was proposed in advance, but it was dependent on public response. Cocchi, "Monarch Releasing Is Changing Its Image," *Box Office* (8 December 1975): 12.
130 Ibid.
131 Richard Eder, "'Snuff' is Pure Poison," *New York Times* (7 March 1976): B24.
132 "Snuff Biz Goes When Pickets Go," *Variety* (24 March 1976): 36.

Snuff was released it had already attained international notoriety. Rona Barret, host of the network show *Good Morning America*, read the reports about snuff movies in *Variety* and was so outraged that she called on the United Nations to investigate.[133] In one instance *Variety* was contacted by Mike Jeffries, an Australian radio personality (Radio 2UE, Sydney), who inquired about *Snuff*, asking, "Whether or not this was the sickest thing you'd ever heard of?"[134]

Ironically, the final scene for *Snuff* was only shot *after* the pre-publicity campaign, in December 1975. Shackleton had been spreading rumours for months in advance but he did not arrange for the filming of the end sequence until he had gotten enough bookings to make it a viable business proposition. According to an article in *Erotica* (December 1976) Shackleton hired a production company that specialized in making industrial films, but which also picked up extra business making low-budget explicit sex movies, to shoot the scene, and a special effects man who normally worked on TV and magic shows to provide the gore effects. Pig guts, lamb hearts, latex fingers and three gallons of stage blood were used to create the unrealistic effects. Shackleton rented a mid-town loft apartment studio that was usually a set for porn films and the scene was shot on 30 December 1975. Further highlighting the fraud, *Erotica* magazine published several behind-the-scenes photographs taken on the set of the 'snuff' scene. One of these showed the 'victim' preparing for her 'murder,' reclining in a hollowed out box of a sunken bed. Two crew members are clearly shown in another picture fitting a prosthetic dummy over the victim, and finally the dummy being pumped full of theatrical blood.[135]

Despite the film's many short comings, due to the marketing campaign and willingness of the public to believe, *Snuff* provoked controversy and became a rallying point for conservatives and militant feminists who needed a focus for their anti-obscenity rhetoric. A film that no one could credit with redeeming social value, but one which epitomised the crusader's apocalyptic rhetoric, *Snuff* was the perfect target.

133 "'Snuff' The Greatest rip-off in porn history," *Erotica* (December 1976): 18–20.
134 "'Snuff' (Sex Murders) Film Now Thought Hoax From Argentina," *Variety* (17 December 1975): 4.
135 "'Snuff' The Greatest rip-off in porn history," *Erotica* (December 1976): 20. A few years later *Homicide Detective* (January 1978) used some of the stills from the final scene of *Snuff* as cover illustrations, even though they did not relate to any of the stories in the magazine.

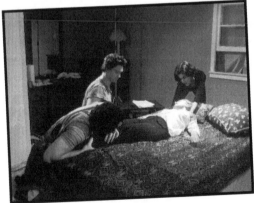

188

Chapter Eight

MADE IN SOUTH AMERICA
WHERE LIFE IS CHEAP

The Transformation of *Slaughter* into *Snuff* and the Indianapolis Premiere

ADVERTISEMENTS FOR *SNUFF* (1976) CLAIMED THAT ONLY IN "LATIN AMERICA, where life is cheap could such a film be made," explicitly linking adult entertainment as a commercial commodity with the unconfirmed contemporary rumours about sex murders for 'snuff' films. The outrageous marketing exploited both the sensational anti-obscenity rhetoric of Raymond Gauer and tabloid newspaper reports from October 1975 claiming police had seized a pornographic film from South America that depicted the actual murder of a young woman. Advance publicity, which made John Leonard of the *New York Times* think that the filmmakers must have gone to "tabloid correspondence school,"[1] circulated in a climate of high public awareness of rape and violent crime, and created considerable interest in a film that would otherwise have passed by unnoticed.

The pre-publicity from distributor Monarch followed a long tradition of outrageous exploitation showmanship. *The Maniacs Are Loose* [aka *The Thrill Killers*] (R. D. Steckler, 1965) was made in Hypno-Vision and in each cinema people dressed up as maniacs would attack members of the audience. *The Wizard of Gore* (Herschell Gordon Lewis, 1970) warned that squeamish people should leave the auditorium and in exhibitions of *Cannibal Girls* (Ivan Reitman, 1972) a bell would ring to warn sensitive members of the audience that an upcoming scene would feature graphic violence and nudity so they could close their eyes. The 'Orgy of the Living Dead' drive-in triple bill[2] offered an insurance policy

---

1   John Leonard, "Commentary: Cretin's Delight On Film," *New York Times* (27 February 1976): A21.
2   *Revenge of the Living Dead* (Willard Huyck and Gloria Katz, 1973), *Curse of the Living Dead* (Mario Bava, 1966) and *Fangs of the Living Dead* (Armando De Ossorio, 1968).

189

to audience members that would provide a lifetime's free incarceration at a mental asylum to anyone who went mad watching the three films. However, Allan Shackleton's campaign updated earlier marketing tactics to reflect the concerns of contemporary America. The publicity campaign, masterminded by Shackleton, had begun six months before *Snuff*'s release, and even though it was exposed as a fraud during that time distribution went ahead.

In December 1975 unnamed sources informed *Variety* that the footage used in *Snuff* was originally shot for a different film project, entitled *Slaughter*, but no one was interested until Shackleton came up with his imaginative marketing plan.[3] A few months before Shackleton acquired the rights to *Slaughter* he had been working with Carter Stevens on a film parody of the *Star Trek* television series. The project was in pre-production when Paramount announced that they were going to make a *Star Trek* film and, after getting legal advice, the project was dropped. Afterwards Shackleton bought the inexpensive *Slaughter* footage with a view to releasing it, hoping to recover the aborted project's preproduction costs.[4]

Whilst *Slaughter* was obviously based on the 1969 Manson Family murders in Los Angeles (the same crimes that were credited with popularizing the term 'snuff'), the advertising campaign primarily exploited newspaper reports citing police seizure of pornographic films imported from South America, and also the exaggerated accusations of Raymond Gauer. The main body of *Snuff* was originally filmed in Argentina in 1970 by Michael and Roberta Findlay to be released under the title *Slaughter*, but it was so bad that it languished on the distributor's shelf. At one point it seemed exploitation impresario Joe Solomon was going to distribute *Slaughter*, but he backed out. After that there were no other distributors interested in the film.[5] Made in Argentina to avoid union costs and regulations, *Slaughter* was filmed without sound because most of the cast spoke no English and it was

3   "'Snuff' (Sex Murders) Film Now Thought Hoax From Argentina," *Variety* (17 December 1975): 4.
4   Mike Ward, "S'nuff Said: The behind-the-scenes scoop on the movie that could only be made in Carter Stevens' studio, where life is cheap!" *About Cult Film* online at http://www.aboutfilm.com/aboutcultfilm/features/snuff.html
5   "'Snuff' (Sex Murders) Film Now Thought Hoax From Argentina," *Variety* (17 December 1975): 4.

easier and cheaper to dub the whole film later.[6] When Shackleton bought the film, he cut the existing conclusion, added an extra scene of his own at the end, and released the resulting film as *Snuff* (1976).[7]

Advertised with an attention grabbing and provocative poster, *Snuff* was a classic example of exploitation promotion. The poster, a black and white photograph of a dead woman cut into four strips by a big pair of scissors, bears the film's title in blood red letters. The blades of the scissors are smeared red and the woman's blood seeps between the cuts in the photograph. The woman in the poster is nude, suggesting it is a pornographic film, while the cuts in the photograph and the blood emphasise the violence.

If the image used on the advertising poster was not provocative enough the accompanying text boasted that *Snuff* was "The bloodiest thing that ever happened in front of a camera!!" — reputedly exceeding anything shown previously in films because, according to the rumours, the film climaxed with a real murder, not a fake one. Tempting potential viewers with the claim that the film was "The picture they said could never be shown," the poster reflects a sense of transgression and taboo commonly found in Mondo movies, which also frequently promised footage of real murders. Of more contemporary relevance, the Zapruder footage had recently been shown to the American public on TV for the first time and the imagery made a lasting impression. The poster also referred to the tabloid rumours about 'snuff' movies originating in Argentina, claiming *Snuff* was "The film that could only be made in South America where life is cheap!" However, the advertising was deceptive, misrepresenting *Snuff*, which in reality was nothing like the poster implied.

At the start of *Snuff*'s twisted narrative an actress, Terri London

---

6   Kerekes and Slater, *Killing for Culture*: 11.
7   Michael and Roberta Findlay were a husband and wife team who made softcore sex films in the 1960s. Michael Findlay was best known for directing the 'Flesh Trilogy', *Touch of Her Flesh* (1967), *Curse of Her Flesh* (1968) and *Kiss of Her Flesh* (1968), in which women are murdered in a number of imaginatively gruesome ways. After their divorce Michael was killed in a bizarre accident in 1977 when he was decapitated by a helicopter rotor blade on top of the Pan Am Buiding in New York City. He was on his way to the Cannes film festival to promote a 3D projector lens which he hoped would revolutionise cinema. Roberta continued making exploitation and explicit hardcore sex films on her own. Eric Pace, "Travellers on Separate Paths Victims of Copter Accident," *New York Times* (18 May 1977): 35.

(Mirtha Massa),[8] goes to Argentina with her producer to make a film and to see her boyfriend, Horst Frank (Clao Villanueva), a wealthy playboy with a degenerate and immoral lifestyle. The majority of the film depicts the activities of a South American cult composed of young women who unquestioningly obey every command of their leader Satan (Enrique Larratelli), who is obviously intended to be a fictionalized version of Charles Manson. In September 1975, some months before *Snuff* was released, Squeaky Fromme attempted to assassinate President Gerald Ford[9] and one associate of the Family was reported in *Time* as saying "If Charlie told a girl, 'Hey, baby, go out and snuff [kill] yourself,' she would do it"[10] — and Satan's girls are just as obedient. Emphasising the power Manson was commonly credited with wielding over his followers, potential members of Satan's gang undergo an initiation of torture to show their commitment and loyalty, and once the women join Satan's gang they are under his complete control, just as the members of the Manson Family were entranced by their guru.

In the course of her visit Terri winds up pregnant either by Horst or his father (Alfredo Inglesias), an international weapons dealer. The film culminates with the followers of Satan attacking Horst's home and killing everyone they find, a re-enactment of the Tate killings in Benedict Canyon. In the final scene Horst's father and Terri are in bed together when two of Satan's gang burst into the room brandishing weapons and, refusing to be bribed by repeated offers of money, shoot the man and, as in the case of Sharon Tate, kill Terri by repeatedly stabbing her in the stomach. At this point the screen goes black and the footage Michael Findlay shot for his film *Slaughter* is finished. Shackleton removed the ending filmed by Mike Findlay and recruited a replacement cast in

---

8   Mirta Massa was an Argentinean beauty queen in the late 1960s who appeared in several films before such as *El Satiro* (Kurt Land, 1970) before making *Slaughter* (1971) and later featured in *Destino de un capricho* (Leo Fleider, 1972) and *La Super Aventura* (Enrique Carreras, 1975). She retired from acting in the 1980s to concentrate on painting.

9   Two attempts were made to assassinate Gerald Ford while he was President of America, both occurring within a few weeks of each other while he was touring in California. The first happened in Sacramento (5 September 1975) when Lynette 'Squeaky' Fromme, one of the Manson Family tried to shoot him. Seventeen days later in San Francisco, Sarah Jane Moore shot at him twice across the street.

10 "The Family That Stays Together," *Time* (15 September 1975) 26–27. The same article in *Time* magazine also identified ties that developed between Manson's Family and the Aryan Brotherhood, noting that two members of the Family and two members of the Aryan Brotherhood were convicted of the 1972 murder of a couple in California.

New York to shoot a short scene which would be the basis for the *Snuff* marketing campaign and the film's subsequent notoriety.

In the extra segment added on by Allan Shackleton, after Terri is stabbed, the camera cuts away to a behind-the-scenes shot of the crew on the set as they begin to pack up at the end of a day's shooting and disperse. The director,[11] dressed in a lilac t-shirt with *Vida es Muerte* ('Life is Death') printed on it, starts a conversation with a female crew member about how much the last scene of the film turned him on, and says he wants to re-enact it when the rest of the crew are gone. Without further ado they start kissing on the bed, even though at least five crew members are still on set and two different cameras are running. Feeling uncomfortable the woman complains that the crew are still recording and in response the director threatens her with a knife. Initially she is unfazed, believing he will not hurt her but, despite the presence of witnesses, the director begins to torture her.

After cutting deep into his victim's shoulder the director then severs her fingertips with wire cutters. Other members of the crew watch, and one female crew member even helps hold the helpless victim down while she is being mutilated. Despite the victim's protestations, a hand is cut off with a power saw and finally the director stabs the corpse of his victim in the stomach and begins to pull out the intestines. The screen goes black as the film runs out and there are no closing credits, only an audio track with one of the crew asking, "Did you get it? Did you get it all?" It is notable that the final scene of *Snuff* is very similar to the description given to the FBI by an unnamed informant in August 1975 of the final 'snuffer' reel.

The absence of onscreen credits is an attempt to establish the authenticity of *Snuff* as a genuine underground pornographic loop, similar to many others which traditionally had no opening or closing credits to protect the identity of the performers from prosecution and public condemnation. Even after the wave of 'porno chic', when the notorious full length hardcore roughie *Water Power* (Shaun Costello)

11 Since there are no cast and crew credits at the beginning or the end of the film the identity of the actor who plays the director or actor is not known. When *Snuff* was released under the title 'The Big Snuff' an actor named Brian Cary is sometimes credited as the director in the final scene but no biographical information is available. Carter Stevens did not know the actors personally and cannot remember their names. Ward, "S'nuff Said" *About Cult Film* online at http://www.aboutfilm.com/aboutcultfilm/features/snuff.html

was released in 1977, it had no onscreen title or credits. The practice was not limited to adult films. In 1973, a few years before *Snuff*'s release, Andy Warhol's art-house film *Blue Movie* (1968) was successfully prosecuted for obscenity. The film lasts ninety minutes, forty-five minutes of which depict a man and a woman experimenting with sex in a small apartment, and concludes with no credits or formal ending. The very act of omitting the credits was subversive and contrasted with the conventional Hollywood star system where performers seek all of the notoriety they can muster. In *Snuff*, anonymity was key.

David Szulkin claimed that Ed French created the special effects for the final scene in *Snuff*,[12] and Allan Shackleton hired Simon Nuchtern to direct the additional footage. The scene was filmed at Carter Stevens' studio in New York. Stevens had a loft apartment on 29th Street, in Chelsea, which he used to shoot commercials and small films. Shackleton rented it and built a set to replicate the bedroom in *Slaughter*.[13] Despite the cheap and unsophisticated gore, film critic Richard Eder still asserted, "The special effects are unsparing."[14] In terms of violence and gore *Snuff* was not noticeably worse than many other contemporary films such as *Death Wish* (Michael Winner, 1974), the psychologically unsettling *Taxi Driver* (Martin Scorsese, 1976), the gruesome *Wizard of Gore* (Herschell Gordon Lewis, 1970), *The Last House on the Left* (Wes Craven, 1972), *The Texas Chain Saw Massacre* (Tobe Hooper, 1974), *Jaws* (Steven Spielberg, 1975) or *Ilsa, She Wolf of the SS* (Dan Edmunds, 1974), all of which were released within a few years of *Snuff*. Despite the attempt to depict graphic violence, the whole 'snuff' scene is entirely unconvincing because the special effects are simply not very well done.

When the victim's fingers are cut off the actress wears a latex glove, and the two fingers the director removes are wax prosthetics while her two real fingers are tucked back into the palm of her hand. When the victim's hand is cut off the actress' real hand is concealed in the

---

12 David A. Szulkin, *Wes Craven's Last House on the Left: The Making of a Cult Classic* (revised edition), FAB, Guildford, 2000: 162. Ed French is best known for his special effects and makeup work on later mainstream films such as *Star Trek IV* (1991), *Terminator 2* (1991), *The Black Dahlia* (2006) and *Valkyrie* (2008).
13 Ward, "S'nuff Said," *About Cult Film* online at http://www.aboutfilm.com/aboutcultfilm/features/snuff.html
14 Eder, "'Snuff' Is Pure Poison," *New York Times* (7 March 1976): B13.

mattress, and it is a wax and latex prosthetic which is amputated. When the director slits open the victim and removes her intestines he intentionally does not open her shirt; had he done so the audience would have seen the fake torso packed with animal intestines and a heart. The most obvious absurdity in the scene is kept for last when the victim is clearly conscious after having her heart removed! In the Parisian Grand Guignol theatrical performances at the turn of the last century, "An eye gouging, disembowelment, stabbing or throat-slitting needs to be performed slowly, with care and precision. If rushed the audience resents being denied the right to relish the moment."[15] But *Snuff* ignores this credo; the effects are cheaply done and the scene hurried. In terms of brutal intensity it is arguable that the murder scene in *Last House on the Left* has still to be surpassed and it is much more realistic than the amateurish acting and special effects in *Snuff*.

Working with a tiny budget the scene for *Snuff* was shot in one day; beginning at 8 am, filming went on past after 2 am the following morning.[16] To save money there were only two trained actors in the scene and the rest of the cast were in actuality the film's crew members. Difficulties arose during the marathon shooting session and at one point the 'victim' had a panic attack, believing that she really was going to be murdered. It was only after Simon Nuchtern calmed her down that the scene was finished. Carter Stevens acknowledged the effects were unrealistic but they were shot very quickly and on a small budget — the phoney blood was made from Karo syrup and food colouring. But he also felt, in respect, that the final scene might seem better and more realistic because the preceding *Slaughter* footage was so bad.[17]

In the opinion of Linda Williams, "The particular obscenity of this last sequence thus resided in a perverse displacement of pornographic hardcore sexual activities, which typically end in penetration, onto the penetrating violation of the body's very flesh."[18] In other words, a foolish attempt by Williams to use her position as an academic to over-analyse Shackleton's exploitation showmanship. The only real

15 Richard J. Hand and Michael Wilson, *Grand Guignol: The French Theatre of Horror*, University of Exeter Press, Exeter, 2002: 38.
16 Ward, "S'nuff Said," *About Cult Film* online at http://www.aboutfilm.com/aboutcultfilm/features/snuff.html
17 Ibid.
18 Linda Williams, *Hard Core*, Pandora, London, 1991: 192.

significance of the marketing campaign behind *Snuff* and the final scene was that it provided an ironic and amusing subversion of the viewer's expectations. If the audience were anticipating hardcore sex and a real murder they would be disappointed, because all they got was minor nudity and bad special effects. Despite this, many people left *Snuff* believing that they *had* seen a real murder.[19] Describing Shackleton as a "consummate showman" with a talent for exploitation films, Stevens estimated that it cost less than $10,000 to buy the *Slaughter* footage and shoot the extra scene. To release it into the National Theatre on Broadway, however, one of the most prestigious cinemas in America, Stevens suspected that Shackleton had paid less than $100,000 and probably closer to $50,000.[20]

Shackleton was not the first to try to convince an audience that they were seeing a real murder. In the early 1960s Dave Friedman and Herschell Gordon Lewis thought too many people were making 'nudie' films and that the market was too crowded and mundane, so they looked for fresh subject matter and picked 'gore'.[21] Stanford Kohlberg, owner of a chain of drive-ins around Chicago, financed their film *Blood Feast* (Herschell G. Lewis, 1963), because he wanted to make a graphically violent film to see if other cinemas would exhibit it.[22] One advertisement for *Blood Feast* warned the audience "You'll Recoil and Shudder as You Witness the Slaughter and Mutilation of Nubile Young Girls — in a Weird and Horrendous Ancient Rite!" while another boasted that there was "Nothing so appalling in the annals of horror!"

Herschell Gordon Lewis, the director of *Blood Feast*, was under no illusions as to what he was doing: "*Blood Feast* I've often referred to as a Walt Whitman poem — it's no good, but it's the first of its type and therefore it deserves a certain position."[23] Until *Blood Feast*, "people died neatly in movies. We made up for years of no blood with

---

19 Avedon Carol, "Snuff: Believing the Worst," in Alison Assiter and Avedon Carol (Eds.), *Bad Girls and Dirty Pictures: The Challenge To Reclaim Feminism*, Pluto Press, London and Boulder, Colorado, 1993: 127.

20 Ward, "S'nuff Said," *About Cult Film* online at http://www.aboutfilm.com/aboutcultfilm/features/snuff.html

21 John Wisniewski, "The Wizard of Gore: Herschell Gordon Lewis Speaks," *Bright Lights Film Journal* (No.34, October 2001) online at http://www.brightlightsfilm.com.34/lewis.html

22 Joe Bob Briggs, *Profoundly Disturbing: Shocking Movies That Changed History*, Plexus, London, 2003: 96.

23 Lewis quoted in Friedman, *A Youth In Babylon*: 347.

a single picture. We did things no one had ever done before."[24] Lewis acknowledged that he viewed filmmaking purely as a business and pitied "anyone who regards it as an art form and spends money based on that immature philosophy."[25] When *Blood Feast* was reviewed in *Variety* it was condemned as "incredibly crude and unprofessional" and "an insult to the most puerile and salacious of audiences."[26] Kevin Thomas of the LA *Times* described it as "a blot on the motion picture business. It is amateurish in every department, and only readers of puerile comic books will go to see this movie."[27] *Newsweek* called the film an "abominable Box Office Spectacular" and, observing the acknowledgements made in the closing credits to the Miami police and sanitation departments, quipped, "Those sanitation men should know garbage when they see it."[28] Dave Friedman later acknowledged being ashamed of the "appalling crudity" of the gore films he made with Lewis and remembered the two of them visiting butchers shops to buy sheep and chicken entrails.[29] However, *Blood Feast* cost $24,500 to make and is estimated to have recouped $7 million over the next fifteen years.[30] That was the sort of box office return Shackleton hoped to emulate.

At the premiere of *Blood Feast* at the Bel Air Drive-In (Peoria, Illinois) Lewis and Friedman were surprised to see a backlog of traffic as they arrived. While laughing amongst themselves because the gore effects looked fake Friedman was approached by a member of the audience who commented, "Man, they sure do make it look real."[31] Thinking quickly, and responding to his showman instincts, Friedman told the patron that the killings *were* real. He was determined to convince the public that the death scenes in *Blood Feast* were real in order to attract interest to the film, but few viewers actually believed Friedman even

24 Lewis quoted in Broeske, "Killing is Alive and Well in Hollywood," Los Angeles *Times* (2 September 1984) Calendar: 19.
25 Lewis quoted in Briggs, *Profoundly Disturbing*: 95.
26 "Blood Feast," *Variety* (6 May 1964).
27 Thomas quoted by Friedman in Dan Scapperotti, "Nudie Pioneer, David Friedman," *Femme Fatales* (v.6 No.10/11, April 1998): 83.
28 "Gourmet Special," *Newsweek* (18 May 1964): 62.
29 Hebditch and Anning, *Porn Gold*: 190.
30 Briggs, *Profoundly Disturbing*: 87. Lewis followed *Blood Feast* with *Two Thousand Maniacs* (1964) and *Color Me Blood Red* (1965) to complete the trilogy, and several years later made *The Wizard of Gore* (1970).
31 Pat Broeske, "Killing is Alive and Well in Hollywood," Los Angeles *Times* (2 September 1984) Calendar: 19.

though the effects were much more explicit than those used in the final scene of *Snuff*.[32] The only people who believed that *Blood Feast* or *Snuff* showed a real murder were those who wanted to believe it was so.

Snuff premiered at the Uptown Theatre in Indianapolis on 16 January 1976 with a self-imposed X rating, and tickets costing $7.50, considerably more than a conventional feature presentation. In preparation Shackleton began his advanced publicity in the city a month before the film's release. An FBI report notes that in mid December 1975 WIBC, a local Indianapolis radio station, broadcast an interview with a representative from the Monarch Releasing Corporation who announced that the city had been chosen as the location for the world premiere of a forthcoming film. Selected as a typical American city, Indianapolis had a suitable mixture of people to be a valid test of the film's playability.[33]

Before the premiere Shackleton gave a press conference that was covered by the local media and reported nationally.[34] However, the local authorities also took notice and District Attorney James Kelley undermined Monarch's marketing strategy and took a direct approach, forcing Shackleton to run a disclaimer acknowledging that *Snuff* was a theatrical production with simulated violence. Furthermore the Indianapolis *Star* and *News* both initially refused to run illustrated adverts for the film, but later compromised, insisting if adverts were published they would have to carry the notice: "This is a theatrical production. No one was harmed or injured during filming." The newspaper's stance created a minor controversy but eventually Shackleton conceded to the demand.[35] DA Kelly was quoted as saying that if the killings were real the film would be impounded as evidence of murder, and if they were faked he believed that the public should be informed. "The reception that Shackleton and his repellent movie get here," noted the Indianapolis *News*, "will say a lot about Indianapolis and America."[36]

The Uptown Theatre in Indianapolis was a small cinema located in a

32 Briggs, *Profoundly Disturbing*: 95.
33 "Snuff Movie (22 January 1976)," FBI, *Snuff Films*, File Number 145–5568.
34 Lynch, "The Facts About the Snuff-Film Rumours," *Oui* (July 1976): 117.
35 Ibid. See also B. J. Gilley, "Movie denies murders are for real," *Montreal Gazette* (21 January 1976): 18.
36 Indianapolis *News* quoted in ibid.

high crime area. There was no pomp or fanfare at the premiere, none of the cast attended and there were no celebrities. *Oui* flew Jay Lynch to Indianapolis for the gala opening of *Snuff*, and he remembered that the audience were primarily men in raincoats along with some college students. He counted the number of people attending each screening and reported that the first screening (6 pm) attracted only sixteen people, the second (at 7.30 pm) eighteen people, and the third (9.15 pm) fourteen people. Even at $7.50 per head the attendance was a financial disaster, but Lynch found it hard to be sympathetic: "Considering the quality of the film, this disaster was well deserved."[37]

Unbeknownst to Lynch, amongst the patrons on the opening night were a doctor and two FBI agents. The official FBI report estimated that there were about nine other people in the audience, of which at least two were local vice cops![38] At the end of the screening the doctor advised the FBI agents that he believed the murder was theatrically staged because there was no arterial blood spurting when the victim's hand was amputated. Also, the removal of the heart is a complex procedure and a lot of connecting tissue and vessels would have to be cut, whereas in the film it was done with too much ease; furthermore the heart was too small to be that of a normal human, causing him to believe it was an animal heart.[39]

Understandably Shackleton was upset by the poor turnout for the premiere.[40] DA Kelley's enforced disclaimer undermined the film's promotional campaign and, with no pickets or protests, the film was unable to attract media attention or draw a substantial audience. Later, as a consequence, Shackleton phoned Kelley in tears complaining that the disclaimer was ruining his business,[41] but it stayed in place and *Snuff* closed within a week. However, in New York there was a different reception: Protests by militant feminist drew attention to the film and ensured continuing box office success both in the city and nationwide.

37　Lynch, "The Facts About the Snuff-Film Rumours," *Oui* (July 1976): 117.
38　"Snuff Movie (22 January 1976)," FBI, *Snuff Films*, File Number 145–5568.
39　Ibid.
40　Lynch, "The Facts About the Snuff-Film Rumours," *Oui* (July 1976): 118.
41　Peter Birge and Janet Maslin, "Getting Snuffed in Boston," *Film Comment* (May–June 1976): 35.

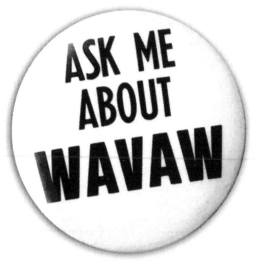

Chapter Nine

IF YOU CAN MAKE IT THERE
YOU CAN MAKE IT ANYWHERE

Reception in New York and the Feminist Response

ALLAN SHACKLETON'S FILM *SNUFF* WAS RELEASED IN NEW YORK CITY IN January 1976 at the Mann's National Theatre, on a playbill with a documentary entitled *The Amish Farm and House*. Socially divided and in the midst of a financial crisis, the city seemed like the logical location for a confrontation between the distributors of *Snuff* and a variety of groups championing specific interests, most notably militant feminists. Released about three months after reports in the New York *Post* and *Daily News*, the public were familiar with the persistent 'snuff' rumours, but not aware of the FBI investigation. In the economic emergency that gripped the city it was easy to believe that some people would do anything to make money.

In the early 1960s New York had been a relatively affluent, ethnically white, blue-collar city. The 1970s were a difficult transitional period and by the 1980s the city was a multi-racial, multi-ethnic, and economically divided white-collar metropolis.[1] In the mid 1970s New York City's fiscal crisis made it the prodigal municipality. With more than $5 billion in short-term debt the city was facing closure in capital markets and the Municipal Assistance Corporation ('Big Mac') and Emergency Financial Control Board agencies were established by the state government to restructure the debts and save the city from bankruptcy. Trapped in a dire situation one edition of the New York *Daily News* (30 October 1975) summarized President Ford's decision to deny the congressional re-authorization of the federal loan guarantees which had rescued New York: "Ford to City: DROP DEAD."

Amidst the depressing economic climate *New York Times* film critic Vincent Canby noted, "As reflected in good movies and bad, serious

---

1   Arian et al., *Changing New York City Politics*: 4.

ones as well as forthrightly foolish, New York City had become a metaphor for what looks like the last days of American civilization."[2] Contemporary films showed the city in a "mess" and run by "fools," reflecting the public's lack of confidence and the perceived economic disarray. In the cinematic New York criminals often held the decent citizens of the city at their mercy, and were often protected by corrupt police and civil libertarians. Congested with traffic, and polluted with toxins,[3] the state of the city could be seen as a symbol of the condition of its inhabitants.

The existence of unsubstantiated 'snuff' rumours contributed to a widespread cultural malaise across America. The story was widely exploited by imaginative journalists such as Bill von Maurer of the Miami *News*, who warned that 'snuff' films were "on their way" because "the first barrier had been hurdled by the merchants of murder." In his opinion, once the US Bureau of Customs cleared *Snuff*, establishing that the film had entered the country legally despite "strong rumours" that the murders in the film were real, a precedent had been set and, "Real or not, that's a foot in the door for the real thing."[4] Unfortunately imagination was no substitute for facts.

When *Snuff* arrived in New York City two FBI agents attended a screening at the National Theatre on 13 February and concluded accurately that the murder in the final scene was "completely staged" and that there was nothing in the film that could be construed as hardcore pornography.[5] However, real or not, even though they had not seen *Snuff*, the film appeared to confirm the worst fears of militant feminists and conservative moralists, and it was a potent symbol in their crusade against pornography. The alleged mixture of sex and violence, culminating in the death of an actress, showed the shocking excesses to which a liberal culture, as prophesied in their rhetoric, could extend. Concerned that if such films really did exist they could jeopardize efforts to establish legitimate markets for pornographic films, the AFAA

---

2   Canby, "New York's Woes Are Good Box Office," *New York Times* (10 November 1974): B1.
3   Ibid.
4   Bill von Maurer, "Snuff films get a foot in the door," Miami (Florida) *News* (2 February 1976): 3B. It would not have been in the Bureau of Custom's jurisdiction to investigate the murder scene in *Snuff*, nor would the scene have been present when the original *Slaughter* footage was imported several years earlier.
5   FBI, *Snuff Films*, File Number 145–5568.

offered $25,000 for a copy of a real 'snuff' film.[6] Outraged by the *Snuff* marketing campaign, Dave Friedman announced, "This is not the kind of film we make or condone."[7]

The AFAA denounced *Snuff* saying, "The depiction of gruesome murder, which is surely the most obscene of all human acts, and implying to the public that it could be for real is obscene, false and misleading." The statement continued addressing wider issues raised by the film:

> Our society has strange values. We who engage in the business of making and showing erotic motion pictures for adults are sometimes scorned, reviled, and in some cases threatened with prison for daring to show adults enjoying sex. Yet those who show killing, maiming and dismemberment are well within contemporary community standards.[8]

Vince Miranda, president of the AFAA, criticised the tactics used by CDL in promoting the existence of 'snuff': "They got a lot of money from people on this, by promising to name names. Only they never did. Every week they'd say, 'Next week we'll tell you all about it!' but next week was the same story. Hell, if you told *me* you were honestly fighting actual murders in films and excessive violence, *I'd* contribute."[9]

The *Variety* review of *Snuff* (25 February 1976) noted the earlier tabloid newspaper stories that had circulated in October 1975 and made it clear that the film had been exposed as a hoax several months previously (in *Variety* and other journals). However, the media and New York public were oblivious and *Snuff* took more than $60,000 in its first week. When asked about the protesters in New York, Shackleton replied, "I was praying they'd show up"[10] — to avoid another disaster like Indianapolis. Hostility towards the film was such that, one night, as Shackleton and a *Variety* reporter sat parked in a car watching the pickets outside a cinema showing *Snuff*, the pair were attacked by a mob that

6 Johnson and Schaefer, "Soft Core/Hard Gore," *Journal of Film and Video* (Summer–Fall 1993): 56.
7 Friedman quoted in Rotsler, "Down With Snuff!" *Adam Film World* (August 1976): 21.
8 Rotsler, "Down With Snuff!" *Adam Film World* (August 1976): 21.
9 Miranda quoted in ibid. As a consequence of the *Snuff* controversy the AFAA called on the MPAA to change the X rating applied to all adult films to 'Adult Only/E', designating erotica, and 'Adults Only/V', designating violence.
10 "Snuff," *Variety* (25 February 1976).

recognised Shackleton, and a policeman had to intervene to free the car so they could escape.[11] For the rest of his life Shackleton understandably felt that the showbiz aspects of *Snuff* were underappreciated.[12] *Variety* did acknowledge the Grand Guignol imagery in Shackleton's publicity campaign; "the film's promotion capitalizes on the same bloodlust that rock star Alice Cooper exploits by tossing a chicken into the crowd and watching it tear the animal apart," conceding that, awful as *Snuff* might be, Shackleton at least "deserves notice for bringing life, such as it is, back into promotion." The review concluded, "All this interest in the pic is not a very pretty picture."[13]

In the *New York Times* John Leonard also pointed out that *Snuff* was a hoax with such poor special effects that even the TV series *Marcus Welby, MD* might have improved upon them. While the murder was not as outrageous a spectacle as advertised, it was still a "contemptible movie," and one Leonard wished did not exist. Despite the hype surrounding the film, he concluded that "Bare breasts, buttered popcorn and blood are all that *Snuff* has to offer."[14] In the same newspaper, a week later, Richard Eder restated that the film was a hoax. "There is a patch of anti-matter on Times Square," wrote Eder, "into which not only public decency disappears, but reality as well. It is a repulsive put-on film called *Snuff*, and it is housed at the National Theatre." He pointed out,

> everything in the film is suspect: the contents, the promotion and possibly even some of the protest that is conducted each evening outside the box office. Nothing is provable, nothing is believable, and although swindles are hardly new in show business, it's been a long time since such a peculiarly poisonous kind of swindle has come along.

Eder described the film as a "horrendously written, photographed, acted, directed and dubbed bit of verdigris showing a group of devil

---

11 "Creator of 'Snuff' Film Dies," *Variety* (24 October 1979): 46. According to Carter Stevens, Shackleton intended to hire fake pickets to generate interest in the film but before he could make the necessary arrangements real pickets appeared. Ward, "S'nuff Said," *About Cult Film* online at http://www.aboutfilm.com/aboutcultfilm/features/snuff.html
12 "Creator of 'Snuff' Film Dies," *Variety* (24 October 1979): 46.
13 "Snuff," *Variety* (25 February 1976). At the time Cooper was well known for his Grand Guignol stage theatrics featuring a torture chamber, guillotine and chicken's blood.
14 Leonard, "Commentary: Cretin's Delight On Film," *New York Times* (27 February 1976): 21.

girls massacring people in Argentina or Uruguay,"[15] a summary which may initially seem harsh but is ultimately an honest, and probably a tactful, description. The public, however, did not listen to the critics and in the first week at the National Theatre (NY), *Snuff* took $66,000, followed by $48,000 in its second. In its third week pickets boosted receipts and the film took $39,000.[16] Prompted by the success of *Emmanuelle* and *Snuff* and concern about the long-term impact on their business, the League of New York Theatres and Producers sent a letter to cinema owners in the midtown district asking them not to show pornographic films — seeing it as a misuse of first-class cinemas. Henry Sabison, director of the League's special projects department, cautioned, "our fear is that once a theatre turns to pornographic films it rarely returns to quality films. It would be another battle lost for the legitimate theatre area as well as for other businesses in the district."[17] The appeal of short term profits and the need to stay in business were important considerations for cinema owners but they also posed a threat to the cultural and moral future of the city.

Rumours surrounding the existence of 'snuff' films were vague and often contradictory, confusing the public and leading to some misunderstanding of what actually constituted a 'snuff' film. CDL and feminist rhetoric emphasised 'snuff' films as violent pornography with explicit sex and murder, but sometimes in the media the emphasis was so heavily placed on murder that it obscured references to pornography. In other instances it was unclear if the victims had volunteered to make the film, aware of the consequences of that choice, or if they had been forced. Public confusion surrounding the 'snuff' rumours was evident when one cinema customer, questioned about the murder of women to make movies, replied "If this is how someone wants to end their life and make some money at the same time, what's the matter with it?"[18] This may express acceptance of the tabloid stories claiming an actress was hired for the film, aware that she was to be killed.

---

15 Eder, "'Snuff' is Pure Poison," *New York Times* (7 March 1976): B13. In *Variety* Howard Jacobson had earlier expressed his scepticism about the decency groups that Shackleton claimed had protested about the film. Jacobson, "If 'Snuff' Killings Are Real, — Film Violence Faces New Test," *Variety* (10 December 1975): 3.
16 "'Snuff' Rides Rumour," *Variety* (10 March 1976): 5.
17 Louis Calta, "Theatre League bids cinemas refrain from using sex films," *New York Times* (25 February 1976): 34.
18 Leonard, "Commentary: Cretin's Delight On Film," *New York Times* (27 February 1976): 21.

Al Goldstein, publisher of *Screw*, adopted a different approach to the *Snuff* controversy:

> I personally feel that Allan Shackleton has the right to make money in any dastardly way he chooses, but what really perturbs me is the dishonesty of *The New York Times* and the *Daily News* and the New York *Post*, who first created the fraud — the concept of 'snuff' movies — and are now cashing their chips over it. They are making lots of money out of ads for 'snuff' movies and, in effect, have created a myth and are now selling that myth.[19]

Unfortunately Goldstein was not aware of CDL's role in the creation of the stories about the existence of 'snuff' films. In *Adam Film World* Dirk Hammond identified the consequences of *Snuff* for the adult entertainment business:

> It is truly unfortunate that sexuality, with all its varied and positive elements should be exploited in the manner of snuff films. After all the battles for sexual freedom, and the commitment of intelligent people everywhere to loosen the bounds of individual morality in a realistic direction, the public will most certainly be revolted and confused by the proliferation of snuff films — if it ever happens. They may well provide the blue noses with the perfect ammunition to halt the advance of sane and decent human sexuality. And maybe that's just what some people out there want — profitwise, that is.[20]

Hammond's hopes for a more open society were not shared by moral conservatives or by a small group of very vocal militant feminists in New York. National recession and the bleak economic situation in the city, reports of the involvement of organized crime in the sex industry, and radical feminist activism combined to create an unsettling image of social decay which seemed to justify Raymond Gauer's apocalyptic rhetoric and made 'snuff' seem like a plausible idea.[21] Militant feminists

19   Lynch, "The Facts About the Snuff-Film Rumours," *Oui* (July 1976): 118.
20   Hammond, "Are Snuff Films For Real?" *Adam Film World* (April 1976): 84.
21   Gage, "Organized Crime Reaps Huge Profits From Dealing in Pornographic Films," *New York Times* (12 October 1975): 1, 68. See also Gage, "Pornographic Periodicals Tied To Organized Crime," *New York Times* (13 October 1975): 1, 43; Kaplan, "Pornography and Pirated Stereo

had for some time depicted women as the victims of a pornography industry dominated by ruthless men. In the book *Sisterhood is Powerful* (1970), Robin Morgan used the slogan "Pornography is the theory: rape is the practice" to summarize her ideological perspective.

The self-imposed X rating implied *Snuff* featured explicit hardcore sex, which it did not. In some interviews Allan Shackleton persisted with that idea, claiming that the film was originally a pornographic film, but the sex scenes were trimmed to conform to US obscenity laws.[22] Militant feminists who had *not* attended screenings of *Snuff* were only familiar with the newspaper reports and assumed that the film did contain explicit sex scenes and accordingly described the film as 'pornographic'. As a consequence the film became a rallying point for feminist anti-pornography campaigners and a symbol of the abusive patriarchy of which they perceived themselves to be victims. Taking to the streets fifty people picketed the cinema exhibiting *Snuff* in Times Square, carrying signs that read 'Murder Is Not Amusing,'[23] and 'We mourn the Death of Our Latin American Sister.' Complaints were lodged with the FBI, the District Attorney's office, the mayor's office, police department and other public officials, and petitions about *Snuff* were signed by liberal writers such as Eric Bentley and Susan Brownmiller, Sol Yurick, Viveca Lindfors, Gloria Steinem and Susan Sontag, and by Elizabeth Holtzman, the Democratic Representative for Brooklyn.[24] Unfortunately the *Snuff* controversy also provoked Andrea Dworkin's first feminist protest, and gave her an issue that she would manipulate for decades.

Recognizing the unusual philosophical position being adopted by the liberals, Jeffrey Hart wrote in the conservative journal *Human Events* that *Snuff* was a "Technicolor advertisement for sadistic violence against women" and it had "propelled them [liberals] to a position indistinguishable from that of wool-hats in West Virginia."[25] The distorted claims surrounding *Snuff* drew unlikely allies for militant

---

Tapes Seized in Raid on Mob-Linked Operation," *New York Times* (12 December 1972): 51; Blumenthal, "Porno Chic," *New York Times Magazine* (21 January 1973): 28–34; Brass, "Peep Porn $$ Titillate Mob," *New York Post* (1 October 1975): 3; "The Porno Plague," *Time* (5 April 1976): 46–51.

22 Tom Teide, "Brutality yes, pornography no?" Fort Scott (Kansas) *Tribune* (18 February 1976): 2.
23 "Fifty Picket Movie House To Protest Violent Film," *New York Times* (16 February 1976): 22.
24 Leonard, "Commentary: Cretin's Delight On Film," *New York Times* (27 February 1976): 21.
25 Jeffrey Hart, "Look who would censor 'snuff' films," *Human Events* (3 April 1976): 8.

feminists. Wardell Pomeroy, coauthor with Alfred Kinsey of *Sexual Behaviour in the Human Female* (1953), believed that "If anything should be censored ... *Snuff* would head the list."[26] Susan Sontag, Martin Duberman and Grace Paley, usually advocates of free speech, called for censorship and prosecution in the case of *Snuff*.[27] However, Nat Hentoff, columnist for the *Village Voice* and a First Amendment absolutist, provocatively remarked that even if the woman's murder were real, "I don't believe anything should ever be shut down."[28]

Militant feminist protesters picketed Mann's National Theatre daily, distributing flyers which made concrete the connection between contemporary news reports about 'snuff' films of a woman murdered in Buenos Aires and *Snuff* advertising, "It is implied in the advertisements of the film currently showing that this may be the same film."[29] Their campaign effectively provided Allan Shackleton with free publicity every day. The feminist protest, later modified to reflect the distributor's denial that a woman really was killed in the film, contended, "Whether or not the death depicted in the current film *Snuff* is real or is simulated, that the murder and dismemberment of a woman's body is [sic] commercial film material is an outrage to our sense of justice as women, as human beings."[30] Ironically, during the *Slaughter* film footage — that is, the film before the tagged on ending — more men than women are killed but most of the protesters had not seen *Snuff*, and did not want to.[31] Meanwhile Shackleton revelled in the controversy and boasted, "Pickets sell tickets," acknowledging his determination to make money from the film, as well as to draw attention to himself in the film business. He also reported that he had received several offers to make a sequel.[32]

In New York protesters criticized Manhattan District Attorney Robert M. Morgenthau for his refusal to either act immediately or to respond

---

26 Pomeroy quoted in "The Porno Plague," *Time* (5 April 1976): 50.
27 Ibid.
28 Hentoff quoted in ibid.
29 LaBelle, "Snuff — The Ultimate in Woman Hating," in Radford and Russell (Ed.), *Femicide*: 191–92.
30 Ibid.
31 Leonard, "Commentary: Cretin's Delight On Film," *New York Times* (27 February 1976): 21. Leonard notes that there were male and female protestors picketing the theatre, "most belonging to activist homosexual organisations."
32 LaBelle, "Snuff — The Ultimate in Woman Hating," in Radford and Russell (Ed.), *Femicide*: 192.

to the phone calls to his office. They also claimed he ignored protests at the cinema, and a petition to his office from prominent citizens, clergy, and social services.[33] During the investigation into *Snuff* the New York police approached Carter Stevens because he had taken photographs of the final scene while it was being shot in his studio apartment, which were then sold to several different adult film magazines and subsequently published.[34] It took Morganthau one month to determine that the murder scene was a hoax, created using "conventional trick photography," and that the actress involved was "alive and well." But, after watching *Snuff*, Morganthau reported, "I'm concerned about the fact that this kind of film might incite or encourage people to commit violence against women."[35] Morgenthau identified and interviewed the 'victim' as an aspiring actress who wanted to make a name for herself but was embarrassed by the controversy surrounding the film and wanted her name withheld.[36] Exposure of the hoax did not ease public concern about the adult film industry or the possible existence of real 'snuff' films. Bill McCarthy, Professor of Criminal Justice and Sociology at the State University of New York, was a police sergeant in the public morals division of the NYPD at the time of the *Snuff* controversy and

33 Ibid: 191–92.
34 Carter Stevens directed *Collegiates* (1973) and *Lickety-Split* (1974) which initially brought him to the attention of the NYPD. A few years later, in the hysteria surrounding *Snuff*, the police wanted him to look at some 8mm loops and give his opinion. He pointed out the camera tricks used and assured the police that the reels were not snuff films. Ward, "S'nuff Said," *About Cult Film* online at http://www.aboutfilm.com/aboutcultfilm/features/snuff.html
35 "Morgenthau Finds Film Dismembering Was Indeed A Hoax," *New York Times* (10 March 1976): 41.
36 "Snuff star butchered only in her performance," Miami *News* (10 March 1976): 3A. Morgethau's investigation concluded that the final scene was shot in a West 29th Street studio. Lynch, "The Facts About the Snuff-Film Rumours," *Oui* (July 1976): 118. Numerous newspapers and magazines reported the results of Morgenthau's investigation, for example Jeff Blyth, "So after all the fuss, this 'murder' is a hoax — and that's official," *Screen International* (13 March 1976): 17; "Actress not 'snuffed out'" *Milwaukee Journal* (10 March 1976): 3, and "'Murder' in film called make believe," Chicago *Tribune* (10 March 1976): 5. The only personal information released was that the actress was twenty-six-years-old and had worked in summer stock and appeared in a few commercials. The 'victim', Tina Austin, was an aspiring actress who appeared in several exploitation films in the late 1970s. She had small roles in films like *Cocaine Cowboys* (Ulli Lommel, 1979), *The Exterminator* (James Glickenhaus, 1980) and *New York Nights* (1980) directed by Simon Nuchtern, who was responsible for filming the final scene of *Snuff*. Austin's acting career never took off and, ironically, her main cause for notoriety is as the mother of American glamour model Nicole 'Coco' Austin. According to Avedon Carole the woman who was allegedly murdered in *Snuff* did make public appearances and was interviewed by the media. Carol, "Snuff: Believing the Worst," in Assiter and Carol (Eds.), *Bad Girls and Dirty Pictures*: 128.

remembered that even after Morgenthau announced the finding of his investigation there was a "frenzy of public demand" calling for the police to infiltrate the porn industry and extinguish the trade in 'snuff' films.[37]

The film also had an important radicalising effect for feminists. Sexual violence was a persistent concern for all feminists and a few years before the release of *Snuff* Mary Daly coined the term 'gynocide' in *Beyond God the Father* (1973) to describe the sexual murder of women[38] — which militant feminist Andrea Dworkin expanded on in *Our Blood* (1976) to include "the systematic crippling, raping and/ or killing or women by men."[39] A few years after *Snuff* Robin Morgan condemned pornography for promulgating "rape, mutilation, and even murder as average sexual acts, depicting the normal man as a sadist and the healthy woman as a willing victim." She continued referring to a trend of "Brutality Chic" that had been embraced by everything from high-fashion magazines to department store window displays, where rock albums carried "gynocidal" images and "'snuff films' and child porn movies play in first-run [movie] houses." [40] Leah Fritz, a former employee of *Screw* magazine, initially considered adult sex films to be trivial until the release of *Snuff* when she changed her mind and came to view pornography as "nothing less than gynocidal propaganda."[41]

The mix of sex and violence was a prominent and potent piece of rhetoric for the feminists, especially Andrea Dworkin who made numerous speeches alleging personal experience of the subject. In October 1974 Dworkin participated in a 'speakout' on sexual issues in New York City (sponsored by NOW) with a controversial paper entitled "Renouncing Sexual Equality." When she was finished some members of the audience were left shaking and crying and Dworkin received a ten-minute ovation. In her speech she evoked pathos with her exaggerated allegations that male sexuality was dependent

---

37 McCarthy quoted in Alan Sverdlik, "The Snuff Movie Myth," New York *Post* (25 February 1999): 050.
38 Daly, *Beyond God the Father: Towards a Philosophy of Women's Liberation*: 73.
39 Dworkin, *Our Blood*: 16.
40 Robin Morgan, "Check It Out: Porn, No. But Free Speech, Yes," *New York Times* (24 March 1978): 27.
41 Judy Klemsrud, "Women, pornography, free speech: A fierce debate at NYU," *New York Times* (4 December 1978): D10.

on victimizing others.[42] In her essay "Pornography and Grief" (1978) Dworkin further expanded her claims, saying the "eroticization of murder is the essence of pornography,"[43] a farcical claim but one on which she based much of her ideology.

Even though Morgenthau identified the victim in *Snuff*, and the film had been exposed as a hoax in newspapers and trade journals, militant feminists continued to exploit her 'murder' as a rallying point to attack pornography. As a result of the protests by congressmen, feminists, film critics and outraged citizens who demonstrated against *Snuff*, the film grossed more than $300,000 in its first eight weeks at the National Theatre.[44] In March 1976 feminists in Monocle, New York, protested at the exhibition of *Snuff*, took their complaint to the District Attorney and an obscenity charge was filed against the theatre owner, Richard Dame. The case dragged on for twenty-one months, and was finally resolved when Dame publicly apologized to all women for showing *Snuff*.[45]

Militant feminists were not quick to celebrate the American bicentennial and Letty Cottin Pogrebin, an editor of *Ms.* Magazine, noted that after the Declaration of Independence in 1776 women were kept powerless. Ignoring his wife Abagail's advice to "Remember the Ladies" (in a letter dated 31 March 1776) John Adams , one of America's Founding Fathers, replied (14 April 1776), "I cannot but laugh ... We know better than to repeal our masculine system."[46] Pogrebin felt like a "wallflower at the bicentennial ball" alienated by "the whole masculine, militaristic flavour of the celebration." She noted the continuing inequality endured by women and called upon them to challenge the American Dream, claiming that since the Declaration women's suffering and exploitation had accelerated:"Even the sexual uses of women are getting more sinister. In addition to rape pornography and prostitution we now have 'snuff films,' presented as a real you-are-there slaughter of a woman hired to 'act' in the movie

---

42 Heidenery, *What Wild Ecstasy*: 112–113.
43 Andrea Dworkin, "Pornography and Grief (1978)" in Andrea Dworkin, *Letters From A Warzone: Writings 1976–1987*, Secker and Warburg, London, 1988: 22.
44 "Not Playing At A Theatre Near You," *Oui* (July 1976): 117.
45 LaBelle, "Snuff — The Ultimate in Woman Hating," in Radford and Russell (Ed.), *Femicide*: 192–93.
46 John and Abagail Adams quoted in Letty Cottin Pogrebin, "Sexism Rampant," *New York Times* (19 March 1976): 32.

— and this is presented as titillating." Pogrebin called upon women to celebrate the American Bicentennial by plotting the next American Revolution, "the one that frees the real silent majority: womankind."[47]

The most outspoken militant feminist of the era, Andrea Dworkin, first delivered her "Pornography: The New Terrorism" lecture at New York University Law School in early 1977, exploiting in it the myth of 'snuff' and making sensational accusations to characterize the whole pornography business. Connecting slavery, the Holocaust, and pornography, the lecture was a distorted tirade intended to be provocative. Pornography, Dworkin claimed, is an instrument of propaganda, a "glove that covers the fist in any reign of terror," and one that sanctioned and incited violence against women. After exploiting the imagery of American slavery and the Nazi concentration camps Dworkin conjured up a scene from her own twisted imagination, of "A woman, nearly naked, in a cell, chained, flesh ripped up from the whip, breasts mutilated by a knife: she is entertainment, the boy next-door's favourite fantasy, every man's pernicious right, every woman's potential fate."[48] Identifying the torture of women as sexually arousing entertainment for men she continued:

> Pornography is the propaganda of sexual fascism. Pornography is the propaganda of sexual terrorism. Images of women bound, bruised, and maimed on virtually every street corner, on every magazine rack, in every drug store, in movie house after movie house, on billboards, on posters pasted on walls, are death threats to the female population in rebellion. Female rebellion against male sexual authority, is now a reality in this country. The men, meeting rebellion with an escalation of terror, hang pictures of maimed female bodies in every public place.[49]

Using inflammatory accusations to challenge the idea that pornography was fun and that it reflected human sexual fantasies, Dworkin claimed "Real women are tied up, stretched, hanged, fucked,

---

47 Pogrebin, "Sexism Rampant," *New York Times* (19 March 1976): 32.
48 Dworkin, "Pornography: The New Terrorism (1977)," in Dworkin (Ed.), *Letters From A Warzone*: 199. Dworkin boasts that she gave the same speech on numerous college campuses, and that in every instance, in the aftermath of her appearance, students organised anti-obscenity protests.
49 Ibid: 201.

gang-banged, whipped, beaten, and [left] begging for more." In her imagination all pornographic films were documentary records of real abuse.[50] Prone to wild exaggeration, Dworkin distorted the content and availability of explicit sex films to draw attention to her divisive ideology. Using extreme imagery as a representative example, she generalised about the sex industry.

Discussing the subject of pornography Susan Brownmiller was asked "where do you draw the line?" to which she replied "I don't have to draw the line. But I can tell you that *Hustler* and 'snuff' are beyond it."[51] Beverly LaBelle, another militant feminist, described *Snuff* as a "pornographic film," and emphasised its symbolic significance by noting it was one of the first to provoke a strong reaction from radical feminists:

> It marked the turning point in our consciousness about the meaning behind the countless movies and magazines devoted to the naked female body. *Snuff* forced us to stop turning the other way each time we passed an X-rated movie house. It compelled us to take a long hard look at the pornography industry. The graphic bloodletting in *Snuff* finally made the misogyny of pornography a major feminist concern.[52]

One notable consequence was the establishment of Women Against Violence Against Women (WAVAW), which claimed to be "an activist organisation working to stop the gratuitous use of images of physical and sexual violence against women in mass media — and the real world." WAVAW aimed to do so through public education, consciousness-raising and mass consumer action. After seeing how successful WAVAW was, a number of prominent feminists, among them Gloria Steinem and Susan Brownmiller, met in New York City in the summer of 1977 to discuss forming a new feminist organisation dedicated to a campaign against 'violent pornography', and advocating censorship.[53]

Continuing to exploit concerns about violent pornography, Andrea

---

50 Dworkin, *Pornography: Men Possessing Women*: 201.
51 Brownmiller quoted in Molly Ivins, "Feminist leaders join anti-smut campaign despite reservations," *New York Times* (2 July 1977): 31.
52 LaBelle, "Snuff — The Ultimate in Woman Hating," in Radford and Russell (Ed.), *Femicide*: 190.
53 Smith, "Violent Pornography & the Women's Movement," *Civil Liberties Review* (January–February 1978): 50–53.

Dworkin tried to use the notoriety of *Snuff* to make a direct connection to real sex crimes in an essay called "A True and Commonplace Story" (1978) by telling two stories in parallel. She began by recounting the case of four women in Rochester, New York, who broke a window to tear down a poster advertising the "sadistic, pornographic" film *Snuff*. The women were arrested and charged with a felony and faced four years in jail, a punishment that Dworkin saw as "transparently more vendetta than justice."[54] To highlight the injustice she recounted another experience from December 1977 when she was flying to Rochester to appear at a benefit for the four women. Dworkin met a young feminist from her hometown whom she engaged in conversation. Subsequently the pair became friendly and met frequently; however, while she was attending college in New England someone attempted to rape the young woman and afterwards she became withdrawn and insecure. Dworkin used the story of the young woman and the feminist *Snuff* trial for two reasons: one was to emphasise the connection she claimed existed between cinematic violence and real sex crimes, the other was to point out the disparity in punishments for the feminists who faced four years in jail for breaking a window in contrast to the would-be rapist who was not punished, all of which highlighted the injustice and hypocrisy faced by women in society.

Amid the militant feminist rhetoric in the debate about sex crimes and violent pornography Robert K. Dornan, national spokesman for CDL, claimed in 1976 that downtown Akron (Ohio) was "probably hopeless" because of the proliferation of porn theatres and adult bookstores.[55] Dornan went to Akron to address Church Women United, and during his speech he decried the film ratings system as a "vicious, lying ripoff," condemning cinema for glorifying criminals and urged "decent citizens" to vote for candidates who campaigned on obscenity issues and advocated strict enforcement of anti-obscenity laws.[56] The escalating concern about sexual violence and widespread awareness of sex crimes, especially rape, made the issue open to manipulation for unscrupulous political gain. Alfred Regnery, son of right-wing publisher Henry Regnery and member of Young Americans for Freedom (YAF),

---

54 Dworkin, "A True and Commonplace Story (1978)," in Dworkin, *Letters From A Warzone*: 107.
55 "Smut Fighter Sees Akron 'Mired' In Porno Films, Publications," *Variety* (25 February 1976): 36.
56 Ibid.

and his wife Christine lived in Verona, just outside Madison, Wisconsin. At Halloween 1976, when Alfred was running for Dane County Attorney, his wife Christine reported that the family home had been broken into during the afternoon by two men, one black and one white. According to her story the men humiliated and tortured her while two of her children slept. She claimed to have been raped with a number of objects including cans of deodorant and hairspray before her assailants escaped unseen.

At the time Alfred Regnery's constituency, Dane County, was a hotbed of radicalism and he tried to manipulate the attack to claim that it was intended as a warning from political opponents to force him to withdraw as a candidate. However, when it became apparent that the police could not verify the basic facts of his wife's story they began to suspect that she had not been attacked. They also found a stash of hardcore pornography in the house that depicted sex acts very similar to those she claimed to have been subjected to by her assailants. Even her own husband had misgivings about the claims and came to believe that his wife's injuries were self-inflicted. Amid the controversy Regnery lost the election but his wife was not charged with filing a false police report because the new county attorney did not want to appear vindictive. Ironically, in 1978, Regnery moved to Washington with his family and joined the staff of right-wing Republican senator Paul Laxalt as a lobbyist for the Family Protection Act.[57]

Politicians exploited the emotive issue of sex crime, condemning it as the result of years of liberal excess and hoping to produce a conservative backlash. *Snuff* began as an insignificant exploitation film, intended to lure audiences to the cinema, but in doing so it became an integral part of a nationwide debate on pornography. To those who had not seen the film, *Snuff* epitomized the decline of traditional values and a nadir of decadence. As a consequence, across America militant feminists joined with political conservatives to condemn and protest.

---

57 Heidenry, *What Wild Ecstasy*: 241–243. See also "Al Regnery's Secret Life: The pathetic career of Reagan's juvenile justice chief," the *New Republic* (23 June 1986) online at http://www.tnr.com/article/politics/al-regnerys-secret-life

Chapter Ten

FROM SEA TO SHINING SEA

Nationwide Distribution of *Snuff*

DESPITE THE DISASTROUS FAILURE OF *SNUFF* IN INDIANAPOLIS, THE SUCCESS in New York ensured that there was enough commercial interest to make nationwide distribution viable. Also in Shackleton's favour was the uncoordinated and inconsistent official response to *Snuff* across local and state jurisdictions. Feminists from the National Organisation for Women (NOW) and Women Against Violence Against Women (WAVAW) complained that the film "advertises and advocates murder of women as sexually stimulating,"[1] but in many cases their protests simply provided Shackleton with more free publicity. Even though the film had been exposed as a hoax in *Variety,* the *New York Times*, and *Time*,[2] and by district attorneys Kelley (Indianapolis) and Morgenthau (New York), and despite the obvious absurdity of the distributors openly promoting a film of an actual on-screen murder, local authorities were not consistent in their actions and the protests that were organized often drew more attention to the film.

The controversy surrounding *Snuff* allowed officials in the twin cities of St. Paul and Minneapolis to come down hard on the exhibition of adult films.[3] During his successful election campaign in 1975 mayor Charles Stenvig emphasised the issue of pornography, promising to crack down on the sex industry, and Shackleton's film gave him the opportunity for which he was looking. *Snuff* was the first film to be prosecuted for two years by anti-obscenity activists in Minneapolis, but the exhibitors won the case and the authorities reluctantly permitted it to be exhibited.[4] The Minnesota Attorney General contemplated

---

1   Kerekes and Slater, *Killing for Culture*: 25.
2   "'Snuff' (Sex Murders) Film Now Thought Hoax From Argentina," *Variety* (17 December 1975): 4; Leonard, "Commentary: Cretin's Delight On Film," *New York Times* (27 February 1976): 21; "The Porno Plague," *Time* (5 April 1976): 50.
3   "'Snuff' Stirs Woe For Other Porno," *Variety* (3 March 1976): 26.
4   "Svenskas Fail To Stop Snuff," *Variety* (10 March 1976): 5.

prosecuting *Snuff* on the grounds of consumer fraud but declined, fearing that it would just provide more free publicity for the film. Exhibitors Ferris and Edward Alexander brought *Snuff* to the American Theatre in Minneapolis and advertised it as being "banned in St. Paul" to draw crowds. City officials sent vice squad officers to view the film twice to assess its content. Even though the final scene was obviously fake one vice officer, Richard Morrill, mystifyingly wrote in his report, "Everything in the final scene appeared to be in fact actually happening to the girl. The dismemberment of her body was so real it made me physically ill."[5]

As a consequence of exhibiting *Snuff* the Alexander brothers were directed by court order to show why the film, along with two other films they were exhibiting at the Rialto Theatre, *Sensations* (Alberto Ferro, 1975) and *Fantasy in Blue* (Roger Kramer, 1975), should *not* be held obscene — a reversal of the usual assumption of innocent until proven guilty. The two contentious pornographic films were quickly replaced with *Wet Wilderness* (Lee Cooper, 1975) and *Fantastic Voyeur* (Cooper Brothers, 1976) but *Snuff* remained at the American Theatre,[6] and the order against the Alexander brothers was later thrown out of court.[7]

In early April, municipal judge Neil Riley described the contents of *Snuff* as acts of "masochistic butchery" that "go beyond the First Amendment," and finding the film obscene he threatened to issue a seizure warrant if it appeared in Minneapolis again.[8] *Snuff* had already been playing for several weeks in Minneapolis, at the Alexanders American Theatre, but the engagement was terminated when the police department sought to confiscate the print. It reappeared at the Franklin Theatre a week later, but was taken off exhibition when the legal situation once again came into question.[9]

Nearby, in neighbouring St. Paul, city officials closed the Strand Theatre on 19 February, a day before *Snuff* was due to open. Kevin Van Feldt, the proprietor, felt that the shutdown was politically motivated because the municipal authorities objected to the exhibition of *Snuff*,

---

5 "'Snuff' Stirs Woe For Other Porno," *Variety* (3 March 1976): 26.
6 Ibid.
7 "Svenskas Fail To Stop Snuff," *Variety* (10 March 1976): 5.
8 "Snuff is Butchery," *Variety* (14 April 1976): 5.
9 Ibid.

and that if he had shown a family orientated film like *Snow White* there would not have been a problem. According to Van Feldt 150 people queued outside the cinema expecting to see the first performance of *Snuff*, and he still anticipated good business when his licence application was approved by the city council. However, aware of the conclusions reached by the FBI investigation, Lawrence Cohen, mayor of St. Paul, directed the city attorney to request that adverts for *Snuff* should clearly indicate that the murder was a theatrical re-enactment.[10] Upon reconsideration by the city council, Von Feldt's application for a licence was grudgingly approved and he immediately announced his intention to exhibit *Snuff* as originally planned.[11]

Lt. David Weida of the Minneapolis police department reflected on the situation created by *Snuff*, and the problem facing law enforcement, saying, "There's nothing to seize. It's not as bloody as *Jaws* and it's not as pornographic as movies they're showing at other theatres." Other officers who viewed the film agreed with Weida and reported the violence was no more severe than that found on TV westerns and, unimpressed with the obvious special effects, they at least acknowledged the promotional showmanship, describing it as a "side show ripoff." But the failure of municipal authorities to ban *Snuff* in the Twin Cities did not curb anti-obscenity campaigners who targeted all aspects of the sex industry, not just adult films.[12]

When *Snuff* arrived in Washington, D.C. Gary Arnold reviewed it for the Washington *Post*, noting the film "earned an undeserved notoriety on the basis of a calculatedly tasteless and devious ad campaign." Condemning it as "tacky, amateurish and fake," he pointed out that *Snuff*'s opening in Indianapolis had been a failure, and the admission price of $7.50 "absurd." He specifically attacked Shackleton's promotional campaign which was

> calculated to mislead morbidly curious or merely credulous segments of the press and public, [*Snuff*] has created so much advance distaste that papers in many cities, including Washington, have refused to run his ads. There's something peculiarly self-defeating about a shock

10 "'Snuff' Case in St. Paul," *Variety* (25 February 1976): 36.
11 "'Snuff' Stirs Woe For Other Porno," *Variety* (3 March 1976): 26.
12 "Svenskas Fail To Stop Snuff," *Variety* (10 March 1976): 5.

exploitation [campaign] so effective it scares away the mass advertising the bogeyman needs.[13]

George Will, conservative columnist for the Washington *Post*, used *Snuff* as a focus for wider social comment and criticism when he identified it as a "grotesque new outlet" for the "pornographic impulse." He took the opportunity to criticise the hypocrisy of the *New York Times* for *not* condemning the series of liberal Supreme Court obscenity decisions that "virtually obliterated all legally enforceable standards of public decency," and then complaining about finding itself in "the middle of the open sewer of pornography that mid-town Manhattan has become." However, he did acknowledge that the main body of *Snuff* was just a "mishmash of shootings and knifings and general mayhem," no worse than TV entertainment before the 9 pm watershed, and no worse than contemporary films such as *The Texas Chain Saw Massacre*.[14]

Additionally, Will used the film's notoriety and linked it to his bleak depiction of Times Square — as "the rotting core of the big apple" and (in the contemporary economic crisis) "home of the city's last growth industry, pornography" — to dramatize the perceived decline of American morality and traditional values. He condemned the moral decay in Times Square as representing a public policy failure which, "like so many liberal policies, was based on nothing more than naïve hope." In his opinion, "Some aspects of American life have become so vulgar that they can hardly be discussed without contributing to the coarsening of American life," and Times Square was such a place. Attributing a symbolic significance to the area, Will claimed a "new sliminess involving children and animals" was being manufactured that offended his moral standards, but in the climate of degeneracy "business is booming." Depicting Times Square as a place where a "pornography supermarket" shared the same building as a major bank, he evoked traditional clichés, claiming it was necessary to "Elbow your way through the dirty men in dirty raincoats in the crowded peepshows, and read the vivid descriptions of current fare."[15] Never

13 Gary Arnold, "More Hoot Than Horror," Washington *Post* (9 March 1976): B5.
14 George Will, "Naive Hopes and Real Decadence," Washington *Post* (28 March 1976): C7.
15 Ibid.

did Will question the social and economic realities that caused the area to become the focal point for the sex industry.

Like CDL and the militant feminists, Will emphasised extreme examples of pornography to suit his existing conservative and moralistic ideology rather than try to comprehend the broad spectrum of the sex industry. Not known for his in-depth knowledge of obscenity, he asserted that pornography was "relatively tame" in 1969,[16] and noted that liberal newspapers opposed censorship and justified a permissive attitude which led to a sharp decline in American values and beliefs. "The insensate pursuit of the urge to shock," Will quoted from the *New York Times*, "carried from one excess to a more abysmal one, is bound to achieve its own antidote in total boredom. When there is no lower depth to descend to, ennui will erase the problem."[17] He opposed that view, citing *Snuff* as the "lowest depth so far" but promising, "human ingenuity will find lower depths to conquer." Apparently ignorant of the Supreme Court decisions in *Miller* (1973), *Paris* (1973), *Hamling* (1974) and *Jenkins* (1974), Will warned his readers that they should:

> Think about this. The path of American law has been steadily downhill to this point: Today pornographers need fear no law, except, perhaps, consumer protection laws which conceivably could righteously insist that films promising a real murder must show a real murder.[18]

Trying to provoke outrage, Will intentionally misrepresented the state of obscenity legislation and American society, distorting the debate but legitimising his reactionary ideology.

In Las Vegas, meanwhile, attorney Carl Lovell had been in contact with the Indianapolis police department and was determined to use Nevada's consumer protection laws against *Snuff* if the promoters tried to claim the murder was real. The El Portal Theatre initially cancelled plans to exhibit *Snuff* due to pressure from city officials, but later rescheduled the film. Lowell pointed out that he did not intend to ban the film unless the murders were real: "I don't want to get trapped

16 Ibid.
17 "Beyond the (Garbage) Pale," *New York Times* (1 April 1969): 46. quoted in Will, "Naive Hopes and Real Decadence," *Washington Post* (28 March 1976): C7. Despite Will's claims the original article adopts a critical conservative tone and does not endorse pornography in any way.
18 Will, "Naive Hopes and Real Decadence," *Washington Post* (28 March 1976): C7.

221

by their public relations department by doing exactly what they want at our expense. They would say it was banned in Las Vegas, giving Las Vegas a bad name."[19] As if that was possible.

Moving westward *Snuff* opened in Los Angeles on 17 March, hosted by Mann Theatres who had already exhibited the film in several other cities. LA *Times* film critic Kevin Thomas was unimpressed with *Snuff* but also lamented that because the film was badly done and cheaply made "it's hard to work up sympathy for those who pay out money hoping to see the filming of an actual murder."[20] Despite a critical mauling in virtually every city, during the first three weeks in New York *Snuff* took $155,000 and was making a lot of money for Mann Theatres at the box office in a number of other places across America. However, an unlikely situation developed in Los Angeles, where both feminists *and* members of the AFAA picketed performances (but for very different reasons).[21]

Where militant feminists identified *Snuff* as a rallying point in their campaign against explicit sex films, the AFAA protested against *Snuff* because they realised it was bad for the developing adult film industry. The media quickly picked up on the story and Dave Friedman offered a $25,000 reward to anyone who could produce evidence that performers were being killed to make X-rated films. In the subsequent thirty years the money was not claimed, and no murder charges were brought.[22] To perpetuate the controversy however, according to William Rotsler, some "unscrupulous" film producers, not members of the AFAA, began a whispering campaign to give further credence to the 'snuff' rumours.[23]

Larry Gleason, a representative of Mann Theatres, was willing to believe that Monarch Releasing orchestrated the cinema pickets: "It's not unusual — any place we've played has had pickets. They may very well have arranged a lot of it. It's a well-promoted movie. The more press it gets, the happier everyone gets." AFAA members denied being involved with Monarch as a publicity stunt, and they condemned *Snuff*

19 "'Snuff' Unreels in Vegas Subject to Many Limits," *Variety* (25 February 1976): 36.
20 Thomas, "Controversial 'Snuff' Opens Run," *LA Times* (19 March 1976) IV: 22.
21 "Snuff Biz Goes When Pickets Go," *Variety* (24 March 1976): 36.
22 Hebditch, *Porn Gold*: 338.
23 Rotsler, "Down With Snuff!" *Adam Film World* (August 1976): 21.

as "the greatest rip off since Watergate."[24] Kevin Thomas in the LA *Times* was not fooled by the publicity surrounding the film and asserted that "It is most patently a fake" with a "nauseating" final scene. Even though there was "minimal sex and nudity," Thomas claimed that to call the film disgusting is to "indulge in extravagant understatement." While he dismissed *Snuff* as "trash" he made the very pertinent observation that "Unfortunately, it's precisely the kind of picture that threatens freedom of expression on the screen by stirring up the proponents of censorship."[25] Completely lacking artistic value *Snuff* was pure exploitation, offensive to conservatives and feminists and a liability to the business plans of the AFAA.

In the midst of protests against *Snuff*, Raymond Gauer again contributed to the controversy he started and was quoted in *Adam Film World* (April 1976) acknowledging he had not seen a 'snuff' film personally, adding: "my undercover guy, though he's never seen one, has talked to enough people to be convinced they exist. Another source is convinced they exist in quantity and that they've been screened in the very 'In' circles in Hollywood."[26] As usual Gauer's comments offered no empirical proof, just hearsay and speculation designed to reassert his original unfounded allegations.

Mainstream interest in 'snuff' was such that two contemporary TV series aired episodes that exploited the panic. In one episode of *The Rookies* entitled 'Blue Movie, Blue Death' (aired 24 February 1976), a young actress is blackmailed into making pornographic films. As a consequence of an undercover operation to investigate a company making explicit sex films it is discovered to be a mafia operation, responsible for the deaths of some of its performers. For dramatic effect, in the course of the episode the audience sees the expression of terror and hears the screams of an actress as she is stabbed to death. A few weeks later, in an episode of *Police Story* entitled 'Open City' (aired 12 March 1976), the making of 'snuff' films is presented as an established fact and two vice squad officers, Daley (Hugh O'Brien) and Gentry (Christopher Stone), come into conflict with a city attorney who is reluctant to investigate violent pornography. The

24 Snuff Biz Goes When Pickets Go," *Variety* (24 March 1976): 36.
25 Thomas, "Controversial 'Snuff' Opens Run," *LA Times* (19 March 1976) IV: 22.
26 Gauer quoted in Hammond, "Are Snuff Films For Real?" *Adam Film World* (April 1976): 84.

police officers are investigating the activities of a group of ruthless East Coast pornographers who are prepared to do whatever is necessary to protect themselves, even if it means kidnapping and murdering a young actress — but thanks to Daley and Gentry she is saved and the criminals apprehended.[27] Ann Myers, a former softcore actress turned producer of adult films, was outraged by the episode: "I love sex films, I *love* sex films. We don't like being lumped with violence films in the mind of the public. *Police Story* makes the public believe we are hand-in-glove with these snuff films. Sex is beautiful but violence is not."[28] The *Police Story* episode, according to AFAA president Vince Miranda, prompted his organisation's picket of *Snuff*.[29]

When a cinema in San Diego advertised *Snuff*, local feminist groups gathered outside about one hour before the first showing, chanting and passing out leaflets. Several TV stations sent camera crews to cover the forty-strong protest but, despite this, or maybe because of it, the theatre manager said that due to all the publicity he would be showing the film for an additional week. However, the following night the playbill was changed and *Snuff* was not shown again. The feminist protesters also paid a visit to the San Diego *Union* newspaper, where they were assured that the newspaper would not carry any future advertisements for *Snuff*. A similar protest by feminists in Colorado around the same time was also successful.[30]

Snuff was booked into the Roosevelt Theatre in Chicago by the Plitt Theatre chain, and was due to open on 12 March, but was cancelled after an editorial in the Chicago *Sun-Times* condemned the film and challenged the film industry at large:

> Neither Plitt nor anyone else ought to show the film here at all. We don't want official censorship. We do want responsible standards of taste and humanity both by Plitt and the community at large. The press agents say the public wants films like *Snuff*. But why play to that perverted taste — or encourage it to begin with?[31]

27 "Not Playing At A Theatre Near You," *Oui* (July 1976): 117.
28 Myers quoted in Rotsler, "Down With Snuff!" *Adam Film World* (August 1976): 21.
29 Ibid.
30 LaBelle, "Snuff — The Ultimate in Woman Hating," in Radford and Russell (Ed.), *Femicide*: 190–91.
31 Chicago *Sun-Times* quoted in "Plitt Cancels Snuff Editorial; Sun-Times," *Variety* (10 March

Later editions of the paper commended Plitt for the decision to cancel screenings but continued to condemn filmmakers, distributors and exhibitors for "pandering to a demand for violence and sadism they themselves have created" and tried to encourage public demonstrations against similar films.[32] Shackleton was surprised, but undaunted by Plitt's decision, describing it as their loss, and noting mild problems in the places where *Snuff* took big box office receipts. While he acknowledged the management of the film chain were entitled to their opinion he added, "I didn't think Plitt would knuckle under like this."[33]

In contrast to the response and success in New York City *Snuff* completed an eleven-day engagement in Boston in March 1976 at a first-run Sack Theatres, a prestigious chain specialising in major Hollywood productions, where it was a complete flop.[34] The decision by Sack to show an exploitation film like *Snuff* reflected the contemporary social and economic conditions. Late in 1974, amidst financial troubles, A. Alan Friedberg replaced Ben Sack as head of the cinema chain and by December the next year revenues were up by eighty per cent despite a fall in operating profits in cinema chains across America due to "spiralling costs, lack of product [new films], and general economic factors."[35] To emphasise the lack of new films Friedberg predicted that Disney's *Snow White and the Seven Dwarfs* (David Hand, 1937) would be the biggest box office film for Christmas 1975, and in December the Sack Theatres were showing *Gone With The Wind* (Victor Fleming, 1939) and *2001: A Space Odyssey* (Stanley Kubrick, 1968). Under Friedberg the Sack Theatres revised their advertising and presentation to exhibit commercial films and attract a wider audience,[36] and *Snuff* was part of the plan to revitalise the business.

1976): 5.

32 Chicago *Sun-Times* quoted in ibid.

33 "Plitt Cancels Snuff Editorial; Sun-Times," *Variety* (10 March 1976): 5. After protests Chicago's largest theatre chain decided not to show *Snuff*. Gene Siskel, "The public snuffs chains chance for a killing," Chicago *Tribune* (14 March 1976) section 6: E2.

34 Birge and Maslin, "Getting Snuffed in Boston," *Film Comment* (May–June 1976): 35.

35 "Ben Sack Chain, One Year Later, Up 80%; Need More Product," *Variety* (10 December 1975): 4.

36 Ibid. Sack opened up a number of multi-screen cinemas and planned to replace two downtown theatres that were to be demolished as part of an urban development project with new cinemas.

Sack Theatres, in conjunction with Allan Shackleton, held two press conferences to publicize the film in Boston. The usual guest list of established media was invited, city and suburban dailies and weeklies, two alternative weeklies and some of the more popular radio stations. However, also invited were representatives from a range of radical publications such as the feminist magazine *Mother Courage*, *Gay Community News*, the *BU Free Press* college paper, and a number of representatives from underground radio stations.[37] At the conference Shackleton seemed determined to provoke outrage by making comments about the 'Dyke Tactics Squad' whom he claimed had protested outside screenings of *Snuff* in Philadelphia: "I never knew real fear until I saw them. Mean. Nasty. Wearing rhinestoned jackets." When any of the representatives expressed their anger during the meeting it was suggested they should organize a protest outside the theatre.[38] The press conferences backfired. No groups picketed the cinema in Boston, and the film did not receive significant coverage in the Boston newspapers apart from a few early reviews, undermining Shackleton's plan. An *ad hoc* group of feminist activists and some women working in the news media organized a successful publicity blackout. Ellen Davis, of the Gay Action Media, noted, "We knew something was fishy about that press conference. People came away asking, 'Why is Sack buying the radical community a free drink?'"[39] The group wanted *Snuff* out of Boston, and the quickest and most effective way to ensure this happened was to make sure it did not get any publicity. In the course of the eleven-day media blackout activists were dissuaded from picketing the cinema or using other "quasi-terrorist tactics." Davis estimates that no more than a dozen people attended each screening and, unable to generate interest through sensational media reports and protests, the exhibitors of *Snuff* had to try to draw an audience from sexploitation patrons, but as in Indianapolis, when the raincoat brigade saw the film they did not like it.[40]

Whilst *Snuff* was still being exhibited in Times Square it was removed from exhibition in New London (Connecticut) after protests.[41]

37 Birge and Maslin, "Getting Snuffed in Boston," *Film Comment* (May–June 1976): 35.
38 Ibid.
39 Ibid: 35, 63.
40 Ibid: 63.
41 "'Snuff' snuffed; Garde withdraws controversial film," the *Day* (New London) (15 March

It was also banned by the Maryland State Censor Board (MCSB), a milestone decision as MSCB had previously only banned films on "porno sexual" grounds, whereas *Snuff* was banned for "psychotic brutality." Predictably, the last five minutes of the film were the source of contention for the censors but Barry Glasser from Monarch argued that to delete the final scene would be "suicide at the box office" because "It's the last five minutes when the film gets its novelty."[42] When MSCB and Monarch were unable to resolve the situation, *Snuff* was banned in the state.

Opening at the Fox Theatre in Detroit on 17 March *Snuff* drew a good audience,[43] taking $50,000 in the first week, but in San Francisco the response was poor and it took only $7,700 in the first week. The reception in other cities was equally erratic. Opening in ten theatres in Los Angeles *Snuff* took a total of $31,800, and in Orange County the exhibition was cancelled after bomb threats.[44] At Rutger's University an Ad Hoc Committee Against Sexism was set up to protest about *Snuff* and it claimed to have influenced the local cinema to stop showing the film by picketing and complaining to the mayor.[45] Having his film banned in Baltimore, Wilmington (Delaware) and Orange County (California),[46] did little to hinder Shackleton's ambitions; *Snuff* was still a box office success in New York, Philadelphia and Los Angeles, amongst other cities.[47]

In the immediate aftermath of the *Snuff* protests militant feminists turned their attention to other exploitation films such as *The Incredible Torture Show* (Joel Reed, 1976), which they claimed promoted violence towards women, and Don Smith of the LAPD remembered that after the 'snuff' hysteria everyone believed that they had seen a 'snuff' film and police departments had to watch suspected films to see if they were real or not. He recalled the loop *Vampira* had to be taken to the coroner's office for an expert opinion, but after one look at the torture

1976): 15.
42 "Maryland Bans Snuff; Distrib Won't Cut The Gory Final Sequence," *Variety* (3 March 1976): 26.
43 "'Snuff' Rides Rumour," *Variety* (10 March 1976): 5.
44 "Not Playing At A Theatre Near You," *Oui* (July 1976): 117.
45 David Astor, "Rutgers Group Fights Pornography," *New York Times* (16 May 1976) section 11: 17.
46 "The Porno Plague," *Time* (5 April 1976): 50.
47 Birge and Maslin, "Getting Snuffed in Boston," *Film Comment* (May–June 1976): 35.

scene the coroner said the intestines removed from the 'murdered' girl were actually from a cow.[48]

Although the film was a blatant fake, the marketing campaign behind *Snuff* capitalised on public fears and curiosity. Shackleton managed to successfully exploit public interest in Charles Manson and the distorted claims made by CDL, and he profited from the outrage generated by militant feminists. In doing so his observation that 'pickets sell tickets' proved accurate. The promotional campaign was successful but met with mixed results across America.

The notoriety of 'snuff' meant mainstream as well as exploitation media sought to take advantage of public curiosity, and the term 'snuff' entered the mainstream vocabulary as a kind of violent pornographic film in which the actress is actually murdered for the audience's entertainment. Building on the controversy, the British distributors of *Snuff* emphasised the outrage caused in America by the film, boasting that it was "The original atrocity shot and banned in New York." They added the outrageous advertising line "the actors and actresses who dedicated their lives to making this film were never seen or heard from again."[49] The exaggerated allegations begun by Raymond Gauer had spriralled out of his control and become an international sensation.

48 Smith quoted in McDowell, "Movies To Die For," San Francisco *Chronicle* (7 August 1994) This World section: 9.
49 British distributors never released *Snuff* theatrically in the UK, but it was available for a time on videocassette.

Chapter Eleven

THE MAN WHO SAW REAL 'SNUFF'

Larry Buchanan and the Exploitation of 'Snuff' Hysteria

AFTER THE FINANCIAL SUCCESS OF *SNUFF* A NUMBER OF OTHER EXPLOITATION films sought to make use of the film's notoriety. The German 'white coater' *Confessions of a Blue Movie Star* (Andrzej Kostenko and Karl Martine, 1974) was re-released in 1976 subtitled *The Evolution of Snuff* — with extra footage inserted to make it more shocking and exploit the controversy surrounding *Snuff*. Originally a documentary about the making of a pornographic film in Germany, *Confessions of a Blue Movie Star* presented some interesting social commentary, the narrator repeatedly pointing out the economic incentives for the performers, many of whom were struggling students looking to make some extra money, but the sex content was tame compared to contemporary hardcore sex films.

Mainly composed of predictable footage of performers being cast and the film being made accompanied by a narrated voice-over, the filmmakers also document the death of Claudia Fielers, a twenty-three-year-old medical student who performs in the film. Committing suicide by poisoning mid-production, Fieler's death gave the documentary a new direction and, when her body was taken back to her hometown for burial, an opportunity to reflect on the effects that modern society and the adult film business had on her life. But more cynically, after Fielers' death the director cast another woman to fill her role so he could complete his film.

A brief segment was inserted at the start of the reissued version of the film, shifting the context of the original documentary and introducing the idea of 'snuff' films. An inarticulate Roman Polanski is interviewed and discusses rumours of 'snuff' films saying that, when sexual taboos on screen were broken, some people thought 'What will we do next?' In his opinion, "obviously the next step is to kill somebody for real." Polanski continues, "such films wouldn't be made if there were no market for them. I think that film only reflects what the world, what society is about. I think that art reflects ... is a mirror of the world."[1] The film also ends with Polanski emphasising the power of cinema: "I think a camera can be as dangerous in the hands of a filmmaker as a bazooka." The screen goes black and the film is over. After a few seconds the screen changes to red and the narrator's voice returns, announcing:

> This documentary would not be complete without showing the following clips. These films were received only moments after the actual documentary had been completed. They are presently under investigation and could possibly be used as evidence in a criminal complaint. We feel, however, they should be shown. Although they are horrendous they serve to complete our evolution of snuff. The exhibition of these film clips should not be construed to suggest or deny any act or intent on the part of the people involved which might amount to the commission of a crime.

Additional footage of an interview with a 'snuff' director who disguises his appearance by wearing a brown paper bag over his head follows. Dressed in a denim jacket, with an iron cross hanging from one pocket, it is obviously Ken Brocker, introduced earlier in *Confessions of a Blue Movie Star: The Evolution of Snuff* as a twenty-five-year-old rock singer and fiancé of one of the performers in the porn film. Broad shouldered and stocky, he is physically similar to Krug (David Hess) from *Last House on the Left* but, ironically, because of the bag he also resembles 'The Unknown Comic', a regular guest on the long-running *Gong Show*, who performed with a brown paper bag covering his head.

The interview with the 'snuff' film director is inter-cut with very short, but graphically violent, clips of Sadie (Jeramie Rain) from *Last House on the Left* stabbing and dismembering Phylis (Lucy Grantham), and then playing with the viscera. This footage was added by Atlas International. A distribution company handling the original *Confessions*

1 Polanski's involvement in the film is emphasised despite his minimal interview material obviously having been culled from another source. The 1989 release of *Confessions of a Blue Movie Star* documentary by Spring Video goes even further, claiming that the documentary not only stars Polanski but that the screenplay was also written by him.

of a Blue Movie Star in Germany, Atlas also had distribution rights for *Last House on the Left*.[2] While the original *Confessions of a Blue Movie Star* documentary emphasised the financial motivation of participants in porn films, the 'snuff' director explicitly says he did *not* do it for the money. Instead, he claims that he and the other participants were stoned, mentally and physically numb, when they filmed their 'snuff' movie, and that it was part of a ritual. Exactly what sort of 'ritual' is not explained, but the connection between rumours of Manson, ritual murder and Satanism is explicit. There is no mention of pornography by the 'snuff' director, his sole focus is on violence.

The Zapruder footage of John F. Kennedy's assassination, and its constant repetition on television, is cited by the 'snuff' director as an example of real murder on screen being used for public entertainment. He also mentions a well-known story about an 'Italian guy', Gualtiero Jacopetti, who, while making *Africa Addio* (1966), reportedly paid a soldier to delay an execution so it could be filmed, and that he also recorded his cameraman being eaten by lions. Similarly the 'snuff' director referred to another unnamed Mondo film where a cameraman is shown being eaten by sharks. But his vague examples are of filmed deaths or executions, not of pornographic films that climax in murder. The scene concludes with the interviewer pointing out that the deaths in the Mondo films were accidental whereas the 'snuff' films were "cold-blooded," to which the director replies, "Not any more cold-blooded than the public wanting to see them." Concluding with an ominous onscreen warning — "The End. And the end of all humanity." — the obviously faked additional segment tacked onto *Confessions of a Blue Movie Star* did nothing to substantiate the existence of 'snuff' films or to dispel the myth; it simply exploited its existing notoriety.

After *Miller* and the 'snuff' rumours, other anti-obscenity activists followed CDL's example and used exaggerated claims about violent and extreme pornography to raise funds. *Time* magazine described the Rev. Billy James Hargis, well known as an anti-obscenity crusader, and leader of the Christian Crusade for Christian Morality, as an "ultra-right Fundamentalist."[3] In January 1976 his Tulsa-based organisation sent out fundraising letters that exploited the backlash against pornography:

2   Szulkin, *Wes Craven's Last House on the Left* (revised edition): 161–162.
3   "The Sins of Billy James," *Time* (16 February 1976): 54.

Dear Friend:

After years of shock and sorrow over the decline of morals and decency in our country, I thought I had become shock proof ... Can you believe it: complete colour films of sexual acts between women and men, including homosexual acts, using your children. Unless you and I act today ... our children and our children's children will be exposed to perversion so sinister that good will become evil and evil will become good.[4]

Focusing on homosexuality and paedophilia, the distorted claims were trying to exploit public fears for the benefit of Hargis, who was in a dire financial situation, and facing a series of serious revelations about his personal conduct.

Hargis founded the Christian Crusade in 1950 to promote his far-right politics and theology and, as the organisation developed, he used radio and TV shows along with the *Christian Crusade Weekly* to promote his ideas. Publishing books such as *Is the School House the Proper Place to Teach Raw Sex?* (1968), which sold 250,000 copies, Hargis promoted an ideology similar to that of CDL. Married with four children, he championed conservative family values, homophobia, vitriolic anti-communism, and a reactionary Christian philosophy. The crowning achievement in Hargis' career was the foundation of the American Christian College in 1970 but, ironically, hypocrisy and sexual misconduct proved to be his downfall.

In October 1974 revelations of sexual misconduct against Hargis surfaced. They began as a consequence of accusations made by a young couple that Hargis had wed in September 1974. While on honeymoon they discovered that they had *both* slept with Hargis, and later more students came forward with similar stories. In total five students at the American Christian College, four of them male, claimed to have had sexual relations with Hargis. He justified the homosexual acts to the young men using the Old Testament relationship between David and Jonathan as a parallel, and threatened to blacklist the youths if they told anyone about what had happened. When confronted with the claims Hargis admitted his guilt.[5] Damaged by the revelations his

4   Letter quoted in ibid.
5   Ibid. See also Edward E. Plowman, "The Rise and Fall of Bill James," *Christianity Today* (27 February 1976): 42–43. Even though he had admitted his guilt Hargis only resigned after the

organisation was desperate to raise funds, hence the distorted claims about the porn business. Similarly CDL, to maintain the anti-obscenity crusade at a national level, had to make sensational allegations to attract enough donations to maintain their campaigns and pay the Viguerie Corporation.

A few months after *Snuff* was released, Jay Lynch published an investigative article entitled "The facts about the snuff-film rumours" in *Oui* (July 1976) that further debunked the claims made by Shackleton and conservative moralists. In the course of researching his article Lynch made dozens of phone calls and talked to many people, but was unable to locate a real 'snuff' film to report on first-hand. Many people told him that they knew someone who had seen a 'snuff' film but when he investigated further the primary sources denied all knowledge. He found no movies or first-hand accounts, just a lot of rumours.[6] The only instance where Lynch was able to locate someone who claimed to have seen a 'snuff' film first hand was when he was following up on information from Robert K. Dornan, a national spokesman for CDL from 1973 to 1976, providing an insight into the providence of CDL information and the veracity of their sources.

Dornan told Lynch that an unreleased film, *Goodbye, Norma Jean*, which purported to depict Marilyn Monroe's early days in Hollywood, featured a scene of a party held in the 1940s where the guests watch a 'snuff' film. An incident that Dornan claimed was based on fact.[7] *Goodbye, Norma Jean* was written, directed and produced by Larry Buchanan, who specialized in exploitation films which he advertised using promotional techniques derived from exploitation king Kroger Babb.[8]

$72,000 insurance policy, taken out on his life by the Christian Crusade, was cashed in and given to him along with a $24,000 annual stipend. He then publicly announced his intention to retire to his farm in the Ozarks because of ill health. However, without the fundraising abilities of Hargis the College soon ran into financial difficulties and faced bankruptcy, mainly because Hargis had retained control of the mailing list from which seventy per cent of the organisation's funds were generated. Early in 1975 he tried to return to the College but in 1976 Hargis was exposed by *Time* for his sexual misconduct. The College could not survive the scandal and closed in 1977.

6 Lynch, "The Facts About the Snuff-Film Rumours," *Oui* (July 1976): 70.

7 Ibid: 86. Dornan appeared in films such as *The Starfighters* (Will Zens, 1964), *To The Shore of Hell* (Will Zens, 1966) and *Hell on Wheels* (Will Zens, 1967) during his brief acting career. From 1965 to 1976 he produced public affairs TV shows and hosted *The Robert K. Dornan Show*. In 1973 Dornan ran unsuccessfully as mayor of LA but was elected Representative 1977–1983. In 1982 he ran for the Senate.

8 His other films include *The Naked Witch* (1961), *Free, White and 21* (1962), *Under Age* (1964),

When Lynch interviewed Buchanan for his article, *Goodbye, Norma Jean* was still unreleased. Buchanan claimed the film was based on his own experiences and furthermore that he had seen a black and white 'snuff' film in the 1940s, one that had been shot on a beach under a pier in daylight featuring two nude "frighteningly underage" girls who stab a wino to death and possibly also castrate him. With further questioning Buchanan's story became progressively more absurd. When asked if there were any ritual elements in the 1940s 'snuff' film, Buchanan said that after the two girls had killed the man they mixed their blood as the sun set and said "We will not copulate with man or beast." Whilst the film was silent Buchanan claimed he had recognized the murder as part of a Society for Cutting Up Men (SCUM) ritual — the same SCUM to which Valerie Solanos belonged, who would eventually shoot and critically wound Andy Warhol — and that the organisation was operating as a vast lesbian underground with chapters in New York, Los Angeles, San Antonio and Chicago. According to Buchanan SCUM began as a gang of teenage girls in San Antonio (Texas), that used blowtorches to castrate and murder middle-aged men at Padre Island in the 1940s, he also informed Lynch that he owned a film property called *SCUM* that he began shooting in the early 1960s but abandoned.[9]

This was not the only one of Buchanan's films to feaure sadistic sexual murder carried out by women on men. Amongst Buchanan's other cinematic credits was a script called *The Cod Squad* about a group of women who had been raped. Realising that the police were doing nothing about the high rates of sex crime and child abuse, the women become vigilantes and castrate offenders who escape legal punishment.[10] Buchanan's script drew on traditional exploitation movie subject matter as well as contemporary concern about sex crimes. Between 1972 and 1973 the number of reported rapes in New York City rose by thirty-eight per cent and similar increases were reported in other cities across America. Women organized rape support groups

---

The Eye Creatures (1965), *High Yellow* (1965), *In the Year 2889* (1966), *Curse of the Swamp Creature* (1966), *Mars Needs Women* (1966), *It's Alive* (1968), *Hell Raiders* (1968), *A Bullet For Pretty Boy* (1970) and *Mistress of the Apes* (1981).

9   Lynch, "The Facts About the Snuff-Film Rumours," *Oui* (July 1976). The film described by Buchanan bears some similarity to the decapitation murders reported by Dornan in his role as CDL spokesman.

10 Gilpin, "The Larry Buchanan Interview (Part 4)," *Bijou Flix* online at http://www.bijoucafe. com/innerviews/buchanan_interview4.htm

as a response in numerous cities and in LA militant women did form an anti-rape squad promising to track down rapists. Once identified they would shave the offenders' heads, cover them with dye and photograph them for posters whilst holding signs that read 'This Man Rapes Women.'[11] However, there were no reports of women murdering men in feminist rituals. The plot synopsis of *The Cod Squad* given by Buchanan sounds very like the description given of the 1940s 'snuff' film which he claimed to have seen, and also a reworking of his *SCUM* screenplay. Although Buchanan claimed to have seen a 'snuff' film in Hollywood, he would not give any more information about exactly where it was screened or who else was present, and he did not report it to the police, believing they would not be interested. His motives for asserting that he had seen a 'snuff' film were questionable and his unwillingness to provide more information undermined his position further. Despite the obviously dubious nature of Buchanan's claims Dornan was willing to accept them as fact without question.

Buchanan also claimed to have seen a second 'snuff' film, this time in the early 1970s, a grainy, badly duplicated film of two girls killing a man, but he could not make out the performers' faces and found it hard to discern what was happening. Because of the condition of the film Buchanan speculated it had been duplicated a dozen times, suggesting that a considerable number of copies existed. But if the quality of the print was so bad,[12] it raises questions about how he could vouch for the film's authenticity.

Another unsubstantiated story Buchanan told Jay Lynch was that after the success of *Mondo Cane* (Gualtiero Jacopetti, 1962) several imitations were quickly produced. For one project a crew was sent to the Andes looking for human sacrifices, but when they were unable to find the real thing as a substitute they bought several children from a poor family and slaughtered them in front of the camera. Predictably Buchanan could not remember the name of the film but noted that early screenings caused so much uproar that the negative and a handful of existing prints were destroyed.[13] In a much later interview Buchanan claimed to have seen a third 'snuff' film in Rio de Janeiro

11   "The Rape Wave," *Newsweek* (29 January 1973): 29.
12   Lynch, "The Facts About the Snuff-Film Rumours," *Oui* (July 1976): 86, 117.
13   Ibid: 86.

where children were bought from their parents and killed.[14] But all his descriptions of 'snuff' movies sound more like the product of his own feverish imagination than specialist sex films.

Buchanan appears to have been emulating Shackleton and numerous other earlier exploitation filmmakers by shamelessly making claims to draw attention to his own film projects, and to make them seem topical, more relevant, and better informed than they actually were. For Buchanan 'snuff' was simply cinematic footage of a real murder, often ritualistic, without any explicit sexual content, and therefore more closely related to urban legend and Mondo sensationalism than pornographic excess. His stories were far-fetched and unsubstantiated, and his motives dubious, but Robert Dornan accepted and repeated Buchanan's claims, adding to their credibility and disseminating them to a wider audience who wanted to believe the worst about society.[15]

When *Texas Chain Saw Massacre* was re-issued in 1976 in the wake of *Snuff*, Stephen Koch described it in *Harper's* as a "vile little piece of sickening crap"; without any redeeming features, it was "simultaneously unpleasant and unimportant."[16] He continued:

> It is a particularly foul item in the currently developing hardcore pornography of murder, fundamentally a simple exploitation film designed to milk a few more bucks out of the throng of shuffling wretches who still gather, every other seat, in those dank caverns for the scab-picking of the human spirit which have become so visible in the worst sections of the central cities.

Inaccurately claiming that *Texas Chain Saw Massacre* was a failure on its first release, that it was not even popular with traditional exploitation audiences, he asserted it had been "rescued" by a branch of "film intelligentsia" — a familiar conservative scapegoat. In fact the Museum of Modern Art had purchased a print of the film for its permanent collection, prompting a commercial re-release and a

---

14   Gilpin, "The Larry Buchanan Innerview (Part 4)," *Bijou Flix* online at http://www.bijoucafe. com/innerviews/buchanan_interview4.htm

15   In the *Celluloid Apocalypse* documentary (Perry Martin 2006) film director John Carpenter reports that he was once offered an opportunity to see what was purported to be a 'snuff' movie, but he declined because he was not interested.

16   Koch, "Fashions in Pornography," *Harper's Magazine* (November 1976): 108, 110.

screening at the Cannes Film Festival.[17]

Barely able to contain his vitriol, Koch declared *Texas Chain Saw Massacre* to be "just another American success story, the ancient tale of exploitation, hype, and the besotted pornographic mind receiving their reward." He compared the "virulent social pathology" in the film to the Manson Family because of the blood cult and the obsession with violence. Claiming that it was best discussed alongside 'snuff' movies because both are "something close to the absolute degradation of the artistic imagination," Koch identified a "sickening logic" behind *Texas Chain Saw Massacre* and 'snuff' films, where "simple intensity" is granted a pre-eminent role. He compared it to André Breton's observation that a simple surrealist act would be to walk into a crowded street and fire a revolver at random into the crowd, and concluded by saying, "the new pornography of murder acquires a prestige because people actually think its hysteria has something to do with artistic liberation."[18] Koch's superficial comparison of *Texas Chain Saw Massacre* to 'snuff' films had no other purpose than to justify his reactionary anti-intellectual rant.

In Europe filmmakers took note of the 'snuff' controversy and quickly put together low-budget films to exploit the American box office hits. After the success of Just Jaeckin's softcore *Emmanuelle* (1974) came a series of Italian films directed by the prolific Joe D'Amato, featuring the 'Black Emanuelle', Laura Gemser, which sought to profit from the reputation and popularity of their predecessor. D'Amato was aware of rumours about 'snuff' films before making *Emmanuelle in America* (1976) and he shot his faked 'snuff' footage on 35mm and intentionally scratched the film to make it look like it was shot on 8mm.[19] However, from the outset D'Amato constructed a morality tale of sex and violence that juxtaposed conventional sexual imagery alongside graphic violence and presented 'snuff' as a sexual novelty for the wealthy.

D'Amato reinvented the character of the hedonist Emmanuelle as

---

17 Ibid: 108.
18 Ibid: 108, 110.
19 *Joe D'Amato and the Black Emanuelles* documentary (Roger A. Fratter, 2002). 'Joe D'Amato' is one of many pseudonyms used by the prolific director Aristede Massaccesi. In other interviews Massaccesi claimed that the 'snuff' footage was shot on Super 8mm, scratched for effect, and then blown up to 35mm so it would not look like the rest of the film.

Emanuelle (single 'm'), an investigative reporter whose job enabled her to travel around the world covering stories for her newspaper. At the start of the film Tony (Guilio Bianchi), a young man intent on murder, abducts Emanuelle, whom he condemns as evil for stimulating the basest human instincts. He complains that there is no morality left and says he wants to teach the world a lesson. A naïve virgin, he blames all of the disasters in the twentieth century on sex; he believes he can redeem his model girlfriend Janet (Stefania Niocilli) with Emanuelle's death, and then they can wed. Trying to calm Tony, Emanuelle starts to give him a blowjob, causing him to drop his gun and run from the car shouting about how much he likes it. His violent urges reflect his repressed sexual desires and once released from them Tony marries his girlfriend Janet, after which all he thinks about is sex. Tony is obviously a satire on conventional reactionary morality that represses human instinct and condemns sex while promoting violence as a solution to problems

Emanuelle's first assignment calls for her to infiltrate the harem of a wealthy businessman, who is also an illegal weapons dealer. Eric Van Deeren (Lars Bloch) has gathered twelve women, each one named for a sign of the zodiac, to service his sexual desires. Van Deeren hates to lose and thinks anything can be bought at the market value, a representation of the American business creed, and with his women he believes that if he pays enough he can experience any kind of eroticism. Unimpressed, Emanuelle mocks him, saying that he is afraid of women and has never known love, adding that he has always had to buy the things he wanted, a continuing theme throughout the film.

Her next assignment takes her to the Caribbean to infiltrate a stud farm, the Chez Fabien Singles Club, a retreat that caters to the sex fantasies of ugly rich women. While at the club Emanuelle stumbles upon a female guest watching a jerky and faded film of soldiers torturing, mutilating, raping and murdering a number of females, the first of several scenes relating to 'snuff' in *Emanuelle in America*. One woman in the film has her buttocks branded while another has her breasts blowtorched, beaten and disfigured. Some of the women are strangled while others are shot in the head and it is clear the film, documenting sexual abuse and murder, is part of the wealthy woman's fantasy. Emanuelle takes pictures of the film with a hidden camera as evidence to use in her report.

Returning to New York, Emanuelle identifies one of the women in the film from a newspaper story as a prostitute thought to be the victim of a revenge killing. Sceptical, her editor asks, "Are you sure it wasn't just a run-of-the-mill pornographic film?" but Emanuelle is convinced the torture and murder is real and she wants to investigate further. An informant tells Emanuelle that the people behind the 'snuff' loops are powerful and wealthy, and that in Washington, D.C. she will find a man, a member of Congress, "who will wallow in this filth and protect it." The Congressman (Roger Browne) in question is an arrogant right-wing conservative who Emanuelle flatters, telling him how intelligent and handsome he is, to win his confidence. His insular and sanctimonious ideology is evident when he complains, "everybody in this country is concerned with what the world thinks of us. When actually we should feel great pride in what we've achieved, for this is the greatest country in the world." And he is sure many people agree with his views, not unlike Nixon and his 'silent majority'.

A flag-waving hawk, the Congressman criticizes the youth of American because "Their heads are stuffed full of crazy ideas and a lot of nonsense." His self-righteous answer to the problem is simple — "What we really need now is another war" — even though America had only withdrawn from the carnage in Vietnam a few years earlier. He adds, "Then they'd come back with their heads screwed on straight." When asked about those who do not come back he pompously and callously replies "the ones who don't will have given some meaning to their lives, sacrificing themselves for their country." He, however, will not be risking his life for his country because he is too old and too wealthy to fight in the pointless war he craves.

The Congressman is quickly established as a hypocrite who does not live up to the traditional values he endorses. Married with a family, he maintains a bachelor pad in Washington, decorated with erotic art that emphasises violent sexual imagery, for entertaining his girlfriends. For the sake of her investigation Emanuelle allows the Congressman, who looks a bit like Hugh Hefner, to seduce her and asks him to show her a new experience because she wants to try something "more stimulating ... far out, forbidden." The first porn loop he shows her is a conventional grainy black and white scene featuring two women and a man. He then promises to show an unimpressed Emanuelle something "really strong," and selects another short and jumpy film.

The scratched and faded images depict similar torture and mutilation as the film at the stud farm with women being flogged and then impaled onto huge wooden dildos. While Emanuelle watches the film the Congressman is more interested in his latest female conquest. The film is over quickly and continuing her act Emanuelle enthuses, "Those pictures were — so real! As if it were really happening! It was all so awful ... but what a turn-on." Coyly she confides that sometimes she dreams of living through something as cruel as torture and murder; "It's the raw horror that excites me." The Congressman tells her that she could "make that dream come true, because things like that really do happen." Emanuelle pretends to be sceptical, dismissing the images as the secret fantasies of a middle-class American girl. But he says he will make her experience her secret fantasies.

After drugging Emanuelle the Congressman takes her to a private plane that flies them to an undisclosed destination. Upon landing she is put into a military jeep and driven through dense jungle to an isolated building. (Because of the jungle location it seems that the plane has taken her to Central or South America, evoking the tabloid newspaper reports in 1975 and the marketing campaign for *Snuff*.) Inside the building Emanuelle sees the torture chamber used in both the film from the stud farm and the one she saw at the Congressman's apartment. She witnesses more women being tortured, an open-ended funnel is inserted into the mouth of a woman and boiling oil poured in; another woman, spread-eagled, has her chest mutilated and her nipples sliced off with a knife.

The special effects used in the torture scenes *are* realistic, and all the more shocking because they appear in the middle of a softcore pornographic film.[20]

20 The scene in *Emmanuelle in America* with the woman being forced to drink a hot liquid through a horn is reminiscent of an illustration used in *Witchcraft Through the Ages* (Benjamin Christensen, 1922) where a tortured soul in a Hieronymus Bosch painting is forced to drink brimstone through a funnel. This image is very similar to the torture device for the 'cleansing of the soul' used in medieval Europe; it was believed that the accused could be cleansed by forcing them to drink boiling oil, water or coals. Cleansing of the soul was carried out as a precursor to other acts of torture where the accused would be punished for their sins. Many of the tortures suffered by the women in the 'snuff' scenes have religious significance. In

In *Porn Gold* (1988), David Hebditch and Nick Anning noted contemporary rumours that documentary footage of torture, filmed by the perpetrators themselves, in General Augusto Pinochet's Chile and Jörge Videla's Argentina, had been incorporated into a commercial film: "There are strong grounds for believing that some very brief sequences of this extremely gruesome material were incorporated into a scene in one of the films in the unending *Emmanuelle* series, which are made in Europe."[21] The remark was obviously intended as a reference to *Emanuelle in America*. A rumour circulated in the 1970s that anti-obscenity activists had film footage recording the rape and torture of male and female civilians by teams of specially trained soldiers. Different reports identified the abuses as being perpetrated alternatively in Argentina, Chile, Honduras, Guatemala or Columbia. No films were ever presented to substantiate the claims and finally, in September 1996, a spokesman for Amnesty International in New York acknowledged that no member of the organisation's staff had ever seen such footage.[22]

In *Emanuelle in America*, Emanuelle is not sure if the torture scene was all a dream, or a nightmare. The Congressman adds to the uncertainty by telling her it was neither, just LSD powder, and that the images were a reflection of her own twisted imagination. Whilst none of it was real he says it was "beautiful all the same." Her question makes the scene seem ambiguous: was it real or did she fantasise it all? However, whilst Emanuelle is supposed to be drugged she remains awake and alert, and if it was just a drug-induced hallucination how would the Congressman know it was 'beautiful'?

---

the *Hortus Delciarum* illuminated manuscript (1167–1185) the tortures of Hell are graphically depicted and these closely correspond to the mutilations carried out upon the women in D'Amato's snuff footage, as do the punishments of the medieval witch-hunts described by Heinrich Kramer and James Sprenger in *Malleus Maleficarum* (1486). Women were more likely to be identified as witches and numerous commentators identify that witch-hunting could easily be seen as woman-hunting. Christina Larner, *Enemies of God*, Chatto and Windus, London, 1981; 100. See also Hans Peter Broedel, *The Malleus Maleficarum and the Construction of Witchcraft*, Manchester University Press, Manchester, 2003; Marianne Hester, *Lewd Women and Wicked Witches*, Routledge, London, 1992; Deborah Willis, *Malevolent Nurture*, Cornell University Press, New York, 1995; Robin Briggs, *Witches and Neighbours: The Social and Cultural Context of European Witchcraft*, second edition, Blackwell, Oxford, 2002: 224–249.

21 Hebditch, *Porn Gold*: 337–338.
22 Heidenry, *What Wild Ecstasy*: 322.

Returning to New York, Emanuelle is convinced that it was all a nightmare, and that she has failed for the first time in her career. However, when her editor develops the film in her mini-camera there are shockingly graphic pictures of women being tortured by men in military fatigues, proving conclusively that what she saw was real. Just as she starts to feel that she has produced worthwhile investigative journalism, the editor tells her that the owner of the newspaper has given specific instructions that no article based on Emanuelle's photographs are to be published, the first time he had given such an order. Trying to placate her, the editor tells her to write the article anyway, as a compromise, and put it into the newspaper's archive, and he promises to publish it at the first opportunity. Emanuelle is unwilling to concede because she is angry knowing that she could have been killed, and disgusted because other girls will be murdered in the torture films, making the newspaper an accomplice to murder if it does not publicise and condemn the atrocities. Frustrated by the situation, Emanuelle quits her job and leaves New York with her boyfriend Bill (Riccardo Salvino). Escaping to an idyllic island they quickly find that decadent Western society has caught up with them in the form of a film crew, who corrupt the primitive natives and force Bill and Emanuelle to run off to avoid being hired as extras.

The 'snuff' movies depicted in *Emanuelle in America* are a comment on state sanctioned violence rather than a condemnation of the adult film industry, and the torture imagery used by D'Amato connects contemporary South American dictatorships to medieval religious persecution. The pseudo-documentary styles used in films such as *Emanuelle in America*, and a few years later *Cannibal Holocaust* (Ruggero Deodato, 1980), exploited public awareness of the 'snuff' hysteria for their own benefit and presented such realistic graphic scenes of violence that the respective directors were forced to prove they had not filmed real murders.[23] However, learning from the

23 Petley, "'Snuffed Out': Nightmares in a Trading Standards Officer's Brain," in Mendik and Harper (Ed.), *Unruly Pleasures: The Cult Film and Its Critics*: 207. It is alleged that *Emanuelle in America* inspired David Cronenberg to make *Videodrome* (1983). D'Amato continued to mix graphic violence and hardcore sex in *Emanuelle and the Last Cannibals* (1977), *Erotic Nights of the Living Dead* (1980) and *Porno Holocaust* (1981). For *Buried Alive* (1979) he was accused of using a real corpse in an autopsy scene instead of special effects and despite being debunked rumours persist that some other horror films, such as *El Jorbado de la morgue* (Javier Agguire, 1972) and *Der Todesking* (Jörg Buttgereit, 1990), used real corpses to improve special effects

mistakes made by Allan Shackleton, *Emanuelle in America* ends with the disclaimer that "the events and characters portrayed in this film are imaginary and any reference to actual people or events is purely casual." Furthermore, one of the actresses in the 'snuff' scenes, the woman who has her breasts cut off, sued Joe D'Amato and forty members of the crew claiming the experience was too brutal and realistic, and that she had been traumatized. As a consequence of her legal action D'Amato's passport was confiscated for five years, meaning he could not leave Italy until he paid her compensation.[24]

Seeing the potential profit, other filmmakers incorporated references to 'snuff' into their marketing campaigns or in actual films. An Italian made film that had previously been released in America as *The Slasher is the Sex Maniac* was subsequently re-edited and re-titled *Penetration* (William Mishkin, 1976) to profit from the notoriety of *Snuff* and the protests about violent pornography. Posters advertised it as "The Ultimate X Crime," one which was "unbelievably explicit! ... graphically violent! A Double turn-on!" In the original, Inspector Capuana (Farley Granger) is a cop trailing a killer, but when re-edited he is hunting for women who are having affairs because they are the victims of a murderer. This created an opportunity to insert additional hardcore porn footage of Kim Pope, Tina Russell and Harry Reems to spice up the film. An obscure Brazilian melodrama, *Snuff — Vitimas do Prazer* [aka 'Snuff — Victims of Pleasure'] (Claudio Cunha, 1977), also told a story about unscrupulous film producers who plan to film the murder of an actress. In order to exploit the popularity of the American *Ilsa* films and the notoriety of 'snuff', Jess Franco's *Greta, the Mad Butcher* was re-titled and released as *Ilsa, the Wicked Warden* (Jess Franco, 1977). In a South American asylum that is run like a concentration camp by chief warden Greta del Pino (Dyanne Thorne) a regime of humiliation and sexual abuse is implemented. Inmates are tortured and mutilated for her amusement and at the film's climax the inmates rebel and corner their tormentor. Catching her unarmed they attack del Pino and, using only their teeth, swarm over her like wild animals tearing her apart. As she dies Dr Regio (Peter Falk), one of her henchmen, films her brutal murder from a hidden room with a look of satisfaction.

---

scenes.
24 *Joe D'Amato and the Black Emanuelles* documentary (Roger A. Fratter, 2002)

One film that was directly influenced by Ed Sanders' book *The Family* and the rumours of 'snuff' films was *Last House on Dead End Street* (Roger Watkins, 1977). Roger Watkins was working as a cameraman at a TV station in 1972 when he read, and became fascinated by, the book, and as a consequence wanted to make a film about the 'snuff' films described in it. The film was actually made in 1973 under the title *The Cuckoo Clocks of Hell*,[25] well before the outrage caused by *Snuff*, but because of legal problems it was not released. For years the film was so obscure that many people who had not seen it denied its existence, but for others who viewed it the film's atmospheric and unsettling tone made it a cult classic. In *Sleazoid Express* Bill Landis and Michelle Clifford harshly condemned *Last House on Dead End Street's* fans, claiming that over time the film had

> developed into a Rosetta Stone for the hardboiled clan of narcissistic misfits who call themselves nihilists. They masturbate to the words of Charles Manson and Anton LaVey; they play-act at Darwinism but are a sexually inept, frustrated crowd. Born followers drawn to negativity and hate, their only turn-on is tragedy, chaos and suffering — though not their own, of course. That'd hurt. Many of these sub-morons like believing that *Last House* is an actual snuff movie because it is filled with a cast of unknowns and made by an anonymous director.[26]

Set in a bleak and foreboding contemporary America, the characters are on the periphery of the sex industry but struggling in the exploitative culture. In *Last House on Dead End Street* the pornography is not revolutionary, nor does it contain any social commentary, it is just a mediocre and tawdry novelty for the wealthy. Jim Palmer (Edward Pixley) meets up with Steve (Steve Sweet) who is under pressure from "certain people" to deliver interesting porn loops. Palmer complains, "The business isn't what it used to be ... Too much competition ... people's tastes have become awfully hard to satisfy," but he is reminded that it

25 "Cuckoo Clocks of Hell: An Interview with Roger Watkins director of cult classic *Last House On Dead End Street*," *Headpress* (No.23, June 2002): 98, 104.
26 Landis and Clifford, *Sleazoid Express*: 149. 'Richard Mahler' was another pseudonym used by Roger Watkins when he made porn films, such as *Her Name Was Lisa* (1979), *Pink Ladies* (1980), *Cosmopolitan Girls* (1981), *Midnight Heat* (1982), *Corruption* (1984), *American Babylon* (1984) and *Decadence* (1988).

is his job to satisfy the customer's desires. Steve represents a group of wealthy clients, rich men in New York City with nothing else to do but watch porn all day. They have become jaded by normal pornography and are looking for something new and unusual. Unimpressed by Palmer's wares, Steve says "I want action, angles, something different that nobody's done before." Ironically the conversation takes place while one of the sex parties that Jim and Nancy Palmer (Nancy Vrooman) host is taking place next door. Nancy is the main entertainment and for her star turn she wears blackface and is whipped by a hunchback (Ken Rouse) in front of her guests, whose responses range from sexual arousal to hysterical laughter. While his wife is being humiliated Palmer waits in another room and conducts his business with Steve.

The protagonist in *Last House on Dead End Street*, Terry Hawkins (Roger Watkins), is a petty criminal just released from serving a year in jail; as a consequence he is bitter and nihilistic and wants revenge on society. Unable to sell stag films that he has made because "nobody's interested in sex anymore," he has to find a new niche in the film market, leading him to make his own 'snuff' films in an old abandoned building. Viewers of Hawkins' films are impressed by their realism, unaware that they look like authentic murders because they *are* real. For Hawkins 'snuff' is an act of revenge on society and his films chronicle the torture and sexual humiliation of those he despises. His films are brutal and ruthless, but they reflect his alienation from society rather than being erotic and arousing. The mixture of sex and violence, presented in a gritty *vérité* style, won *Last House on Dead End Street* fans but also attracted harsh criticism, earning the film cult status.

Concern about graphic sex and violence resurfaced again with *I Spit On Your Grave* (Meir Zarchi, 1978), a film about Jennifer (Camille Keaton), a young writer who escapes to the country for solitude so she can work on her book. Passing through a small town near to the house she has rented she meets a number of local men, the same men who later rape her and leave her for dead. Their actions are callous and ruthless, and after Jennifer is raped by three of the men a fourth beats her up. The rape scenes are not shown graphically, nor are they depicted in an erotic manner — furthermore, there are extended scenes detailing the aftereffects of rape, emphasising the pain and injury Jennifer suffers. Following the rape and assault in Jennifer's house the perpetrators send Matthew (Richard Pace), a mentally backward delivery boy, to kill her so she cannot report the crime. Unable to commit the deed, Matthew smears some of her blood onto the knife instead and pretends to have carried out their orders.

Dressed in black, contrasting sharply with the brilliant white of the church interior, Jennifer goes to ask God for forgiveness before she takes revenge on her attackers. Ordering groceries from the local store, which Matthew has to deliver, Jennifer begins to implement her plan. Matthew is nervous beforehand, frightened of what awaits him, but Jennifer calms him and lures him to a clearing beside the river, only to hang him. Next she drives to the gas station where Johnny (Eron Tabor), a married man with two children who was the first to rape her, serves her. Taking him to a deserted area Jennifer pulls a gun and in a panic he tries to claim that the rape was her fault, that she provoked the attack because of the way she was dressed. Pretending to be convinced by his argument she takes him home for a bath, cuts his penis off and locks him in the bathroom to bleed to death. Later Jennifer burns his body and clothes in the furnace. The last two rednecks, Stanley (Anthony Nichols) and Andy (Gunther Kleeman), are killed in the river. One is dispatched with an axe and the other is cut up by the outboard motor of the boat, completing her plan for revenge.

Film critics Gene Siskel and Roger Ebert[27] published damning reviews in the Chicago *Sun-Times* and *Tribune*, before launching a wider attack on *I Spit On Your Grave*. Ebert condemned the film as "garbage," "reprehensible" and "vile," arguing that it lacked "grace, humour, or even simple narrative skill." In his opinion "Its skeleton of a plot existed only as an excuse for a series of violent scenes in which a woman was first ravaged by a pack of four demented men, and then took her vengeance against them." He claimed it was the most disturbing cinematic experience he had seen in more than twelve years as a critic,[28] and Siskel filmed a piece for CBS news in which he stood outside the United Artists Theatre in Chicago with a TV crew and described the film to customers entering.

27 Roger Ebert wrote the screenplays for Russ Meyer's *Beyond the Valley of the Dolls* (1970), *Up!* (1976) and *Beneath the Valley of the Ultra-Vixens* (1979). The violent climax of *Beyond the Valley of the Dolls* is based on the Manson murders, and in *Up!* there are two rape scenes.
28 Ebert, "Why Movie Audiences Aren't Safe Any More," *American Film* (March 1981): 54.

In a 1980 episode of the film review show *Sneak Preview* devoted to 'women-in-danger' films, Gene Siskel noted his belief that the increase of violence against women in films

> has something to do with the women's movement in America in the last decade. I think that these films are some sort of primordial response by some very sick people saying 'Get back in your place women!' The women in these films are typically portrayed as independent, as sexual, as enjoying life. And the killer, typically — not all the time but most often — is a man who is sexually frustrated with these new aggressive women, and so he strikes back at them. He throws knives at them. He can't deal with them. He cuts them up, he kills them.[29]

But none of these claims could be made about *I Spit On Your Grave*, which reversed many of the traditional gender roles. Roger Ebert's campaign only helped publicise the film and in retrospect Meir Zarchi noted "It was good for me, good publicity; it sells more movie tickets and it brought the film to the attention of a lot of people."[30] This was another protest that backfired, drawing more attention to the film rather than condemning it to obscurity.

The theme of 'snuff' films received its highest profile treatment in *Hardcore* (Paul Schrader, 1978). In the film Jake VanDorn (George C. Scott), a member of the Dutch Reformed denomination — strict Calvinists from Grand Rapids, Michigan — is forced to go in search of his runaway daughter Kristen (Ilah Davis). VanDorn first hires Andy Mast (Peter Boyle), a private detective, and then teams up with Niki (Season Hubley), a young prostitute, to aid him in his search. The only lead produced by Mast's investigation is a porn loop called 'Slave of Love' and when VanDorn watches the film in a seedy adult theatre he is initially uncomfortable seeing his daughter nude and becomes progressively more emotional when she has sex with two men. Finally distraught and crying, he shouts for the film to be stopped.

---

29 Ibid. The specific films mentioned included *Prom Night* (Paul Lynch, 1980), *Don't Go In The House* (Joseph Ellison, 1980), *The Howling* (Joe Dante, 1980), *Terror Train* (Roger Spottiswoode, 1980), *The Boogeyman* (Ulli Lommel, 1980), *He Knows You're Alone* (Armand Mastroianni, 1981), *Motel Hell* (Kevin Connor, 1980), *Silent Scream* (Alan Gibson, 1980) and, ironically, *I Spit On Your Grave* (Meir Zarchi, 1978).
30 Zarchi quoted in Balun, *Horror Holocaust*: 23.

Ironically, porn star Marilyn Chambers auditioned for the role of VanDorn's daughter in *Hardcore*, but the casting director told her "You don't look like a porno queen. You look too clean and wholesome."[31] The film was also semi-autobiographical for director Paul Schrader who came from Grand Rapids and grew up in a strict Calvinist family. However, according to John Milius, Schrader

> was this character who had fallen from his Calvinist grace, and was really enjoying his time in hell, sampling every part of it. He loved perversion, but all sexuality in some way was a failure for him. One night, when he was making *Hardcore*, I noticed his wrists were marked. He explained, 'I went to Mistress Vicky and she hung me up and cuffed me. I could only take it for three minutes.' Like he wasn't a true pervert. He couldn't take it for half an hour like a real-man pervert. The same thing with being gay, he failed at that too, couldn't get it up for the boys.[32]

VanDorn's quest to find his daughter takes him out of the conservative religious community he is familiar with and on a journey into mainstream America. It is no accident that Mast repeatedly refers to VanDorn as 'Pilgrim'. His feelings enshrined in religious dogma, VanDorn makes it clear on several occasions that he does not care about mainstream America, or anything outside his own insular community. Waiting in an airport VanDorn explains the TULIP doctrine that is central to his religious beliefs to Niki. 'T' stands for 'Total Depravity', a bleak assessment of human nature that understands original sin means all men are totally evil and incapable of good, an idea that Niki playfully tells him represents "negative moral attitudes." The rest of his dogma is no more humane. 'U' refers to the idea of 'Unconditional Election' whereby God is understood to have chosen a certain number of people to be saved and 'L' is 'Limited Atonement', meaning only a specified number of people will be atoned and permitted to go to Heaven. Emphasising the idea of predestination 'I' denotes the 'Irresistible Grace' of God that cannot be resisted or denied, and 'P' is for 'Perseverance of the Saints', which asserts that once you are in Grace you cannot fall from the numbers of the elect. Embracing this

31 Hubner, *Bottom Feeders*: 306.
32 Biskind, *Easy Riders, Raging Bulls*: 382–383.

elitist ideology unquestioningly, VanDorn believes that his destiny has been decided from the start of time. He is committed to a belief in the omniscience of God; however, while he is sure of his fate most of humanity is doomed.

Immersed in the sex industry, VanDorn's strict traditional values are challenged and in response he condemns the culture around him: "It's this culture based on sex. Sold on sex. Magazines. Music. TV. Buy this because of sex. Use that because of sex. Kids, they think it is normal. They think they're supposed to talk dirty." Pertinent observations but never does he question his beliefs or acknowledge sex is a natural part of human life; he even tells Niki that he does not think it is an important part of life.

VanDorn's quest leads him to search for an enigmatic figure named Ratan (Marc Alaimo) whom he believes is keeping his daughter against her will. When questioned Andy Mast is evasive about the identity and whereabouts of Ratan and his description is more like that of a mythical figure or a bogeyman than a real person. Catering for his customers' desires, he could provide slaves or child prostitutes, or arrange to have people raped or murdered. Niki's summary is more succinct when she says Ratan "deals in pain." He is an entrepreneur in a free market satisfying public demand by selling services to people who can pay his price. The economic system at the core of American society is based on supply and demand and *Hardcore* shows how far Ratan will go to make money.

At one point VanDorn pays $100 to see a screening of an exclusive film in a small smoke filled room above a brothel. While it is never referred to as a 'snuff' film, it is intended to be pornographic and does culminate in murder. Including VanDorn there are only three people in the audience and they do not communicate with each other in any way, nor do they even look at each other. The short film they see is made in black and white without sound, but Tod (Gary Rand Graham), Ratan's business associate, plays an audiotape of Mexican music to accompany it. There is no nudity or graphic sex in the film, and it is obviously intended for people with very specialized tastes who are willing to pay a lot of money. Totally devoid of the graphic sexual activity prevalent in contemporary pornography, there is not even a hint of softcore nudity; the audience for the film are people who see violence as more erotic than sex, their jaded tastes placated by watching the suffering of others.

The 'snuff' film shows a young girl dressed in a mask and black leather boots sitting on a bed, a traditional establishing shot for many pornographic loops, with a Chicano boy standing close by. Since Ratan and Tod have just returned from Tijuana it is assumed that this is where the film was made. The boy chains the girl's ankles to the end of the bed and then stands back as Ratan, dressed in a white suit, enters the scene. He immediately stabs the boy in the stomach and, after removing the girl's mask, slits her throat. As she sees the knife and realises what is about to happen the girl screams in terror. Everything in the film takes place in one room and is captured by one camera, and since Ratan is committing the murder it is assumed that Tod is the cameraman. Incensed by the film and fearing for Kristen's safety, VanDorn realises he needs to find Ratan and save his daughter. After locating Tod in a brothel and beating him viciously VanDorn learns the whereabouts of Ratan, and when he arrives at the El Matador bar he easily identifies his quarry by the same white suit worn in the 'snuff' film. VanDorn is injured in the confrontation but in a panic Ratan tries to escape, only to be shot dead by Andy Mast outside the bar.

Schrader used the idea of 'snuff' to develop a wider social critique, but many people chose to see the film as a further acknowledgement that real 'snuff' movies must exist in the corrupt and depraved adult film business. In *Hardcore*, similar to *Last House on Dead End Street*, 'snuff' is an outrageous form of pornography catering to specialized interests, but the emphasis is placed on murder for entertainment and the explicitly sexual component stressed by CDL is understated. Ratan embodies a ruthless extreme of capitalist economics, and when he is shot it initially appears that the foe has been vanquished and the evil symbolically eradicated, leaving VanDorn the triumphant hero. However, *Hardcore* subverts the happy ending by demonstrating that it is VanDorn's moralistic ideology and the inarticulate and repressed society as a whole that need to be challenged. The quest comes to an end not with the death of Ratan but when VanDorn is finally reunited with his daughter in the basement of the bar.

Rather than run to her father and saviour, Kristen pulls away, frightened that he will hit her and when cornered, she tells him she wanted to leave Grand Rapids and no one made her do anything against her will. Kristen wanted to escape from the life she had in Grand Rapids because she felt her father did not care about her: "I didn't fit into your goddamned world. I wasn't pretty or good enough for you. You never approved of any of my friends. You drove them all away! I'm with people who love me now. You robbed my life." Unprepared for such a reunion VanDorn breaks down and admits he never really knew how to show his love for her, no one ever showed him how, and his "damnable pride" got in the way. In an ironic reversal of roles at the end of his quest he has to ask his daughter to take him home. His behaviour, and self-righteous belief in his own salvation, drove his daughter away from him. Trawling through the sexual underworld, *Hardcore* provides more social critique than sexual thrills and constructs an indictment of reactionary religious values similar to those held by Billy James Hargis, CDL and other anti-obscenity crusaders.

"Vida es Muerte"

Chapter Twelve

HOLY GRAIL OF PORNOGRAPHY

The Aftermath of the 'Snuff' Hysteria

AFTER SEEING THE PREMIERE OF *SNUFF* IN 1976 JOURNALIST JAY LYNCH WENT back to Chicago to update the information he had gathered and prepare to write an article for *Oui* magazine. He contacted the LAPD and was told by Lloyd Martin of the administrative vice unit, "To my knowledge, there is no snuff movie investigation being conducted by the Los Angeles Police Department — and if such an investigation were in progress I certainly would know about it." At the same time Lynch tried to contact Joseph Horman, the New York police officer frequently quoted in tabloid newspapers, but was told that the detective was on extended leave in LA for two months. Ironically, Horman was away making a movie,[1] an appropriate place for a man of his talents. For Lynch the investigation came to a dead end. Shackleton's film *Snuff* was obviously a fake, no real 'snuff' films could be located, and no law enforcement agencies were actively engaged in investigating 'snuff' films. It had become obvious that the spectre of 'snuff' was simply a rhetorical tool used by anti-obscenity crusaders, conservative moralists and militant feminists to serve their ideological interests in a bitter cultural war.

In the mid 1970s the outrageous Larry Flynt replaced Russ Meyer and Hugh Hefner as Charles Keating's nemesis. The arrival of *Hustler* magazine in 1975 challenged *Playboy's* middle-class pretensions to sophistication; "The last remnant of the centrefold's beleaguered immodesty was ripped away with the arrival of *Hustler*, a monumentally lowbrow magazine which offered its readers a gynaecologist's eye view

---

1   Lynch, "The Facts About the Snuff-Film Rumours," *Oui* (July 1976): 118. Joseph Horman led a crackdown on organized crime at a time when it was infiltrating the porn business in the early 1970s and quickly rose through the ranks of the NYPD. His experience of the criminals and his knowledge of the pornography business meant that he would have been well placed to hear rumours circulating about actual 'snuff' movies being made or sold. But William Sherman's 1980 book *Times Square,* about Horman and his time working in the vice department of the NYPD, does not mention snuff at all. In October 1975 Horman, by then a Detective-Sergeant, requested a transfer out of the Organized Crime Control Bureau.

of the nude."[2] For many people life would never be the same again, especially not for Charles Keating.

In July 1976, amidst the *Snuff* hysteria, *Hustler* caused public outrage by commemorating the nation's bicentennial by publishing a cover photo of a woman's groin barely covered by a skimpy stars and stripes bikini bottom with a glimpse of pubic hair. This was not the image conservatives wanted to use to promote 200 years of nationhood. The same month Larry Flynt was indicted in Cincinnati, Keating's hometown, for pandering, obscenity and organized crime and faced a possible $10,000 fine and twenty-five years in jail. The trial began in February 1977 before Judge William Morrissey who, along with both prosecuting attorneys, Simon Leis Jr. and Fred Catolano, was a conservative Catholic.[3] Leis was a close associate of Keating and when previously, in May 1972, Flynt had been charged with discharging a firearm within Cincinnati city limits Leis prosecuted the case. Basing the prosecution case on Flynt's lack of character Leis got a conviction, even though the evidence exonerated Flynt.[4]

'Organized crime' was a very serious charge to face in Ohio. The law was enacted to combat Mafia activities, but it was so loosely phrased it could be applied to *any* group of five or more people who conspired to participate in *any* illegal activity. Flynt was charged along with Al Van Schaik (production manager), Jimmy Flynt (Larry's brother) and Althea Leasure, with *Hustler* magazine cited as the fifth conspirator! Paradoxically, even though Althea, Jimmy and Al were acquitted, Larry Flynt was found guilty on all counts, fined $11,000 and sentenced to serve between seven and twenty-five years in jail, the maximum sentence. In his autobiography Flynt asked, quite pertinently, if the others were acquitted with whom did he conspire? Undeterred, Flynt appealed and his conviction was overturned.[5] The conviction was, however, a symbolic achievement for anti-obscenity crusaders who could claim an initial victory and then later condemn the 'liberal' courts when the decision was reversed.

Charles Keating and his associate Simon Leis (as played by James

2 Miller, *Bunny: The Real Story of Playboy*: 226.
3 Flynt, *An Unseemly Man*: 134.
4 Ibid: 124.
5 Ibid: 127, 154–155.

Cromwell and James Carville) appear in the dramatization *The People vs. Larry Flynt* (Milos Foreman, 1996), instigating criminal prosecutions against Larry Flynt (Woody Harrelson). After acquittal on organised crime charges Flynt addresses a rally of Americans For A Free Press, an organisation Flynt personally funded, and observes the hypocrisy within American society:

> Murder is illegal. But you take a picture of somebody committing a murder that puts you one the cover of *Newsweek*, you might even win a Pulitzer prize. And yet sex is legal. Everybody's doin' it, or everybody wants to be doin' it. Yet you take a picture of two people in the act of sex or take a picture of a woman's naked body and they'll put you in jail.

Here was a double standard that showed American society evidently valued violence more than intimacy. He continued, questioning the dominant social values of conservatives by presenting a slideshow juxtaposing images of naked women against photos of torture victims and mutilated corpses. He comments:

> You know, politicians and demagogues like to say sexually explicit material corrupts the youth of our country and yet they lie and cheat and start unholy wars. Look, they call themselves men but they are sheep in a herd. I think the real obscenity comes from raising our youth to believe that sex is bad and ugly and dirty, and yet it is heroic to spill our guts and blood in the most ghastly manner in the name of humanity. With all the taboos attached to sex it's no wonder we have the problems we have, its no wonder we're angry and violent and genocidal, but ask yourself the question: What is more obscene, sex or war?

In a sense Flynt was deconstructing the 'snuff' myth by asking who it was that found violence more appealing than sex and the answer suggested that it was moral conservatives. After the graphic news reporting of violence against the civil rights movement, the escalation of the Vietnam War, and Nixon's covert expansion of the conflict in South East Asia into Cambodia, to many pornography seemed like a minor issue. But sex, when tied to violence and presented as a threat to family values, was an emotive area.

255

Outrageous from the outset, *Hustler* featured clandestine photosets of Jackie Onassis (August 1975), a middle aged woman (September 1975), 'Joe or Josephine', a hermaphrodite (February 1976), and a pregnant woman (April 1976). Always looking for the next topical and shocking opportunity, in April 1977 *Hustler* published seven nude photographs of Shere Hite, which had been taken in 1968 when she was a model, entitled "The Hite Report Exposed." The same year Flynt also offered TV news anchorwoman Barbara Walters $1 million to pose nude for *Hustler*. A few years later, around the time of the Jerry Falwell Campari advert of 1983, Flynt offered $1 million to any top TV or film actress who would pose for his magazine and also proposed producing an adult film where a medically certified eighteen-year-old virgin would be deflowered.[6] Despite the acquittal in Ohio, Flynt was determined to prove a point and his conflict with Keating escalated, almost out of control.

In March 1977 Larry Flynt spoke at the Sigma Alpha Epsilon fraternity house at the University of Cincinnati. The following month, on 12 April, one of Charles Keating's daughters, a student at the university, was abducted at midday from the campus and raped. Keating believed that Flynt had named her during his speech at the frat house and offered to pay to have the girl embarrassed.[7] Whilst he produced no evidence, Keating held Flynt personally responsible for his daughter's rape and went so far as to accuse Flynt of organizing the attack during a televised interview in 1988.[8]

On 13 May 1977 a 'Rally for Decency' was held in Cincinnati to celebrate Larry Flynt's conviction three months earlier for pandering obscenity and engaging in organized crime. Ironically, Keating condemned "corporations that have no God but money,"[9] vilifying pornographers for their avarice when it was pursuit of money that drove his own lifestyle. Instead of revelling in the victory over Flynt however, Keating's rhetoric attacked church leaders for not being strong enough in the fight against obscenity. As a consequence, and on a very personal note for Keating, their inaction had "permitted the roaring lion

---

6   Binstein and Bowden, *Trust Me*: 164.
7   Ibid: 122.
8   Ibid: 102.
9   Corn, "Dirty Bookkeeping," *New Republic* (2 April 1990): 15.

to destroy the lamb."[10] During the address he told the story about his daughter's rape, which reinforced his existing beliefs about the dangers of pornography. Keating announced he was tired of legal arguments: "There is no difference between Bridgitte Bardot taking off her clothes in movies and children doing it," he asserted, "It's all pornography; it's just a matter of degree."[11] The obscenity issue had become even more personal and his patience with the legal process had worn thin.

Eleven months after Keating's daughter was raped, on 6 March 1978 Larry Flynt was shot in Gwinnett County, Georgia. The shooting was carried out in a very professional manner and a number of conspiracy theories circulated claiming that the Mafia, FBI or CIA was responsible. A prominent adversary, Flynt was frequently condemned by Keating in speeches because of the contents of *Hustler* magazine, but after the shooting Keating was uncharacteristically quiet about the event. A colleague of Keating, an executive who had worked with him for years, informed journalist Charles Bowden that Keating viewed the attack on his daughter as a rape-for-hire orchestrated by Flynt, and the executive could understand why Keating would want revenge but found his response to the shooting uncharacteristic: "Charlie liked to brag about things no matter whether he did them or he wanted to lay claim to doing them. I can't even remember him saying anything about Flynt, about the Flynt shooting." Other colleagues noted the silence and remembered one of Keating's sons even thought his father paid to have Flynt shot. Murder would be a mortal sin for a devout Catholic such as Keating but Flynt did not die in the attack, instead he was crippled for life. In 1988 Charles Bowden interviewed Keating and asked about the rape of his daughter and Flynt's shooting. Keating took Bowden aside and quietly acknowledged both events. When he spoke about Flynt spending the rest of his life in a wheelchair he did so calmly, but with an intensity and determination that was reminiscent of his fanatical religious beliefs.[12]

---

10 Binstein and Bowden, *Trust Me*: 120.
11 Ibid: 122. He also complained about another modern development, hotels offering porn to guests, which provided another source of temptation, but available anonymously and in private thanks to new technology.
12 Ibid: 123–124. In 1984 John Paul Franklin confessed to shooting Larry Flynt in 1978. Franklin was a member of the Ku Klux Klan and the American Nazi Party who violently opposed integration and miscegenation and was suspected of a number of other race-related crimes. Incarcerated in Wisconsin at the time it is suspected that Franklin made the confession in the

The election of Ronald Reagan in 1980 marked the beginning of a *very* conservative decade in American politics and society, and religious values such as Keating's were championed by conservative Republicans and Democrats to justify draconian social policies. CDL remained active and sent out numerous provocative and alarmist direct-mail letters to raise funds. One letter, circulated in 1981, warned recipients, "If you absolutely do not care whether children are raped and sexually abused, then read no further." The claims were sensational, as the 'snuff' letter had been five years previously, "Child molesting is about to become AN ACCEPTED PART OF AMERICAN LIFE. If this is allowed to go any further, does anyone doubt that God will destroy us? If we do allow this to go any further, does anyone doubt God *should* destroy us?"[13] As usual the wild accusations were not supported by any factual evidence. Also in the 1980s, amidst a CDL fundraising campaign, Keating wrote in a letter to members and potential donors, "Back then Hefner's *Playboy* was amongst the worst," but the situation had grown worse and, "Now, twelve-year-old kids pick up the family phone and listen to lurid descriptions of incest, child sexual brutality — even kids having sex with the family pet." Another sensational and distorted allegation designed to provoke outrage and help CDL raise funds.[14]

Keating also continued to maintain a high public profile and as a consequence one of his business interests, Lincoln Savings and Loan Association (LSLA), made unorthodox grants to a number of people and groups. After meeting Mother Theresa in 1981 during her visit to Gallup, New Mexico, Keating lent her his private helicopter to visit a remote Indian reservation and donated $1 million to establish a convent in Phoenix.[15] Donations made by Keating to Mother Theresa and Father Bruce Ritter came from American Continental Corporation (ACC) funds, not out of his own pocket.[16] At least $400,000 was given

hope that he would be moved to Georgia. A possible motive for the attack was the photosets of interracial couples published in *Hustler* magazine. "Man is Convicted of Killing Interracial Couple in Wisconsin in '77," *New York Times* (15 February 1986): 6; Richard Severo, "Former Klansman Indicted In Bombing of a Synagogue," *New York Times* (8 March 1984): A18.

13   Corn, "Dirty Bookkeeping," *New Republic* (2 April 1990): 15.
14   Claudia Dreifus, "The Keating Papers," *Playboy* (June 1993): 52.
15   Jeffrey, "The Man Who Bought Washington," *American Spectator* (February 1990): 18.
16   Binstein and Bowden, *Trust Me*: 13. Ritter's organisation, Covenant House, was praised by President Ronald Reagan in his 1984 State of the Union speech and the following year he served on Attorney General Meese's Commission on Pornography. In 1989 Father Bruce Ritter faced

to Father Bruce Ritter, whose Covenant House also received almost $34 million in questionable loans. Effectively Keating was generously giving away other people's money. As an organisation CDL gave Keating a national soapbox for his crusade, and created lucrative employment for members of his family and sympathetic right-wing lawyers, and provided conservatives with a platform for mounting attacks on the First Amendment. The influence developed by CDL was evident when successful lobbying in Congress led to the passage of anti-phone sex legislation. CDL also issued a guide for "The Preparation and Trial of an Obscenity Case" and provided a think tank dedicated to obscenity issues for the Justice Department. Once an anti-obscenity campaign was conceptualized by CDL it was implemented by some of their members in their role as Justice Department lawyers. Bruce Taylor, CDL general counsel, made clear the format needed for the Meese Commission (1986) and named the authorities that could be called on for an anti-pornography opinion, many of who were appointed by Reagan.[17]

When Reagan's administration established the Meese Commission[18] Keating showed his enthusiasm and support saying, "This is the start of the NEW SEXUAL REVOLUTION ... Our NEW SEXUAL REVOLUTION gives the beauty of sex back to husbands and wives as part of God's plan for the human race."[19] In the Los Angeles *Times* Keating explained that to "bring America back to moral health, we need now to vomit these vermin [pornographers] and let them roll down the gutters into

---

the first in a series of accusations that he molested teenage boys. After additional allegations of financial improprieties Ritter was forced to resign from his post at Covenant House. Fifteen young men accused Ritter of abuse and provided detailed information. The claims were never brought to court. Ritter retired to upstate New York where he lived until his death in 1999.

17 Dreifus, "The Keating Papers," *Playboy* (June 1993): 52–53.

18 Promising a return to traditional values and morality President Ronald Reagan ordered his Attorney General Edwin Meese to set up a Commission on Pornography as a response to Lyndon Johnson's earlier commission into adult entertainment. The Commission, commonly known as the Meese Commission, was heavily criticised for being more ideological than objectively scientific. When delivered in 1986 the finished report was almost 2,000 pages long and amongst its recommendations called for a greater enforcement of existing laws and harsher punishments for obscenity convictions. The report drew considerable criticism for its factual inaccuracies, naïve acceptance of porn myths, obvious conservative bias and unrealistic proposals. Revelations that Traci Lords had been appearing in adult films while underage gave the Meese Commission an opportunity to rescue their floundering crusade. Wilcox, Brian L. "Pornography, Social Science, and Politics: When research and ideology collide." *American Psychologist* 42 (October 1987): 941–943.

19 Keating quoted in Corn, "Dirty Bookkeeping," *New Republic* (2 April 1990): 15.

the sewers where they belong."[20] Sensing a change in fortune Keating was not reluctant to show his excitement. Marjorie Heins, director of the ACLU Arts Censorship Project, noted, "There appears to have been a kind of revolving door between the CDL and the Justice Department during the Reagan years." Worryingly, she added, "Justice was using materials prepared by CDL in its training and making extensive use of CDL people as speakers. The two groups appear to have shared the identical religious-right anti-sex agenda. This relationship fostered a hysteria about freedom of expression on sexual topics."[21] Her observation was made frightening by the ill-founded and sensational claims constructed by CDL to attract attention to the organisation's ideology and raise funds.

Away from the anti-obscenity rhetoric Keating liked to be surrounded by beautiful women. He personally hired those who worked around him, all of whom were young, usually blonde, and buxom. He was also known for walking round the ACC offices peering down the blouses of secretaries and staring at their cleavages. Whilst he did not specifically instruct female employees to get breast implants, Keating's preferences were well known, and a predictable series of events developed. After a period of time working for ACC a female member of staff would find a bonus of $5,000 in with her pay-cheque, and a few weeks later, on a Monday morning, she would come into work with significantly enlarged breasts. The situation was repeated so often that a local plastic surgeon offered ACC staff a special discount, and on one occasion a woman who worked at ACC went to the plastic surgeon only to find the waiting room filled with co-workers. Despite his fanatical moralising about sex, if a visitor to ACC did not show any signs of appreciating the secretaries Keating would later tell the staff that the visitor was "queer,"[22] a reflection of the homophobic attitudes which led him to believe that homosexuals should be put in prison.[23]

Despite his superficial moral superiority, Keating's corrupt business practices were in part subsidizing CDL and it became known as "Charlie's

20 Keating's comments in the Los Angeles *Times* quoted in ibid.
21 Dreifus, "The Keating Papers," *Playboy* (June 1993): 54.
22 Binstein and Bowden, *Trust Me*: 61–62. When Russ Meyer read in the LA *Times* about Charles Keating's breast fixation he was so amused that he reprinted extracts from the article in his autobiography, *A Clean Breast* (2000), and below he placed a picture of his own grinning face between two huge breasts with the sarcastic caption "*Et Tu*, Charlie." McDonough, Jimmy, *Big Bosoms and Square Jaws: The Biography of Russ Meyer*, Vintage, London, 2006.
23 Ibid: 120.

charity," with hundreds of thousands of dollars being funnelled from the LSLA and ACC to CDL. In 1984 alone more than $450,000 was acquired,[24] and during a three-year period in the mid 1980s Keating shifted $840,000 from the LSLA to CDL.[25] People in Arizona who wanted to do business with LSLA were expected to buy tickets for the annual CDL fundraiser ball. Carolyn Warner, who was involved in Arizona State politics, was invited to attend a CDL ball but felt uncomfortable at the event because "The sad stories about depravity against children that were told were almost lurid, as if there were a secret pleasure derived from this."[26] In the fall of 1985, a $1,000 per plate charity ball organized by CDL raised more than $1 million to support the organisation's activities, but some of the organisation's supporters were donating money for mystifying reasons. Commodity broker Conley Wolfswinkel donated a cheque for more than $50,000 and then told Keating that he loved porn and watched it a lot. Undeterred, Keating took the cheque anyway and smiled.[27]

In April 1989 the US government alleged that ACC took approximately $95 million from LSLA investors, seized the company and declared it insolvent. At the time Keating was chairman of both the LSLA and its parent company the ACC. A few months later, in July 1989, CDL became the Children's Legal Foundation (CLF) and thereby distanced itself from the crimes of its founder. No doubt with intended irony Keating's biographers Michael Binstein and Charles Bowden described the type of financial fraud committed by Keating as a "kind of rape."[28] As a consequence of the Financial Institutions Reform, Recovery and Enforcement Bill (1989) the US government were committed to bailing out the savings and loan banks, at a cost to the taxpayers of $300 billion over the next thirty years[29] — diverting funds from important social spending such as education, housing and employment programmes. Charles Keating was convicted in 1993 on seventy-three counts of racketeering, fraud and conspiracy and sentenced to twelve years in

---

24 Dreifus, "The Keating Papers," *Playboy* (June 1993): 52.
25 Schlosser, *Reefer Madness and Other Tales from the American Underground*: 200.
26 Dreifus, "The Keating Papers," *Playboy* (June 1993): 52–53.
27 Binstein and Bowden, *Trust Me*: 204.
28 Ibid: 11. ACC also owned the Cresent Hotel Group that opened a 605-room hotel in Scottsdale (Arizona) in October 1988. The hotel boasts that there is no porn on sale in the gift shops nor available on cable in any of the rooms.
29 Jeffrey, "The Man Who Bought Washington," *American Spectator* (February 1990): 21.

jail, but in 1999 made a deal with prosecutors and pleaded guilty to four counts of fraud; in return his sentence was reduced to time served.

In the years following the release of *Snuff*, militant feminists also maintained their rhetoric without substantiating any of the provocative claims. In her essay "Erotica vs. Pornography" for *Ms.* (November 1977) Gloria Steinem reported that 'snuff' movies were driven underground partly because the "graves of many murdered women were discovered around the shack of just one filmmaker in California." But she did not document the important details of who, when, and where. Grasping to validate her accusations Steinem also noted that movies that *simulated* torture and murder were still produced,[30] a desperate effort to imply that such films were in some way related to 'snuff'; Either a film is a 'snuff' movie or it is not.

The "last screening" of a 'snuff' movie, according to Steinem, was at the monthly showing of a pornographic film by a "senior partner in

30 Steinem, *Outrageous Acts and Everyday Rebellions*: 223. Steinem does not name the filmmaker or give any more information about the location or date the bodies were discovered. The case she is referring to is that of Fred Berre Douglas who was arrested in 1977 after claims were made that he had photographed the murders of several young women. Public awareness of claims about 'snuff' movies led one journalist to coin the term 'snuff shots' to describe the photographs that Douglas allegedly took of his dying victims, Theo Wilson, "Clues in the desert: were models slain for photos?" Chicago *Tribune* (23 July 1977): S2. The police investigation was prompted by information from a woman known only as 'Diane' who said that Douglas had shown her the graves of two prostitutes he claimed to have murdered and dismembered during a photo session. Allegedly Douglas wanted Diane to recruit more women as models for his lesbian bondage photographs. In support of her claims 'Diane' led police to the place where Douglas stashed some of his paraphernalia "Search centres on fifteen victims of sex-model 'snuff' films," Modesto *Bee* (24 July 1977): A5; See also "Authorities hunt bodies of models feared dead," Sarasota *Herald-Tribune* (24 July 1977): 11. The intention was that Douglas would photograph Diane as she tortured and murdered the models. "Police hunt victims of alleged sex killer," Tri-City *Herald* (24 July 1977): 10. Investigators searched a thirty-acre site in the desert looking for the remains of possible victims of "an alleged scheme to torture and dismember women posing for nude photographs." But they found no bodies and no photographs or films of the alleged murders materialized "Victims sought in sex-torture filming," Modesto *Bee* (23 July 1977): A3; "Hunt fails to find porn film victims," The Pittsburgh *Press* (25 July 1977): A4; See also "Jekyll–Hyde snuff film murder?" Modesto *Bee* (26 July 1977): A1. In 1978 Douglas' first murder trial ended with a hung jury, he pleaded guilty to a lesser charge of conspiracy to commit assault and was sentenced to six months in jail and three years probation. In 1984 the snuff allegations resurfaced when Douglas was convicted of murdering two teenagers, Beth Jones and Margaret Kreuger, and burying their bodies in the Anza Borrego Desert in San Diego County, the following year he was sentenced to death. See "'Snuff film' conspiracy alleged; two teen-age girls found murdered," St. Petersburg *Independent* (6 August 1983): 2A; and "2 sought in deaths of teens" Palm Beach *Post* (7 August 1983): A12. Some aspects of the Douglas case sound similar to the crimes committed by Leonard Lake and Charles Ng and they are often confused by commentators, but the murders committed by Lake and Ng were not discovered until the mid 1980s.

a respected law firm." The organisation is unnamed, and the audience a group of friends, amongst them lawyers and judges. One of the attendees allegedly told Steinem that many in the audience were embarrassed by what they saw, but none protested or reported the event to the police.[31] Inexplicably the informant chose to report the incident to a strident anti-pornography feminist like Steinem rather than to the authorities, but Steinem did not report it to the police either, missing out on the opportunity to have the incident officially documented. Had it been formally investigated by the police and the existence of 'snuff' movies established, Steinem and other militant feminists, along with anti-obscenity activists, would have had a solid basis for their claims and no one would have been able to ignore their rhetoric.

Earlier in 1977 a concerned businessman wrote to the FBI after seeing *Snuff* at a theatre in Tokyo. Describing the main body of the film as "unremarkable," he was nevertheless revolted by the final scene that made him physically sick. Convinced that the murder was real, the businessman seemed to want the Bureau to acknowledge they were aware of the film, and to be told it was a fake.[32] A few weeks after receiving the letter FBI Director Clarence Kelley wrote a reply to the businessman to reassure him that the Bureau had already investigated the film and found no actual killing had taken place.[33] When Allan Shackleton died in 1979 *Variety* published an obituary, once more noting that he had fabricated rumours about the seizure of a 'snuff' film and planted them in the New York *Post* and *Daily News* in 1975.[34] His showmanship still went unappreciated, and the 'snuff' myth continued to be manipulated by militant feminists.

Despite the *complete* exposure of Shackleton's publicity campaign, Andrea Dworkin continued to make unsubstantiated accusations about 'snuff' films. In *Pornography: Men Possessing Women* (1979) she claimed that in 1975 organized crime sold 'snuff' films to "private collectors of pornography." How she would know this is not made clear. In the films, "women actually were maimed, sliced into pieces,

---

31   Steinem, *Outrageous Acts and Everyday Rebellions*: 230.
32   "Snuff" (dated 28 March 1977) in FBI, *Snuff Films*, File Number 145–5568–14.
33   Letter from Clarence Kelley (18 April 1977) in FBI, *Snuff Films*, File Number 145–5568–15.
34   "Creator of 'Snuff' Film Dies," *Variety* (24 October 1979): 46.

fucked, and killed," and according to Dworkin's graphic and twisted imagination 'snuff' provided "the perfect Sadean synthesis."[35] This is exactly the image Raymond Gauer and CDL were trying to convey when they created the 'snuff' panic. Dworkin's claims about pornography were shocking and sensational for anyone not familiar with the subject, as were Keating and Gauer's allegations, going far beyond graphic depictions of the consensual sex which dominated the pornography business. Instead she distorted perceptions by focusing on allegations of torture and murder, bestiality and child abuse, exploiting the myths about pornography. Her polemics were absurd, badly informed dogma, and intended to be provocative.

Even after *Snuff* had been exposed as a hoax and the actress who played the murder victim identified and interviewed, the misleading allegations continued. In *Pornography and Silence* (1981), Susan Griffin repeated Laura Lederer's accusation that a model in LA was tortured, her murder filmed and subsequently advertised nationally,[36] an obvious reference to *Snuff*. "A whole trade in such films goes on underground," she added, embellishing far beyond the known facts, "and men pay huge sums of money to see films which, it has been said to them, has captured a real death of a real woman."[37] In the desperate attempts to demonise pornography other absurd claims were made up by militant feminists, such as Gloria Steinem who wrote in *Ms.* (May 1980):

> Since *Deep Throat*, a whole new genre of pornography has developed. Added to the familiar varieties of rape, there is now an ambition to rape the throat. Porn novels treat this theme endlessly. Real-life victims of suffocation may be on the increase, so some emergency room doctors believe.[38]

Not all women agreed with the wild allegations being made by militant feminists. Outspoken proponent of sex education Annie

35 Dworkin, *Pornography: Men Possessing Women*: 71. She repeats the allegation in Dworkin, "Pornography Is A Civil Rights Issue (1986)," in Dworkin, *Letters From A Warzone*: 305.
36 Lederer, "Then and Now: An Interview With a Former Pornography Model," in Laura Lederer (Ed.), *Take Back the Night: Women on Pornography*, William Morrow, New York, 1980: 57–70.
37 Griffin, *Pornography and Silence: Culture's Revenge Against Nature*: 116.
38 Steinem quoted in McCarthy, "Pornography, Rape, and the Cult of Macho," *The Humanist* (September–October 1980): 15.

Sprinkle ridiculed the anti-pornography feminists in her *ABC Study of Sexual Lust and Deviations* (1983) with the poem 'Spread Shot':

We have a desire
to spread our thighs
For everyone to
cast their eyes.
No one has the right
to make that taboo.
So Women Against Pornography
fuck you![39]

When, in August 1983, *Snuff* returned to the Eighth Street Playhouse in Greenwich Village (New York), it was a thoroughly debunked film, but still a cinematic curiosity and a symbolic rallying point. The owner of the Playhouse, Steven Hirsch, was quickly forced to discontinue the film after a coalition of women's groups protested. The National Organization for Women (NOW) was prominent in opposing *Snuff* and executive director Jennifer Brown claimed the depiction of violence toward women in the film was especially dangerous because its audience primarily comprised adolescent boys and young men. Members of the coalition phoned the theatre to complain and protested outside, distributing flyers and disrupting business. As a consequence of the protests a recorded message at the theatre informed patrons: "Tonight is your last chance to see *Snuff*. Some members of this community have found this film offensive, and we don't want to offend anyone."[40]

Unwilling to let the issue drop, a few years later Dworkin appeared as a witness before the Meese Commission (1986), asserting "There *are* snuff films"[41] without explaining what they were, substantiating her claim, or being challenged by the committee. She admitted that she had never seen a 'snuff' film, and hoped that she never would,[42] but in her 'expert' testimony Dworkin claimed to have spoken with journalists whom she trusted (none are named) as well as women who

39 'Spread Shot' reprinted in *Caught Looking*: 81.
40 Johnson and Anderson, "'Snuff' Is Snuffed," *New York Times* (6 September 1983): B4.
41 "Victim Testimony," *Final Report of the Attorney General's Commission on Pornography*: 199.
42 Dworkin, "Pornography Is A Civil Rights Issue (1986)," in Dworkin, *Letters From A Warzone*: 278.

had seen 'snuff' movies. Continuing her wild claims, Dworkin reported that she had contemporary information that prints of 'snuff' films were being sold in the Las Vegas area for between $2,500 and $3,500, that it was possible to buy a seat for a screening of a 'snuff' film for $250, and "in one part of the country" prostitutes were being forced to watch 'snuff' movies before being compelled to perform heavy sadomasochistic acts. While Dworkin's testimony went unchallenged, Deanna Titon, a panel member, pointed out that the examples given were "extreme cases" and would involve crime.[43]

A decade after popular interest in *Snuff* had faded, in her book *Age of the Sex Crime* (1988), Jane Caputi continued the militant feminist rhetoric, asserting that 'snuff' is the name for a type of porn film "which depicts (or purports to depict) the actual torture, mutilation and murder of an actress."[44] Possibly the most ridiculous accusation came more than twenty years after the film's release, in *Dangerous Relationships* (1998), when Diana Russell used *Snuff* as an example of "femicidal pornography" — but from the description given it is obvious she did not even take the time to watch the film. "In the final scene," Russell claims, "a man rips out a woman's uterus and holds it up in the air while he ejaculates." No doubt the imagery contained important symbolism for militant feminists but the scene she described did *not* appear in the film. She adds, "Some people claim that the violent scenes were simulated while others believe they were real"[45] (apparently unaware, or just not interested in Morgethau's investigation which identified and interviewed the actress who played the murder victim).

When it became obvious that no 'snuff' films were going to be found, militant feminists tried to broaden their definition of 'snuff' in a desperate attempt to find something they could demonise. Appropriating the provocative terminology, Diana Russell referred to

---

43   Ibid: 304–304, 307. Dworkin claimed that if a 'snuff' movie were found on the "commercial pornography market" it would be "protected speech." She says this is the position of the New York City DA who said that as long as the person making the film was convicted of murder the film would be "protected speech." Dworkin, "Pornography Is A Civil Rights Issue (1986)," in Dworkin, *Letters From A Warzone*: 306.
44   Caputi, *The Age of the Sex Crime*: 91n.
45   Russell, *Dangerous Relationships*: 98. Russell is so badly informed that she repeatedly claims that the release of *Snuff*, and the resulting hysterical feminist protests, occurred in 1979, when they actually took place three years earlier in 1976.

slasher films as "simulated snuff" and "softcore snuff,"[46] creating her own personal oxymoron, the equivalent of 'simulated murder' and 'softcore murder': If 'snuff' films existed they were significant because, for the first time, allegedly a real murder was filmed as entertainment. If the murder was only simulated, as they have been throughout cinematic history, then there was no reason for outrage because the film had not really broken any social taboos.

Outside the rhetoric of militant feminists and their attacks on the adult film business, rumours of ritualistic 'snuff' movies also continued to circulate. Maury Terry explored the idea that at least one of the 'Son of Sam' murders was filmed in *The Ultimate Evil* (1987), an idea that was reinforced by one of his informants, referred to as 'Vinny' to protect his identity. Vinny had "more than a suspicion" that the group behind the 'Son of Sam' crimes, the '22 Disciples of Hell', had filmed some of the killings. He refers to the members of the group as "a regular jet set of the occult," with mainly white-collar jobs,[47] run by Ray Radin, someone whom David Berkowitz referred to as 'Manson II' because he had been a member of Manson's group in California. Radin ran a pornography operation producing private sex films, stills and videotapes, as well as operating a call girl ring (using college girls) and was identified as being at the top of the occult group's hierarchy on the east coast.[48]

46 Ibid: 105. According to Russell, in slasher films it is usually females who are killed. Hence she calls them 'woman-slashing' films. The film Russell picks to highlight her criticism of slasher films is *Maniac* (William Lustig, 1980). Ironically, Russell is not aware that William Lustig began his filmmaking career in the adult film business.
47 Terry, *The Ultimate Evil*: 590, 625. This accusation was not uncommon. During the long running investigation into the Zodiac murders in California rumours circulated that one of the suspects had filmed some of the murders and left the movie reel in the safe keeping of a trusted friend. See Robert Graysmith, *Zodiac*, Titan Books: 221.
48 Ibid: 535, 643. The 'Son of Sam' Killings took place between July 1976 and July 1977. There were eight attacks and of the thirteen victims six died. The last attack took place on 31 July 1977 and David Berkowitz was arrested ten days later in front of his apartment on Pine Street, north Yonkers. In a televised interview with Maury Terry in the 1990s Berkowitz named John and Michael Carr as two of the other shooters in the 'Son of Sam' crimes. John Carr died in February 1978 and Michael Carr died on 4 October 1979. Roy Radin was murdered in 1983 and his body found in Death Valley. He had been shot in the head twenty-seven times and then a stick of dynamite was placed in his mouth and ignited to blow his face off. William Mentzer is currently serving life without possibility of parole in California state prison (at Lancaster) for the murders of Roy Radin and, in 1984, prostitute June Mincher. Mentzer supposedly knew Charles Manson around 1969 and is referred to by Maury Terry as 'Manson II' in *The Ultimate Evil*.

Maury Terry went as far as to name Ronald Sisman as a member of the group who was at the scene of the Moscowitz-Violante shooting, and that Sisman either did the filming, or assisted whoever was doing the filming from the back of a yellow Volkswagen van.[49] David Berkowitz, who was identified as the 'Son of Sam' killer, reported that on 31 July 1977 Tommy Zaino and his date were the original targets for the 'Sam' group but the plan had to be changed when Zaino moved his car from under the streetlight to a darker spot. When Stacy Moscowitz and Robert Violante pulled into the parking spot below the streetlight they became the new targets of the shooting, which happened at 2.50 am near Dyker Beach Park, Brooklyn. The illumination of the streetlight was necessary if the murder was to be filmed with any clarity or detail. In Terry's theory Violante and Moscowitz walked past the gunman in the park, a better opportunity to kill them without witnesses if murder was the only intention, but the killer waited and conducted the murder in the street, under the light, where there were witnesses.[50]

Roy Radin was well known for his huge collection of pornography and Terry believed he wanted to add a 'snuff' film, with the emphasis placed on murder rather than explicit sex, to his collection. Later Terry changed his opinion and came to suspect that the 'Son of Sam' murders were filmed to circulate within the Church of Satan, but of the ten copies of the film rumoured to be in existence none were ever located.[51] Adding to his suspicions, in 1979, whilst in jail, Berkowitz requested an article relating to the murder of Susan Reinert, a Philadelphia schoolteacher, being investigated by the FBI, alleging he had information that her murder was part of an occult ritual that had been filmed.[52]

49   Ibid: 594. Sisman was a thirty-five year old Canadian whom police described as a photographer, procurer and drug dealer (cocaine). Ronald Sisman was reportedly killed by the group execution style, along with Elizabeth Plotzman, and the apartment they were in ransacked for the tape of the Moscowitz-Violante murder (30 October 1976). Sisman thought he was going to be charged with drug dealing and he was going to copy the stills and video for the police. Terry, *The Ultimate Evil*: 592–94.
50   Ibid: 596–97.
51   McDowell, "Movies To Die For," San Francisco *Chronicle* (7 August 1994) This World section: 9. It is evident from the execution of the crime that if the perpetrators were intending to make a snuff movie it was not going to be particularly pornographic.
52   Terry, *The Ultimate Evil*: 596–97. The story of Reinhart's murder became the basis for Joseph Wambaugh's novel *Echoes in the Darkness* (1987). J. C. Smith, principal of the high school where Reinert taught, was convicted of the murder but the verdict was overturned in

Criminal investigations into the Atlanta Child Murders, Leonard Lake and Charles Ng, and Henry Lee Lucas and Ottis Toole led to allegations or confessions that they had filmed the murders being committed, but none could be described as 'snuff movies' even though media reports frequently used the term. Leonard Lake and Charles Ng in California *did* make videos of themselves torturing and sexually abusing women whom they later killed, but they did not record the actual murders. Toole claimed to have joined a cult called the Hand of Death in the early 1980s, kidnapping young women and children in Texas to transport them across the border to Mexico where the women would be used in 'snuff' movies and the children killed in human sacrifices. However, he also contradicted himself, saying that virgins were kept for sacrifice, and non-virgins were used for 'snuff'. After the cult was done with the victims Toole boasted that he would get the bodies to eat.[53] In one of his stories Toole remembered seeing a 'snuff' movie being made where a woman was put into a guillotine and beheaded, but he does not mention any sexual content. His descriptions of Satanic rituals, human sacrifices, and cannibalism sound more like scenes from Grand Guignol or something out of a clichéd Dennis Wheatley novel, undermining their believability.[54] The notion that Ottis Toole filmed a murder was used in *Henry: Portrait of a Serial Killer* (John McNaughton, 1986) where characters based on Henry Lee Lucas and Toole use a stolen video camera to record a home invasion and capture the murder of the occupants. The scene concludes with Toole trying to rape a dead woman. Toole repeatedly re-watches the tape, with a morbid fascination reflecting his twisted psyche. Unfortunately, whilst the sensational confessions made by the real life Lucas and Toole were prominently reported by the media, the subsequent process by which they were wholly discredited was not.

Convicted murderer Kenneth 'Mad Dog' McKenna acknowledged producing and distributing kiddie porn in Florida, and also claimed to have handled what he called 'kiddie snuff'. Naming two films, *Gator Bait Ten* (ten girls being ripped apart by starving alligators) and *Snake*

September 1992.
53 Barton,, "An Interview With Ottis Toole: The Cannibal Kid," *The Konformist* (August 2000) online at http://www.konformist.com/2000/cannibal-kid.htm
54 Ibid.

Pit (a ten-year-old girl being fed to a twenty-foot long anaconda), McKenna saw himself as a businessman only interested in the money and if his claims are to be believed he made $100,000 from each film.[55] Elsewhere, Hugh Gallagher, editor of *Draculina* magazine, reported that amongst the mail he received was a letter from someone who claimed to work as a contract killer in Chicago, to be involved in a Satanic cult that sacrificed teenage girls, and to have participated in making three 'snuff' films.[56] But the claims, all unsubstantiated, refer to films that document death or murder similar to the depictions found in Mondo movies, but have no sexual component.

Mainstream television writers continued to recognize the value of mentioning 'snuff' movies and, looking for ratings, the pilot episode of the TV series *Gideon Oliver* was a two-hour film called 'Sleep Well, Professor Gideon' (John Patterson, 1989) in which Oliver (Louis Gossett Jr.), a professor of anthropology, investigates the death of an ex-girlfriend who was probing the activities of a Satanic cult. In the course of the episode the meandering story brings Oliver into contact with the adult film business and mentions the cult making 'snuff' movies. Despite having no factual basis, the snuff myth had been accepted into the mainstream of popular culture.

While the rhetoric of anti-obscenity campaigners was prominent and substantial coverage was given to 'snuff' movies during the late 1970s and early 1980s one fundamental problem remained: none had ever been found. Writing in 1984 Joseph W. Slade noted, "To date, despite a thorough investigation by the FBI, despite a large reward posted by the publisher of the sex tabloid *Screw*, and despite frenzied searches by collectors of the bizarre no authentic snuff film has come to light."[57] Across America there was no organized official response to 'snuff' rumours and in 1980 the LA City Attorney's office circulated a memo

55 Schaefer, "Howling in Hell," *Fatal Visions* (No.14, May/June 1993): 36–38. McKenna was a hit man, racketeer, white slaver, pornographer and pimp who began his career as a child with the Irish gangs in Chicago where he claimed to have killed fifteen people by the age of twenty-one. He viewed crime as a business and claimed to have routinely distributed child pornography and 'kiddie snuff'. The interview was conducted by Gerard Schaefer, a convicted killer on Death Row in Florida, and a suspect of numerous other murders. Schaefer was also the author of *Killer Fiction* (1997).
56 Kerekes and Slater, *Killing for Culture*: 222.
57 Slade, "Violence in the Hard-Core Pornographic Film: A Historical Survey," *Journal of Communication* (v.34 No.3, 1984): 148–163: 148.

noting that films with scenes of bestiality, snuff, or sex with minors would be subject to arrest and prosecution. Urination, defecation and sadomasochism were also deemed taboo and liable to be subject to police censorship.[58] A few years later Alan Sears, executive director of the Attorney General's Commission of Pornography (1985–1986), confidently asserted: "Our experience was that we could not find any such thing as a commercially produced snuff film." In a Commission that was "all-inclusive and exhaustive," Sears said with confidence, "If snuff films were available, we'd have found them."[59] Being interviewed about 'snuff' movies in the late 1990s John MacKinnon, a senior special agent with the US Customs Service asserted: "Whether it's snuff starring adults or snuff starring children, I haven't seen any." He added, "It's just not out there."[60] Despite the official denials some individuals made statements that kept the possibility of the existence of 'snuff' films alive, such as Sergeant Don Smith of the LAPD vice squad who acknowledged:

My feeling is that if snuff existed on film or video it would be so far underground the average person would never see it. For years there's been talk of a Las Vegas dealer selling snuff films for $100,000 a pop. For that you get the original film. I've never believed this, but with all the unsolved murders in this country, it makes you wonder. Certainly, the possibility is there.[61]

At the end of his research Rider McDowell claimed to have been contacted by an FBI agent based in Southern California who openly contradicted the Bureau's official position by claiming, "on a very limited basis, circulated within a very small community of people, snuff movies do exist." Ironically, the agent who sought out McDowell also added: "If I told you how I know, it would jeopardize our investigation and compromise our efforts. The last thing we want to do at this

58 Hebditch and Anning, Porn Gold: 340.
59 McDowell, "Movies To Die For," San Francisco Chronicle (7 August 1994) This World section: 8. Ironically, after the Meese Commission Alan Sears joined CDL as an advisor. Claudia Dreifus, "The Keating Papers," Playboy (June 1993): 54.
60 Sverdlik, "The Snuff Movie Myth," New York Post (25 February 1999): 050.
61 Smith quoted in McDowell, "Movies To Die For," San Francisco Chronicle (7 August 1994) This World section: 10.

juncture is tip our hand, and my experience is that the media talks too much."[62] However, a few years later, in 2000, FBI agent Ken Lanning[63] was reported as saying that whilst he was keeping an open mind about the existence of 'snuff' films his experience had made him sceptical.

> I can't definitively speak for what may be going on in some obscure part of the world ... I can only deal with the fact that for over twenty-five years I've been hearing stories about snuff films, and I've literally met hundreds of people who know somebody who saw a snuff film. There's always this one-step removed part of the story.[64]

Lanning referred to 'snuff' as the "Holy Grail of pornography" because the FBI had been trying to find a 'snuff' film since 1975, but had been unable to acquire one despite investigating repeated rumours and reports.[65] This raised questions about how much of a cost was the 'snuff' investigation to taxpayers? And how many man-hours were spent tracking down leads and following up on unsubstantiated claims?

Feminist author Avedon Carol concluded an essay on the 'snuff' myth with a deceptively simple observation, that "the idea of snuff films is a very scary one; but perhaps more scary is the fact that, even when the evidence is that no snuff film exists, we are still so willing to believe in it."[66] Her remark could equally be levelled as a criticism of Raymond Gauer[67] and the CDL as well as Andrea Dworkin and the militant feminists who promoted the belief that such films existed. Carol also raised the pertinent question, "doesn't it do more harm than

---

62 FBI agent quoted in ibid.
63 At the time of the snuff panic Ken Lanning was an FBI agent, and he retired in 2000. He is now part of the Academy group. During his time at the FBI his areas of interest included occult crime/ritual abuse, hostage negotiation and crimes against children.
64 Fisher, "'Snuff' Films: Urban Myth or Grim Reality?" APBNews (17 April 2000) online at http://apbnews.com/media/gfiles/snuff/index.html
65 Ibid.
66 Carol, "Snuff: Believing the Worst," in Assiter and Avedon (Eds.), Bad Girls and Dirty Pictures: 130.
67 Gauer continued his involvement with anti-obscenity campaigns after the 'snuff' panic but he also achieved notoriety when he commissioned the creation of the kneeling Santa Christmas decoration in the early 1980s. The statue was sculpted by Rudolph Vargas at the request of Gauer who was, ironically, concerned by the secularization of Christmas.

good to tell men that they are *supposed* to be rapacious villains?"[68] A concise and articulate challenge to the divisive, partisan feminism promoted by Brownmiller, Steinem and Dworkin.

It seems entirely possible that the claims made by conservatives and militant feminists in the 1970s and 1980s, that 'snuff' films existed and sold for a high price, would encourage someone to make such a film for financial reasons. An unnamed hardcore porn filmmaker acknowledged that there could be a potential audience for such films, saying, "certain elements of our society will go to any lengths for kicks. These are the real weirdos, and most of us stay away from them. They have money, and human life to them is nothing. They figure they can buy anything."[69] Snuff would, therefore, if it existed, be a privilege of the wealthy and jaded, an expensive and rare item to be bought in the capitalist free market. Ken Lanning acknowledged that advances in home video technology increased the possibility that a 'snuff' film would be made, "It's just a matter of time before one is made and it surfaces. Camcorders make the scenario possible."[70] If it is inevitable and a 'snuff' movie is made — will the tabloid newspapers, conservative moralists and feminists be happy? Al Goldstein warned ominously that if the rumour about 'snuff' films, created by conservative anti-obscenity crusaders and perpetuated by militant feminists, goes on for long enough, "eventually some asshole will do it for real."[71]

---

68 Carol, "Snuff: Believing the Worst," in Assiter and Avedon (Eds.), *Bad Girls and Dirty Pictures*: 130.
69 Unnamed filmmaker quoted in Hammond, "Are Snuff Films For Real?" *Adam Film World* (April 1976): 43, 84.
70 Lanning quoted in McDowell, "Movies To Die For," San Francisco *Chronicle* (7 August 1994) This World section: 10.
71 Lynch, "The Facts About the Snuff-Film Rumours," *Oui* (July 1976): 118.

AUTHOR BIOGRAPHY

Stephen Milligen has written articles on American history and popular culture for the *Irish Journal of American Studies* and about the adult film industry for *Headpress*. Needing a change of scene his next research project is a study of Irish giants in eighteenth and nineteenth century popular culture.

https://www.facebook.com/Drstephenmilligen

SELECTED BIBLIOGRAPHY

Allyn, David, *Make Love Not War. The Sexual Revolution: An Unfettered History*, Little Brown and Company, New York and London, 2000.

Arian, Asher, et al., *Changing New York City Politics*, Routledge, New York and London, 1991.

Assiter, Alison, *Pornography, Feminism and the Individual*, Pluto, London, 1989.

Bailey, Fenton, and Randy Barbato (Dir.), *Inside Deep Throat* documentary (2005).

Balun, Chas., *Horror Holocaust*, Fantaco, Albany, New York, 1986.

Barry, Kathleen, *Female Sexual Slavery*, New York University Press, New York and London, 1979.

Barton, Blanche, *Church of Satan*, Hells Kitchen Productions, New York, 1990.

Bataille, Georges, *Eroticism*, Marion Boyars, London and New York, 1987.

Beale, Paul (Ed.), *A Dictionary of Slang and Unconventional English*, Routledge and Kegan Paul, London, 1984.

Binstein, Michael, and Charles Bowden, *Trust Me: Charles Keating and the Missing Billions*, Random House, New York, 1993.

Biskind, Peter, *Easy Riders, Raging Bulls*, Bloomsbury, London, 1999.

Boulware, Jack, *Sex, American Style*, Feral House, Venice, California, 1997.

Briggs, Joe Bob, *Profoundly Disturbing: Shocking Movies That Changed History*, Plexus, London, 2003.

Brownmiller, Susan, *Against Our Will*, Secker and Warburg, London, 1975.

———, "Let's Put Pornography back in the Closet," in Laura Lederer (Ed.), *Take Back the Night: Women on Pornography*, William Morrow, New York, 1980: 252–255.

Buchanan, Larry, *It Came From Hunger! Tales of a Cinema Schlockmeister*, McFarland and Co., Jefferson (North Carolina) and London, 1996.

Bugliosi, Vincent, and Curt Gentry, *The Manson Murders: An Investigation Into Motive*, Penguin, London, 1989.

Cameron, Deborah, and Elizabeth Frazer, *Lust To Kill: A Feminist Investigation of Sexual Murder*, Polity Press, Cambridge, 1988.

Cameron, Deborah, and Elizabeth Frazer, "Cultural Difference and the Lust to Kill," in Penelope Harvey and Peter Gow (Ed.), *Sexual Violence*, Routledge, London and New York, 1994: 156–171.

Caputi, Jane, *The Age of the Sex Crime*, Women's Press, London, 1988.

———, "The Sexual Politics of Murder," in Pauline B. Bart and Eileen Geil Moran (Eds.), *Violence Against Women: The Bloody Footprints*, Sage, Newbury Park and London, 1993: 5–46.

———, "Advertising Femicide: Lethal Violence Against Women in Pornography and Gorenography," in Jill Radford and Diana E. H. Russell (Eds.), *Femicide, The Politics of Woman Killing*, Open University Press, Buckingham, 1992: 203–221.

———, and Diana E. H. Russell, "Femicide: Sexist Terrorism Against Women," in Jill Radford and Diana E. H. Russell (Eds.), *Femicide, The Politics of Woman Killing*, Open University Press, Buckingham, 1992: 13–21.

Carol, Avedon, "Snuff: Believing the Worst," in Alison Assiter and Avedon Carol (Eds.), *Bad Girls and Dirty Pictures: The Challenge To Reclaim Feminism*, Pluto Press, London and Boulder, Colorado, 1993: 126–130.

Clover, Carol J., *Men Women and Chainsaws: Gender in the Modern Horror Film*, BFI, London, 1996.

Cohodas, Nadine, *Strom Thurmond and the Politics of Southern Change*, Mercer University Press, Macon, Ga., 1993.

Commission on Obscenity and Pornography, *The Report of the Commission on Obscenity and Pornography*, Bantam, New York and London, 1970.

Curry, Christopher Wayne, *A Taste of Blood: The Films of Herschell Gordon Lewis*, Creation, London, 1998.

Daly, Mary, *Beyond God the Father: Towards a Philosophy of Women's Libertation*, Beacon, Boston, 1973.

Daley, Brittany A. et al (Ed.), *Sin-A-Rama: Sleaze Sex Paperbacks of the Sixties*, Feral House, Los Angeles, 2005.

Davis Jr., Sammy, *Hollywood in a Suitcase*,

Berkley, New York, 1981.

Davis Jr., Sammy, *Why Me?* Michael Joseph, London, 1989.

Dean, John W., *The Rehnquist Choice: The Untold Story of the Nixon Appointment that Redefined the Supreme Court*, Free Press, New York and London, 2001.

de Grazia, Edward and Roger K. Newman, *Banned Films: Movies, Censors and the First Amendment*, R. R. Bowker, New York and London, 1982.

———, *Girls Lean Back Everywhere: The Law of Obscenity and the Assault on Genius*, Vintage, New York, 1993.

Diamond, Sara, "Pornography: Image and Reality," in Varda Burstyn (Ed.), *Women Against Censorship*, Douglas and McIntyre, Toronto and Vancouver, 1985: 40–57.

Dickstein, Morris, *Gates of Eden: American Culture in the Sixties*, Harvard University Press, Cambridge and London, 1997.

Domingo, Chris, "What the White Man Won't Tell Us: Report from the Berkeley Clearing House on Femicide," in Jill Radford and Diane E. H. Russell (Ed.), *Femicide, The Politics of Woman Killing*, Open University Press, Buckingham, 1992: 195–202.

Duggan, Lisa, Nan Hunter and Carole S. Vance, "False Promises: Feminist Antipornography Legislation in the US," in Varda Burstyn (Ed.), *Women Against Censorship*, Douglas and McIntyre, Toronto and Vancouver, 1985: 130–151.

Dworkin, Andrea, *Our Blood: Prophecies and Discourses on Sexual Politics*, Women's Press, London, 1976.

———, *Pornography: Men Possessing Women*, Women's Press, London, 1981.

———, *Right-Wing Women: The Politics of Dislocated Females*, Women's Press, London, 1983.

———, *Letters From A Warzone: Writings 1976–1987*, Secker and Warburg, London, 1988.

———, and Catherine MacKinnon, "Questions and Answers," in Diane E. H. Russell (Ed.), *Making Violence Sexy: Feminist Views on Pornography*, Open University Press, Buckingham, 1993: 78–96.

———, "Pornography and Grief," in Drucilla Cornell (Ed.), *Feminism and Pornography*, Oxford University Press, Oxford, 2000: 39–44.

Echols, Alice, *Daring To Be Bad: Radical Feminism in America 1967–1975*, University of Minnesota Press, Minneapolis, 1989.

Ellis, Bill, *Raising the Devil: Satanism, New Religions, and the Media*, University Press Kentucky, Lexington, 2000.

Ellis, Kate, et al, *Caught Looking: Feminism, Pornography and Censorship*, Real Comet Press, Seattle, 1988.

Ellis, Richard, "Disseminating Desire: Grove Press and 'The End[s] of Obscenity'," in Gary Day and Clive Bloom (Ed.), *Perspectives on Pornography*, Macmillan, London, 1988: 26–43.

Emmons, Nuel, *Manson in His Own Words*, Grove Press, New York, 1986.

FBI, Snuff Films, File Number 145–5568.

———, File Number 145–6617.

———, File Number 95–281728.

Final Report of the Attorney General's Commission on Pornography, Routledge Hill Press, Nashville, Tennessee, 1986.

Flynt, Larry, *An Unseemly Man*, Bloomsbury, London, 1997.

Friedman, David F., *A Youth In Babylon: Confessions of a Trash Movie King*, Prometheus, New York, 1990.

Friedman, Josh Alan, *When Sex Was Dirty*, Feral House, Los Angeles, 2005.

Frost, Robert C. "William J. Brennan and the Warren Court," in Mark Tushnet (Ed.), *The Warren Court in Historical and Political Perspective*, University Press Virginia, Charlottesville and London, 1993: 123–136.

Funston, Richard Y., *Constitutional Counter Revolution?* Schenkman, New York and London, 1977.

Gagnon, John H., and William Simon, "Pornography — Raging Menace or Paper Tiger?" in Paul C. Rist (Ed.), *The Pornography Controversy: Changing Moral Standards in American Life*, Transaction, New Brunswick, New Jersey, 1975: 85–95.

Gain, Edward, *They's Rather Be Right: Youth and Conservatism*, Macmillan, New York and London, 1963.

Genovese, Michael A., *The Nixon Presidency: Power and Politics in Turbulent Times*, Greenwood, Westport, Connecticut, 1990.

George, Bill, *Eroticism in the Fantasy Cinema*, Imagine Inc., Pittsburgh, 1986.

Gever, Martha, and Marg Hall, "Fighting Pornography," in Laura Lederer (Ed.), *Take Back the Night: Women on Pornography*, William Morrow, New York, 1980: 279–285.

Goodall, Mark, *Sweet & Savage: The World*

Through the Shockumentary Film Lens, Headpress, London, 2006.

Greene, Doyle, *Lips Hips Tits Power: The Films of Russ Meyer*, Creation, London, 2004.

Griffin, Susan, *Pornography and Silence: Culture's Revenge Against Nature*, Women's Press, London, 1981.

Gubar, Susan, and Joan Hoff (Ed.), *For Adult Users Only: The Dilemma of Violent Pornography*, Indiana University Press, Bloomington and Indianapolis, 1989.

Haskell, Molly, *From Reverence To Rape: The Treatment of Women in the Movies*, New English Library, London, 1975.

Hawkins, Gordon, and Franklin E. Zimring, *Pornography in a Free Society*, Cambridge University Press, Cambridge and New York, 1988.

Hebditch, David, and Nick Anning, *Porn Gold: Inside the Pornography Business*, Faber and Faber, London, 1988.

Heidenry, John, *What Wild Ecstasy: The Rise and Fall of the Sexual Revolution*, Simon and Schuster, New York, 1997.

Heins, Marjorie, *Sex, Sin and Blasphemy: A Guide To America's Censorship Wars*, New Press, New York, 1993.

Henry, Alice, "Does Viewing Pornography Lead Men to Rape?" in Gail Chester and Julienne Dickey (Ed.), *Feminism and Censorship*, Prism, Dorset, 1988: 96–104.

Hicks, Robert D., *In Pursuit of Satan: The Police and the Occult*, Prometheus, Buffalo, New York, 1991.

Hubner, John, *Bottom Feeders*, Doubleday, New York, 1993.

Huer, John, *Art, Beauty, and Pornography: A Journey Through American Culture*, Prometheus, Buffalo, New York, 1987.

Itzin, Catherine (Ed.), *Pornography: Women, Violence and Civil Rights*, Oxford University Press, Oxford, 1992.

Kalman, Laura, *Abe Fortas*, A Biography, Yale University Press, New Haven and London, 1990.

———, "Abe Fortas: Symbol of the Warren Court?" in Mark Tushnet (Ed.), *The Warren Court in Historical and Political Perspective*, University Press Virginia, Charlottesville and London, 1993: 155–168.

Kerekes, David, and David Slater, *Killing for Culture: An Illustrated History of Death in Film from Mondo to Snuff*, Annihilation Press, 1993.

———, *See No Evil: Banned Films and Video Controversy*, Critical Vision, Manchester, 2000.

Kipnis, Laura, *Bound and Gagged: Pornography and the Politics of Fantasy in America*, Duke University Press, Durham, 1999.

Kirby, Tim (Dir.), *The Zapruder Footage: The World's Most Famous Home Movie* documentary (1993).

Kolker, Robert Phillip, *A Cinema of Loneliness*, Oxford University Press, Oxford and New York, 1988.

Kuh, Richard H., *Foolish Figleaves? Pornography in-and out-of Court*, Macmillan, New York, 1967.

Kyle-Keith, Richard, *The High Price of Pornography*, Public Affairs Press, Washington, D.C., 1961.

LaBelle, Beverly, "Snuff — The Ultimate in Woman Hating," in Jill Radford and Diane E. H. Russell (Ed.), *Femicide, The Politics of Woman Killing*, Open University Press, Buckingham, 1992: 189–194.

Landis, Bill, and Michelle Clifford, *Sleazoid Express*, Simon and Schuster, New York, 2002.

LaVey, Anton, *Satanic Bible*, Avon, New York, 1969.

Lederer, Laura (Ed.), *Take Back the Night: Women on Pornography*, William Morrow, New York, 1980.

———, "Then and Now: An Interview With a Former Pornography Model," in Laura Lederer (Ed.), *Take Back the Night: Women on Pornography*, William Morrow, New York, 1980: 57–70.

Lee, Martin A, and Bruce Shlain, *Acid Dreams. The Complete Social History of LSD: The CIA, the Sixties, and Beyond*, Grove Press, New York, 1992.

Lyons, Arthur, *Satan Wants You: The Cult of Devil Worship*, Hart-Davis, London, 1970.

MacKinnon, Catherine A., *Only Words*, HarperCollins, London, 1994.

———, and Andrea Dworkin, *In Harm's Way: The Pornography Civil Rights Hearings*, Harvard University Press, Cambridge and London, 1997.

Mathijs, Ernest, and Xavier Mendik (Ed.), *Alternative Europe, Eurotrash and Exploitation Cinema Since 1945*, Wallflower, London and New York, 2004.

McDonough, Jimmy, *Big Bosoms and Square*

Jaws: The Biography of Russ Meyer, Vintage, London, 2006.

McNair, Brian, Mediated Sex: Pornography and Postmodern Culture, Arnold, New York and London, 1996.

McNeil, Legs, and Osborne, Jennifer, The Other Hollywood: The Uncensored Oral History of the Porn Film Industry, Regan Books, New York, 2005.

Miller, Richard B., "Violent Pornography: Mimetic Nihilism and the Eclipse of Differences," in Susan Gubar and Joan Hoff (Ed.), For Adult Users Only: The Dilemma of Violent Pornography, Indiana University Press, Bloomington and Indianapolis, 1989: 147–162.

Miller, Russell, Bunny: The Real Story of Playboy, Corgi, London, 1985.

Millet, Kate, Sexual Politics, Virago, London, 1993. [Originally 1970]

Muller, Eddie, and Faris, Daniel, Grindhouse: The Forbidden World of Adults Only Cinema, St. Martins, New York, 1996.

Murray, Bruce, Fortas: The Rise and Ruin of a Supreme Court Justice, William Morrow, New York, 1988.

Navasky, Victor S., Kennedy Justice, Atheneum, New York, 1971.

Ogersby, Bill, Playboys in Paradise: Masculinity, Youth and Leisure-style in Modern America, Berg, Oxford and New York, 2001.

"The Old in the Country of the Young," Time (3 August 1970) reprinted in Raymond Lee and Dorothy Palmer (Ed.), America in Crisis, Winthrop, Cambridge, Mass., 1972: 406–412.

Palmer, Randy, Herschell Gordon Lewis, Godfather of Gore, McFarland, North Carolina, 2000.

Panigutti, Nico, "Gaultiero Jacopetti," in Stuart Swezey (Ed.), Amok Journal: Sensurround Edition, Amok, Los Angeles, 1995: 140–168.

Partridge, William L., The Hippie Ghetto: The Natural History of a Subculture, Holt, Rinehart and Winston Inc., New York and London, 1973.

Petley, Julian, "'Snuffed Out': Nightmares in a Trading Standards Officers Brain," in Xavier Mendik and Graeme Harper (Ed.), Unruly Pleasures: The Cult Film and Its Critics, FAB Press, Guildford, 2000: 204–219.

Posner, Richard A., and Katherine B. Silbaugh, A Guide To America's Sex Laws, University of Chicago Press, Chicago and London, 1996.

Quarles, Mike, Down and Dirty: Hollywood's Exploitation Filmmakers and their Movies, McFarland, Jefferson, North Carolina, 1993.

Reich, Charles A., The Greening of America, Penguin, Harmondsworth, Middlesex, 1971. [Originally 1970]

Reichley, A. James, Conservatives in an Age of Change, Brookings Institute, Washington, D.C., 1981.

Ritchie, Jean, The Secret World of Cults, Angus and Robertson, London, 1991.

Roberts Jr., Edwin A., The Smut Rakers: A Report In Depth On Obscenity and the Censors, The National Observer, Silver Spring, Maryland, 1966.

Rotsler, William, Contemporary Erotic Cinema, Penthouse/Ballantine, New York, 1973.

Russell, Diana E. H., "Pornography and the Women's Liberation Movement," in Laura Lederer (Ed.), Take Back the Night: Women on Pornography, William Morrow, New York, 1980: 301–306.

———, Sexual Exploitation: Rape, Child Sexual Abuse and Workplace Harassment, Sage, Beverly Hills and London, 1984.

——— (Ed.), Making Violence Sexy: Feminist Views on Pornography, Open University Press, Buckingham, 1993.

———, "Pornography and Rape: A Causal Model," in Drucilla Cornell (Ed.), Feminism and Pornography, Oxford University Press, Oxford, 2000: 48–93.

———, Dangerous Relationships: Pornography, Misogyny and Rape, Sage, London, 1998.

Sanders, Ed, The Family: The Story of Charles Manson's Dune Buggy Attack Battalion, EP Dutton, and C., New York, 1971.

Schaefer, Eric, Bold! Daring! Shocking! True!: A History of Exploitation Films, 1919–1959, Duke University Press, Durham and London, 1999.

Schlosser, Eric, Reefer Madness and Other Tales from the American Underground, Allan Lane, London, 2003.

Schoell, William, Stay out of the Shower: The Shocker Film Phenomenon, Robinson, London, 1988.

Schrek, Nikolas, The Satanic Screen, Creation, London, 2001.

See, Carolyn, Blue Money, David McKay and Company, New York, 1974.

Simon, Adam (Dir.) An American Nightmare documentary (2000).

Skal, David J., The Monster Show: A Cultural

History of Horror, Plexus, London, 1994.

Skinner, James M., *The Cross and the Cinema: The Legion of Decency and the National Catholic Office for Motion Pictures, 1933–1970*, Praeger, Westport (Conn.) and London, 1993.

Slade, Joseph P., "Pornographic Theatres Off Times Square," in Paul C. Rist (Ed.), *The Pornography Controversy: Changing Moral Standards in American Life*, Transaction, New Brunswick, New Jersey, 1975: 119–139.

Snitow, Anita, "Retrenchment Versus Transformation: The Politics of the Anti-Pornography Movement," in Varda Burstyn (Ed.), *Women Against Censorship*, Douglas and McIntyre, Toronto and Vancouver, 1985: 107–120.

"'Snuff' The Greatest rip-off in porn history," *Erotica* (December 1976): 17–20.

Sontag, Susan, *Styles of Radical Will*, Vintage, London, 1994. [Originally 1969]

Stallybrass, Peter, and Allan White, *The Politics and Poetics of Transgression*, Cornell University Press, 1986.

Starr, Marco, "J. Hills is Alive: A Defence of I Spit On Your Grave," in Martin Baker (Ed.), *Video Nasties: Freedom and Censorship in the Media*, Pluto Press, London and Sydney, 1984: 48–55.

Steinem, Gloria, *Outrageous Acts and Everyday Rebellions*, Jonathan Cape, London, 1984.

Steiner, George, "Night Words: High Pornography and Human Privacy," in Paul C. Rist (Ed.), The *Pornography Controversy: Changing Moral Standards in American Life*, Transaction, New Brunswick, New Jersey, 1975: 203–213.

Steinfels, Peter, *The Neoconservatives*, Touchstone, New York, 1980.

Stoller, Robert J., *Perversion: The Erotic Form of Hatred*, Marsfield Library, London, 1986. [Originally 1975]

Stoller, Robert J., *Porn: Myths for the Twentieth Century*, Yale University Press, New Haven and London, 1991.

Svoray, Yaron, *Gods of Death: Around the World, Behind Closed Doors, Operates an Ultra-Secret Business of Sex and Death. One Man Hunts For the Truth About Snuff Films*, Simon and Schuster, New York, 1997.

Szulkin, David A., *Wes Craven's Last House on the Left: The Making of a Cult Classic* (revised edition), FAB, Guidford, 2000.

Talese, Gay, *Thy Neighbor's Wife*, Doubleday, New York, 1980.

Turan, Kenneth, and Stephen F. Zito, *Sinema*, Praeger, New York, 1974.

Warren Jr., Earl, "Obscenity Laws — A Shift to Reality," in Paul C. Rist (Ed.), *The Pornography Controversy: Changing Moral Standards in American Life*, Transaction, New Brunswick, New Jersey, 1975: 96–116.

Waters, John, *Shock Value*, Thunder's Mouth Press, New York 1995.

Wentworth, Harold, and Stuart Berg Flexner (Ed.), *Dictionary of American Slang*, second supplemental edition, Thomas Y. Crowell, New York, 1975.

Weyr, Thomas, *Reaching For Paradise: The Playboy Vision of America*, Times Books, New York, 1978.

Wicker, Tom, *One of Us: Richard Nixon and the American Dream*, Random House, New York, 1991.

Williams, Linda, *Hard Core*, Pandora, London, 1991.

Williams, Tony, *Hearths of Darkness: The Family In American Horror Film*, Associated University Press, London, 1996.

Williamson, Bruce, "Porno Chic," *Playboy* (August 1973) in Peter Keogh (Ed.), *Flesh and Blood*, Mercury House, San Francisco, 1995: 10–28.

Willis, Ellen, *Beginning to See the Light: Pieces of a Decade*, Alfred A. Knopf, New York, 1981.

Wilson, James Q., "Violence, Pornography and Social Science," in Paul C. Rist (Ed.), *The Pornography Controversy: Changing Moral Standards in American Life*, Transaction, New Brunswick, New Jersey, 1975: 225–243.

Woodward, Bob, and Armstrong, Scott, *The Brethren*, Simon and Schuster, New York, 1979.

Zinn, Howard, *A People's History of the United States*, Longman, New York and London, 1980.

Zucher Jr., Louis A. and R. George Kirkpatrick, *Citizens For Decency: Antipornography Crusades as Status Defence*, University of Texas Press, Austin and London, 1976.

INDEX

INDEX

INDEX

285

INDEX

A HEADPRESS BOOK
Hardback first published by Headpress in 2014. Paperback edition 2015.

{t} 0845 330 1844   {e} headoffice@headpress.com

**'THE *BLOODIEST* THING THAT *EVER* HAPPENED
IN FRONT OF A CAMERA'**
Conservative Politics, 'Porno Chic' and *Snuff*

Text copyright © Stephen Milligen
This volume copyright © Headpress 2014
Cover design: Mark Critchell <mark.critchell@googlemail.com>
Layout: Ganymede Foley
Headpress diaspora: David Kerekes, Thomas Campbell, Caleb Selah,
Giuseppe, Dave T., Jennifer Wallis

The moral rights of the author have been asserted.

**A CIP catalogue record for this book is available from
the British Library**

**ISBN 978-1-909394-08-7 (*pbk*)
ISBN 978-1-909394-09-4 (*ebk*)
NO ISBN (*hbk*)**

NO ISBN SPECIAL EDITION

1 HEAD PRESS Est 1991

Headpress. The gospel according to unpopular culture.

**NO ISBN special edition hardbacks and other items
are available exclusively from World Headpress**

WWW.WORLDHEADPRESS.COM